The Porter-Woods Debate

On

Orphan Homes and Homes for the Aged

Between

Guy N. Woods, Memphis, Tennessee

and

W. Curtis Porter, Monette, Arkansas

Held in

Indianapolis, Indiana, January 3-6, 1956

ISBN 1-58427-041-1

Guardian of Truth Foundation
P.O. Box 9670
Bowling Green, Kentucky 42102

INTRODUCTION TO WOODS-PORTER DEBATE

January 3 through January 6, 1956, one of the most significant debates in the history of the church of our Lord was held in the city of Indianapolis, Indiana. The Garfield Heights congregation of that city acted as the very gracious hosts for the occasion, and the disputants were Brother Guy N. Woods and Brother W. Curtis Porter. Neither of these men needs to be introduced to members of the church of Christ in our age. Brother Woods makes his home in Memphis, Tennessee, but is seldom there, for he is almost constantly engaged in meetings and debates all over the brotherhood. He is a veteran of more than one hundred debates and was admirably suited to the task before him in this one. Brother Porter is also a veteran debater and evangelist. His home is in Monette, Arkansas. No man could have been chosen who was better equipped to defend his position than Brother Porter. Certainly these two men give to this debate a uniqueness and a quality that lesser men could not have reached. We feel the issues were thoroughly examined and as strongly stated as they possibly could be when these two men finished with the debate.

Each session of the debate lasted slightly over two hours. The speakers spoke for twenty minutes at a time and each man had three speeches each evening. This proved an excellent arrangement for keeping the issues before the speakers and the audience.

Brother Woods represented the Garfield Heights congregation in the debate. This congregation is located at 2842 Shelby Street in Indianapolis. Brother Will L. Totty, evangelist for this church for the past seventeen years, moderated for Brother Woods and acted as gracious host for the entire debate. His conduct in this role was heartwarming and greatly appreciated by all. Brother Porter represented the Belmont Avenue congregation, located at 1002 South Belmont Avenue in Indianapolis. Brother Cecil Douthitt was his moderator.

The propositions discussed scarcely varied throughout the entire four nights of the discussion. The first two nights Brother Woods affirmed: "It is in harmony with the scriptures for churches to build and maintain benevolent organizations for the care of the needy, such as Boles Home, the Tipton Home, and other orphan homes and homes for the aged that are among us." The last two nights Brother Porter affirmed the negative position that: "It is contrary to the scriptures for churches to build and maintain benevolent organizations for the care of the needy, such as Boles Home, the Tipton Home, and other orphan homes and homes for the aged that are among us."

It is customary in an introduction such as this to say, "The spirit was fine etc., etc." I think to do so here would leave a false impression with those who will read this book. The two disputants were veterans who have long loved one another as brethren and respected one another's abilities. Their attitudes and conduct were exemplary. The surface appearance of all who attended (350 to 400 preachers plus elders, members, and visitors, bring the total to around 800 each evening) was cordial and congenial. However, beneath the surface there seemed to be an antagonism and a party spirit which did not augur good for the continued peace and harmony of the body of Christ. Our prayer is that these impressions were wrong and that those who attended, as well as all who read this book, may turn often to Rom. 8: 9, that the spirit of Christ and the unity it promotes might not be lost.

It would be unforgivable if we failed to mention the great contribution made to this book by Sister Nadene Welch. She made the tape recordings of all the speeches and then undertook the monumental task of typing from the tapes all of the manuscripts. This difficult task she performed in record time. Her tireless work during the debate and afterward is, I am sure, greatly appreciated by all concerned.

A unique addition to this debate was a series of morning sessions, three in number, in which all were invited to speak on whatever subject they desired. Each of these sessions was preceded by a speaker who delivered a thirty minute discourse. These speakers were chosen without regard to agreement or disagreement with the issues involved in the debate or other issues facing the church today. Brother

Allen Sommer, Brother Carl Ketcherside, and Brother E. R. Harper were the morning speakers. After these speeches Brother Bill Heinselman was given the difficult task of acting as chairman of the discussion period. He handled it like a veteran and the conduct of the sessions was excellent. We appreciate the spirit which prompted the Garfield Heights elders to use every means possible for getting the issues involved placed before the brotherhood in the clearest and fairest manner possible.

All of us owe a debt of gratitude to the Gospel Advocate Company for making this debate available to the public. We believe that this book will be one of the most read publications in our brotherhood for many years, and I am sure I speak the sentiments of both disputants when I beseech all who read it to do so with a prayer for unity on their lips, sincerity in their hearts, and a desire in their minds to know the truth and that only.

ROY F. OSBORNE, JR.
416 Lewis Avenue
San Leandro, Calif.

February 16, 1956

WOODS-PORTER DEBATE

FIRST PROPOSITION

It is in harmony with the Scriptures for churches to build and maintain benevolent organizations for the care of the needy, such as the Boles Home, the Tipton Home, and other orphan homes and homes for the aged that are among us.

Affirmative: Guy N. Woods
Negative: W. Curtis Porter

Woods' First Affirmative

Brethren Moderators, Brother Porter, Brethren and Sisters, and Friends:

I rejoice that in the providence of God I am privileged to be here tonight in the affirmation of the proposition which Brother Totty has read. I am grateful to this fine congregation for the invitation to participate in this discussion; and, if I know my heart, I have no other motive, no other purpose, in coming than simply to contend for the truth as I believe it to be set out on the sacred page of God's Word. I am also happy to have Brother W. Curtis Porter as a participant in this discussion. I feel sure that Brother Porter is as able as any man who could be selected to defend the position which he has espoused in the debate; and I, therefore, trust that this may be a profitable and interesting discussion for all.

I am likewise sure that this congregation is not interested, nor would it be edifying for us to spend a great deal of time—or, for that matter, *any time*—in discussion of alleged changes that either of us may, or may not, have made. I know not what course he intends to follow along that line; but, so far as I am concerned, unless he makes it necessary, I shall confine myself to a discussion of the Scriptures, at least with reference to the basis on which the matter is to be considered.

I would like to say in the outset, before I begin the affirmation of the proposition, that I think it not necessary to spend a lot of time in definition. It seems to me that the proposition is clear and explicit and sets out exactly what my obligation is. But just a word or two with reference to some of the terms in the proposition. "It is in harmony with the Scriptures for churches to build and maintain benevolent organizations for the care of the needy, such as Boles Home, the Tipton Home, and other orphan homes and homes for the aged that are among us." By the word "harmony" I mean concord or agreement; by "church," congregations composed of the Lord's people; by "build and maintain," to establish and support; and by "benevolent organizations," charitable enterprises. Right here I would like to spend a moment or two in discussing the word "organization." It is derived from the verb "organize," and the term is defined: "To give organic structure to." The intransitive verb is defined as, "To become systematized or constituted into the whole of interdependent parts." This word is of various usage in our literature. For example, all of us have used it in times past to describe the Missionary Society and other movements which rival the church and are, therefore, wrong. I think instances of that usage may be found in the literature of all of us who have written. Brother David Lipscomb once said: "Christ never organized any organization except his churches. In these, as members of his body, his children must work. No Sunday school, or Missionary Society, or charitable organization outside of his church has ever been authorized. No Christian has a right to work in any of these human organizations." Yet, Brother Lipscomb established and was a part of a Christian school and was a charter member of Fanning Orphan Home until his death. All of us have used this word in two senses: First, we have used it to describe institutions that rival the church of our Lord. And then, in the second place, we have used it to describe the functioning of the church through its members. When I speak of organizations tonight in the sense that my proposition mentions such, I mean merely the *means by* which, or *through* which, the church works in order to accomplish that which God has ordained.

By "care of the needy," providing for the destitute. And then, by that part of the proposition that says, "Boles, Tipton, and other homes among us," I mean to designate the particular type of care that is under consideration in this debate.

Note please what my proposition does not require. In

the first place, it does not necessitate a defense of any *abuses* of the principle involved, nor am I obligated to defend any isolated practices that are characteristic of the homes in the past, in the present, or in the future. The principle involved is simply this: Is it right for the church of our Lord, through its members, to build and maintain homes, such as these, for the purpose of caring for the homeless and the aged? That, friends, is basically the question that is under consideration here tonight. My first argument then will run as follows: First—but before I introduce this, let me explain a thing that might perhaps otherwise lead you to wonder tonight. I do not know what Brother Porter's position is. I have not the slightest idea at the present time just how he thinks that the care of the needy is to be accomplished. I am going, herefore, to presume that it is my obligation to prove every point that I shall introduce here tonight. If, on some of these matters, it should develop that there is agreement, I shall rejoice that such is so. But that will explain the detailed manner in which I shall proceed.

The care of the needy is a New Testament doctrine. In Eph. 4: 28 Paul said, "Let him that stole steal no more: but rather let him labour, working with his hands the thing which is good, that he may have to give to him that needeth."

In James 1: 27 we are told that "pure religion and undefiled before God and the Father is this, To visit the fatherless and widows in their affliction, and to keep himself unspotted from the world."

In Acts 20: 35 Paul said, "I have shewed you all things, how that so labouring ye ought to support the weak, and to remember the words of the Lord Jesus, how he said, It is more blessed to give than to receive."

Now, these passages, friends, set out an obligation. This obligation is not a temporary matter, nor is it to be administered on a so-called emergency basis only. In Mark 14: 7 our Lord said—and note this carefully, please—"For ye have the poor with you always, and whensoever ye will ye may do them good." If it be admitted that there is an obligation to the poor, it must be conceded that that obligation obtains always, because Jesus said the poor are always here. One of two things then must follow; either we do not sustain an obligation to the poor, or else that obligation is not on an emergency basis.

This responsibility toward the care of the needy extends to the church. In 1 Tim. 5: 16 the apostle Paul said, "If any woman that believeth hath widows, let her relieve them, and let not the church be burdened; that it may relieve them that are widows indeed." Now, note what is there said, "that it," i.e., *the church,* "may relieve them that are widows indeed." That, friends, plainly declares that there is a responsibility on the part of the church toward needy widows.

Now, get this, please. The Scriptures do not designate the manner or method which we are to follow in carrying out the duty here enjoined. If it does mention such, then Brother Porter can settle this question and stop the debate by producing the details. Obviously, he cannot do this; and so it follows that, notwithstanding the obligation stated, the manner or method of procedure is not there. Get this principle, please. When a duty is imposed and the manner by which it is to be accomplished is designated, the manner or method is as important as the duty itself. But where the method is not indicated, the procedure is in *the realm of expediency;* and we must then follow the plan which appears to be the best at the time.

In 1 Pet. 4: 11 Peter says, "If any man minister, let him do it as of the ability which God giveth." That is a principle readily recognized.

I should like to call attention just here to a very obvious difference between the old and the new covenant. The old covenant dealt in the most minute detail with obligations. An example of this may be found in Ex. 40 and Lev. 1 where God not only specified the obligation, but also gave detailed procedures. He even told the way in which the offering was to be laid on the fire in the most detailed and minute manner. Under the new covenant, only fundamental matters are stated; and it is up to us to follow the methods best suited. That is a principle that has long been recognized.

I have a chart that I want to put on the screen here, chart number ten; and you will observe the principle. It is a familiar one, and hence there is no particular point in arguing this at length. You will note here the essential

CHART No. 10

THE ESSENTIAL AND THE INCIDENTAL:

THE ESSENTIAL	THE INCIDENTAL
• Go	• Walk, Ride, Fly
• Teach	• Radio, Classes, Charts
• Baptize	• Bap., Pool, Creek
• Lord's Supper	• Cups, Plates, Tables
• Contribution	• Baskets, Hats
• Praise	• Song Books, Parts
• Care of Needy	• Type of Home, Location, Size, No. of Needy, etc.

and the incidental. On the essential side, the command to go; but the manner of going is not indicated. We may walk, ride, or fly. We are commanded to teach. That is the essential. The incidental: radio, classes, charts. We are commanded to baptize. We may baptize in a baptistry, a pool, or a creek. The Lord's supper is given. The cups, the plates, the tables are incidentals. The contribution is the essential. Whether we pass baskets or hats is incidental. We are commanded to sing, to make melody; and songbooks and parts are incidentals. And the care of the needy is the obligation; and the type of home, the location, the size, the number of needy is not indicated. That is the principle, and that will be sufficient for the chart just at this particular time.

It so happens that our Brother Porter has a very splendid discussion along this line in a debate with Brother Waters, a man who opposed individual communion service. Brother Porter has this stated so well that I prefer to read it from him. I am reading from page 67 of the *Porter-Waters Debate,* and this is Brother Porter, now, speaking: "In the third place, I want to call your attention to an argument that I want to base upon what I shall call 'law and expediency'; and I wish that I had an extra blackboard that I might put a diagram on it, but we haven't." Now hear: "Some people have opposed the use of a baptistry upon the same ground that Brother Waters opposes these things that we are discussing tonight. But the command to baptize involves a place in which the baptizing must be done. There must be something to contain the water in which the immersion must be accomplished. Whether it's within the banks of a river, or whether it's within the walls of a baptistry, or wherever it may be, are but incidental matters, but those things fall within the realm of Scriptural principles."

Now, that, friends, is a splendid statement of the matter. Let us just paraphrase this. He will agree with me that there is an obligation to care for the needy. Now look: Just paraphrase his statement and see how well it fits. "Some people have opposed the use of an *orphan home* upon the same grounds that Brother Porter and I are discussing these things here tonight. But the command to care for the needy involves *a place* in which the needy must be cared for. There must be *something* to contain the needy, in which the care is administered. Whether it is within the walls of an *orphan home,* or whether it is within the walls of a *private home,* or wherever it may be, are but incidental matters. But those things fall within the realm of Scriptural principles." Now, that, friends, is a statement that I cannot improve upon from Brother Porter. The care of the needy

CHART No. 9

"REMEMBER THE POOR"

Gal. 2:10

THIS REQUIRES

FOR THE ORPHAN:

- A Place
- Food
- Clothing
- Education
- Supervision
- Medical Care

FOR THE AGED:

- Shelter
- Food
- Clothing
- Medical Care

requires two things: First, resources essential to the discharge of the duty, and occasion for such discharge.

Let us have chart number nine, please. This will indicate to you what is involved in that for which I am contending this evening. Here, if you please, is chart number nine.

Observe what it says. In Gal. 2: 10 Paul said that the other apostles would that they should remember the poor, by which, of course, he simply meant to take care of their needs. Now, this requires for the orphan: First, a place; second, food; and third, clothing; an education, supervision, and medical care. For the aged it requires shelter, food, clothing, medical care. Now, I ask Brother Porter if this is involved in the need of which I am speaking. If he admits that it is, then I ask him to tell me what situation obtains when you supply that. One of two things must be done now. He must deny that we have an obligation, or else he must say that obligation can be scripturally presented in some other fashion than that of an orphan home.

But let me read a little farther from Brother Porter. Here, he is replying to what Brother Waters said about instrumental music. "But instrumental music, which he introduced, is not parallel with those ideas, for the simple fact that when the Lord said to immerse or bury, whether you bury or baptize a man in a baptistry, in a lake, in a pond, or wherever you may be, you are doing nothing but baptize."

BROTHER WATSON: "Three minutes."

Thank you. "And whenever you lay by in store of your means, if you put it in a hat, a box, or a basket, you do nothing but give, and that's what the Lord says. And whenever you eat the bread, whether it's in the plate or out of the plate, you do nothing but eat. And whenever you drink, whether it's out of one container or a dozen containers, you're doing nothing but drink." Now, Brother Porter was reasoning correctly there. What was his point? That the means for doing a thing inheres in the command. Now then, he must take the position in this debate that the means do not inhere, at least the means characteristic of the orphan home which I am tonight defending.

He may say that such is on a par with the Missionary

Society. I wish, before my time is out in this very first speech, to introduce this question. That is chart number two, please. And I think in the two remaining minutes we will have the time.

You will understand that I am merely introducing the subject here. I have here on this side, the Missionary Society; and on the other side, the church. Now, a Missionary Society is composed of churches, individuals, and non-members. And, the Missionary Society operates in the field of missions, hospitals, and schools, and papers, and orphan-

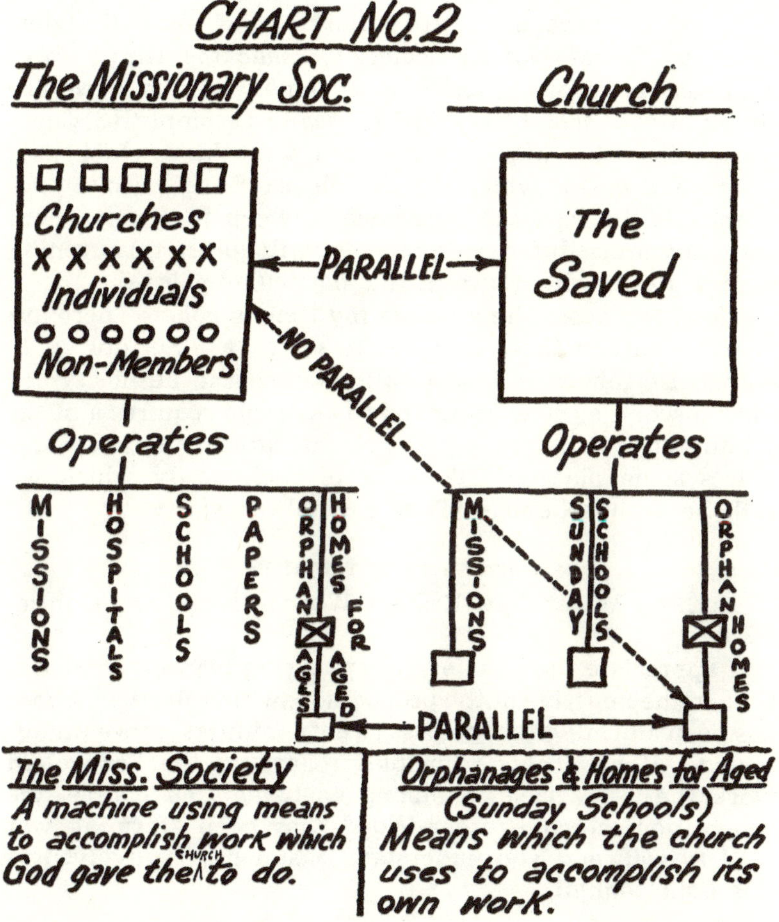

ages, and homes for the aged, whereas the obligation of the church is with reference to missions, and teaching, edification, and the care of the needy in orphan homes. Now, it is ridiculous to say that there is a parallel between the orphan home and the Missionary Society. They do not operate in the same realm. There is a parallel between the orphan home *that* the Missionary Society operates and the orphan home *that* the New Testament church operates, and there is a parallel between the church of the Lord and the Missionary Society. Now, get this difference, please. The difference between the Missionary Society and the orphan home is this. Let's raise it just a little, please. I have a word left out here, and I will supply it, and you will understand it. The Missionary Society is a *machine using means,* whereas the orphan homes and homes for the aged are simply *means which the church uses* to accomplish its own work. It is the difference between a machine which uses means and means which the church itself uses. Now, that, friends, is the essential difference between the two. There are many other differences, but that will suffice this evening to indicate the difference at this particular point.

Now, one other thing before my time is gone. There are many details in these duties with which the Scriptures do not deal. Inherent in the obligation is the authority for their discharge. The command to assemble requires a place, a building, or equipment, just as the care of the needy requires some place to take care of such needy which we call the orphan home. (Time called.)

Porter's First Negative

Brethren Moderators, Brother Woods, Ladies and Gentlemen:

I appreciate the privilege of appearing before you at this time in the negative of the proposition, which Brother Woods has been affirming for the past twenty minutes, as we undertake to discuss these principles regarding the benevolent work that is carried on among us today. Of course, the proposition which Brother Woods has been affirming was read to you; and you understand just what is involved in this issue tonight.

Brother Woods and I have been close friends through the years, and I am sure we will continue to remain close friends even after this discussion is over. And, of course, Brother Totty told you also that I was here in a meeting some years ago; and I remember with interest that meeting in which I engaged with the Garfield Heights church; and I am glad to be back upon this occasion to enter into this period of discussion at this time.

There are a number of things that I would like to say. Of course, we are limited in the amount of time that we have, and just two or three things I might mention. Unity, I am sure, is a thing that is greatly to be desired. David said, "Behold how good and how pleasant it is for brethren to dwell together in unity!" (Psalm 133: 1.) Paul, in 1 Cor. 1: 10, admonished the Corinthian brethren "that there be no divisions among" them, but that they "all speak the same thing" and "be of the same mind and the same judgment." Yet, of course, I am sure that both Brother Woods and I agree that peace at any price would not be desirable. And, as a result, we are engaged in this discussion tonight regarding the principles of benevolent work that should characterize the church today.

I want you to understand also in the very beginning of this discussion that there is no place for an appeal to prejudice or to emotionalism. It isn't a matter of whether or not we believe in caring for orphans or otherwise. I am sure of the fact that I believe in caring for the orphans and for the aged and for the needy as much so as does Brother Woods. Anything along that line would, of course, be entirely contrary to the demands of the issue, for we are concerned about what the Scriptures teach regarding these matters.

I appreciated very greatly the splendid way in which Brother Woods went into a discussion of these principles in the speech that just preceded this. And it is not, as though he would seem to indicate, purely and simply a discussion of "methods." There is more involved in it than this—not merely "methods," but a discussion of "organizations." In fact, his proposition says that "it is in harmony with the Scriptures for churches to build and maintain benevolent organizations"—not merely some sort of systematic arrangement, or some systematic approach, or procedure, or something of that kind; or some method, or some manner, or some mode. But the question concerns that of *organizations.* Actually, the proposition says that "The churches may build and maintain benevolent organizations for the care of the needy." And, of course, that will be discussed more as we go on during these four nights.

But I have some questions I want to hand to Brother Woods; and if someone will hand him this set, please, as I read them, I shall appreciate it.

1st. What is the significance of the word "corporation"?

2nd. What is the meaning of "a body corporate and politic"?

3rd. What "organizations in the church" have brethren "formed" in the past "to do the work the church itself was designed to do" that you opposed as "unnecessary and sinful"?

Now, as Brother Woods stated a while ago, we are not concerned about changes or things of that kind. We are not going to spend a lot of time discussing that. But I am concerned about *what kind of organizations* brethren had *formed* in the past to do the work that the church was assigned to do that he regarded as unnecessary and sinful.

No. 4. What organizations "similar" to "Missionary Societies" did brethren form "for the purpose of caring for orphans" in which you saw "grave danger"?

Now, we want to know what those organizations were. There were some similar; brethren had formed them. I shall demand that Brother Woods tell us what they were. Name some of them, Brother Woods, when you come up here. We shall demand that you do it. Now, we are going to stay after you till you do something about it.

And in the fifth place, or the 5th question. Would you endorse a centralized Sunday School Corporation, chartered under the laws of the state, placed under a Board of Directors, with a President, Vice-President, Secretary and Treasurer, to do the work of edification for churches throughout the brotherhood?

6th. If your answer to question number five is "No,"

then upon what basis do you endorse a similar arrangement for the benevolent work of churches throughout the brotherhood?

No. 7. Do churches have a right to build and maintain missionary organizations, chartered under the laws of the state, with the same officers and arrangements that are characteristic of our Benevolent Organizations, through which to do their work of evangelism?

8th. What New Testament teaching causes you to oppose the idea of churches supporting our Christian Colleges, but, at the same time, causes you to endorse the idea of churches supporting our Benevolent Organizations?

Now, I shall pass to the speech that Brother Woods made and pay my respects to the things that he said. And, as he stated regarding himself, I may also state that I am here simply in the interest of what I am fully convinced is *the truth.* And we intend to discuss those things.

Concerning the definition of his proposition, the only thing I might call attention to is his definition of the words "benevolent organizations." He defined that to mean "charitable enterprises." Well, I want to know just what sort of form those enterprises take. Are they organizations in the sense you used the term, Brother Woods, back yonder in the past when you opposed certain benevolent organizations that were among us then? When upon those occasions you said there was grave danger in matters of that kind—organizations formed for the purpose of caring for orphans? Or did you mean just what you mean here? He said concerning the Missionary Society that it is an organization and, of the sense, that it is an institution that rivals the church; but that he is using it simply in the sense that it refers to a "means" by which our work is done, and not to an organization in the sense of the Missionary Society. But there will be more about that, of course, as we go further along.

He tells us the proposition does not require him, or necessitate him, to defend the abuses that may be carried on in such benevolent organizations, or even to defend some isolated practices that may be carried on; and I am not insisting that he do defend those things. The thing I am insisting that he defend is that he has set up a human organization, a Benevolent Organization that is human in its origin, without any divine authority for its existence, to do the work which God has assigned the church to do. And so we shall have some use for that as the discussion continues.

Coming to his arguments, in the main, the first argument, he said, was based upon the fact that he did not know just how Brother Porter would proceed, or what he thinks about this matter; and, therefore, he would go into details about it. He introduced the idea that there are the needy to be cared for. To care for the needy is a New Testament doctrine. He gave us Eph. 4: 28, in which Paul told the Ephesian brethren to "labor with their hands" that they "might have to give to him that needeth." And, James 1: 27, "To visit the fatherless and widows in their affliction, and to keep himself unspotted from the world." And, in Acts 20: 35, "It is more blessed to give than to receive." These statements, he says, set out for us an obligation. I am sure that Brother Woods and I could shake hands on that. Nobody is disputing an obligation. That isn't even involved in the question tonight. It is not a matter of whether we have an obligation to care for the needy. It isn't that. It is through what organization are we to do the work? Is it to be done through our Benevolent Organizations, or organizations similar to them? Or through what organization are we to work? It is more than just recognizing an obligation that rests upon us or endeavoring to prove that there is an obligation.

Furthermore, he tells us it is not a matter of an emergency. It is not set up on an emergency basis, for in Mark 14 and 7 Jesus said, "The poor you have with you always." Well, I am not so much concerned about the word "emergency." It depends entirely upon what definition he may give to that word. Certainly, there is a *need*, and that is the thing that is involved. And we are concerned about taking care of, or giving aid to, or relieving those who are in need, whether it came about suddenly or otherwise. I am not so much concerned about that. There is a need there that brings an obligation.

Then he says this obligation extends to the church, and gave us 1 Tim. 5: 16, in which Paul instructed Timothy concerning certain widows who were to be taken into the care of the church. Some could not be who had relatives to support them, and that obligation rested upon them; and Paul declared that they should discharge that responsibility and "let not the church be charged" with it, "that it may relieve" those who are "widows indeed." Why, certainly I believe that the church has an obligation to relieve widows indeed; but that isn't the question. That isn't the question in Eph. 4: 28, James 1: 27, Acts 20: 35, Mark 14: 7, or 1 Tim. 5: 16. The question is, Brother Woods, do these verses authorize you or me or the churches of the Lord Jesus Christ to set up human organizations through which it is to be done? Do the churches have a right *to build* and *maintain human organizations* through which this work is to be done, through which this obligation is to be met? It is not whether there is an obligation, Brother Woods. That is not it. Do churches have a right to build and maintain human organizations through which *to meet* those obligations? That is the issue, Brother Woods. You knew that, didn't you? Now, that is the issue; and so we are going to hold you to the issue. Discuss and tell us whether or not the church has a right to build and maintain human organizations through which this work (that God has assigned the church) to do. Can these obligations be met scripturally through human organizations, set up by men, unauthorized by the God of heaven? Remember, you said one time something about "boards and conclaves unknown to the New Testament." That is what we are talking about. Tonight you are contending for "boards and conclaves unknown in the New Testament," in which once there was "grave danger," and which could not be formed without it becoming "unnecessary and sinful." So we are concerned about those organizations.

But he tells us the Scriptures do not designate the "method" by which the work is to be done. He went on to say when the manner, of the work that is given to us, is designated, then the manner of it becomes just as binding, or just as necessary, as the work itself, or the commandment itself. But if the method is not designated, then it is left up entirely to us; and we can use any means which seems to be best according to our discretion of it. Well, we are going to try that on something else and see if Brother Woods is willing to stand hitched on it. And I have copied some statements here from Brother Woods (I have the books in my brief case there), and should he question them, I will produce them. And this one, at least, comes from the *Gospel Advocate* of January 11, 1945, concerning the "how."

"Equally conclusive is the argument drawn from the Great Commission. An analysis reveals that it embraces the following fundamental phases:

"What? Go teach—go preach.

"Which? The gospel.

"Who? The apostles, and, by implication, all of us today. (2 Tim. 2: 2.)

"Where? Into all the world.

"When? After enduement from on high.

"Why? To be saved; to have remission of sins.

"How?——"

A long blank is drawn after that word "how," Brother Woods. And then he comments on it and says:

"Answer to six of these questions regarding our responsibility in obeying the behests of our Savior are specifically set forth; one may search in vain for detailed instructions touching the manner of procedure for the last. The 'how' is nowhere specifically set forth."—An article by Brother Woods in the *Gospel Advocate,* January 11, 1945, page 22.

Then on the same page he said: "The specified details of the commission include the what, which, where, when, who and why. These are essentials. *The how is not given."*

Now then, Brother Woods says, regarding this other matter, when the method is not specified, when the how is not detailed to us, then it is left up entirely to us. Anything that seems to be to us the best thing that meets our judgment, or according to our discretion, we are privileged, or authorized to use. Brother Woods, will you work that on the Missionary Society in you next speech? Will you apply that to the Missionary organization? You say in the matter of preaching the gospel under the Great Commission, the details are not given as to how it is to be done, the manner is not set forth; and, therefore, it is left up to us to choose any way we want to. The Christian Church preachers for years have made that very same argument and said "that authorizes our Missionary Organizations." No details are given; so we have them. And they have them just like you got your Benevolent Organizations, Brother Woods. Notice that.

In First Pet. 4: 11, "If any man minister, let him do it as of the ability which God giveth." And certainly we agree upon that.

He had a difference between the Old Testament and the New, in one of which were some detailed matters, and the

CHART No. 10

THE ESSENTIAL AND THE INCIDENTAL:

THE ESSENTIAL	THE INCIDENTAL
• Go	• Walk, Ride, Fly
• Teach	• Radio, Classes, Charts
• Baptize	• Bap., Pool, Creek
• Lord's Supper	• Cups, Plates, Tables
• Contribution	• Baskets, Hats
• Praise	• Song Books, Parts
• Care of Needy	• Type of Home, Location, Size, No. of Needy, etc.

other, simply fundamental truths. Well, upon those fundamental truths of the New Testament, then, Brother Woods, can you accept a Missionary Organization, just as you accept a Benevolent Organization? If not, why?

Then he introduced chart number ten, on Essentials and Incidentals. He read from the Porter-Waters Debate, in that connection, referring to essentials and incidentals like baptizing and partaking of the Lord's supper and things of that nature, as he had on the chart. And I might make this statement just here, that my position tonight on incidentals is exactly the same that it was when I met Brother Waters in that debate. And all the incidentals involved in there did not involve human organizations, Brother Woods, and I did not introduce a statement there to support any human organization of any kind, not even a Sunday School Organization. When we were discussing Bible classes, I did not try to sustain a *Sunday School Organization.* An organization, set up and chartered under the laws of the state, to do the work of edification is not parallel to our Bible classes. Nobody knows it better than Brother Woods does. And those means and those incidentals will not involve that organization; neither does it involve the one that he is defending tonight. It is more than a means or an incidental.

He tells us then of two things that would be required. First, there is a need; and second, there must be the resources. That came on chart number nine.

And in that connection he endeavored to show something about it for the orphans. There had to be a place, and food, and education, supervision, and medical care; and for the aged there is required a shelter, and food, and clothing and medical care. Certainly so. And all those will come within the realm of the duty, of the obligation; but in neither of them do I find a human organization listed—not even on your chart, Brother Woods. You find no place, even on your chart, for a human organization to do either of them, or any of them, because you were dealing with incidentals.

He read again from the *Porter-Waters Debate* regarding instrumental music, and that I said these are not parallel to the Lord's supper, in which we have plates and cups and things of that nature. Certainly so. Because a plate or no

CHART NO. 9

"REMEMBER THE POOR"

Gal. 2:10

THIS REQUIRES

FOR THE ORPHAN:

- A Place
- Food
- Clothing
- Education
- Supervision
- Medical Care

FOR THE AGED:

- Shelter
- Food
- Clothing
- Medical Care

plate, or a hundred cups or one cup, as far as the container is concerned, are but means. They are not human organizations; and *they are not parallel* to what Brother Woods is defending tonight. He is defending *human organizations.* It is not a means; it is not merely a method, or a manner, or mode. It is an organization. And I was not defending an organization in that speech from which he read in the debate there with Brother Waters some years ago.

Now, his chart number two, which was the final chart that he used, on which he drew the distinction between the Missionary Society and the church.

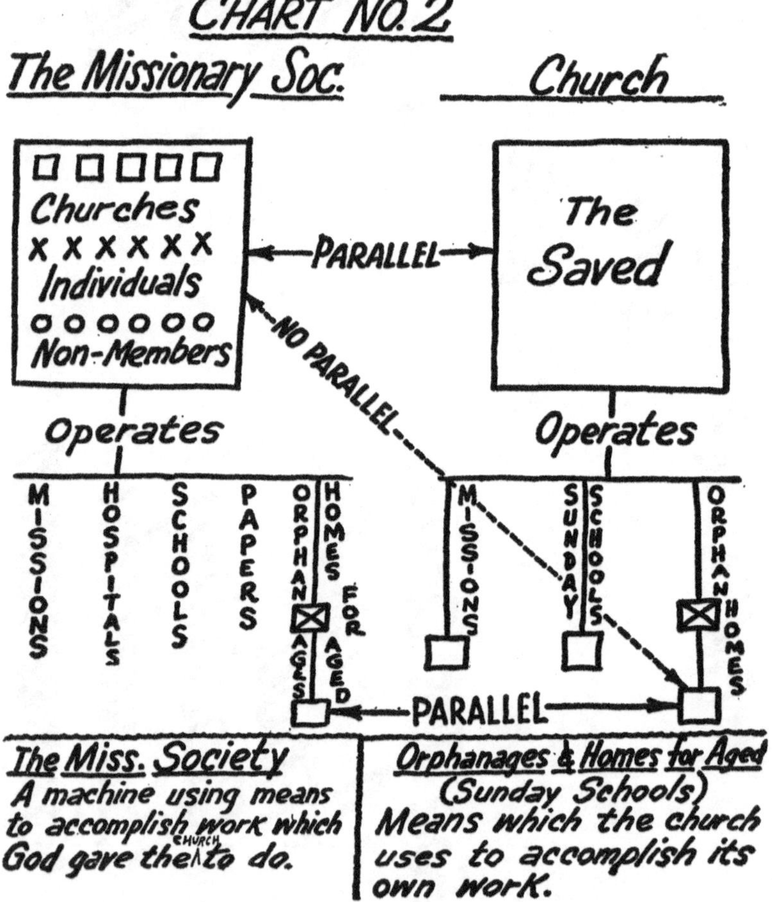

The Missionary Society contained certain things; and the church contained certain things; and they operated in different fields. They were parallel in some points, but not in all. And so he put them down like this: The Misssionary Society is a machine *using means;* and the orphan home is simply *a means.* Now, Brother Woods, will you tell me: Does the Orphan Home *use means?* Does it? You made the difference *between* the Orphan Home and the Missionary Society *in the fact that* the Missionary Society *employs means,* or *uses means,* to get the *work done;* but that *isn't true* with the Benevolent Organization. It is only a *means itself.* Now, you tell me: Does the Benevolent Organization *use means?* Do *they have* some method, some mode, some manner, to follow after you get the organization set up? I would just like to know about that.

(Time called)

And I thank you very kindly.

Woods' Second Affirmative

Brethren Moderators, Brother Porter, Ladies and Gentlemen:

I am happy to be back before you now for the second affirmation of the evening; and I am glad to take up Brother Porter's speech, item by item, and statement by statement, and deal with it thoroughly. I regret, however, that Brother Porter does not see fit to pursue the same course that I outlined in the beginning; for, instead of taking up the matter from a scriptural standpoint, the first thing he did was to bring in a number of statements that I made in times past, which may, or may not, have anything whatsoever to do with this question insofar as the scriptures are concerned. What I, or anybody else, may have said does not enter into what the scriptures teach on this question. What has Brother Porter done tonight? Instead of taking up the matter from a scriptural standpoint, he has based his whole contention on some statements which he alleges are in conflict with what I am holding here tonight. Now, even if he were right,—which he isn't—that doesn't meet the issue on this question. Now Brother Porter has to have something to say and something to do here, and that is the course that he follows. He leaves me no alternative but to follow him, and I am going to introduce this for the purpose of showing that Brother Porter is the fellow who needs to get busy and explain his statements.

I have here a letter which Brother Porter wrote, dated January 27, 1955. Not 1939, way back yonder fifteen or twenty years ago, but within this past year; and here is what he said: "Of course, Paul's instructions to Timothy regarding widows that should be taken care of by the church is pretty definite. If, however, there are enough old folks in Memphis to justify a home, old folks—I mean, who have no relatives to care for them, I suppose the Memphis churches could maintain a home for such if they sustain the same relationship to the home; but if a brotherhood project is to be set up to take care of old folks from all over the nation, I doubt the wisdom of such an undertaking."

Brother Porter believes we can organize and take care of all the old folks in Memphis, all the churches participating, provided that all sustain the same relationship to the home. There is just one way they could sustain the same relationship to the home, and that is for the home to be under a board, a conclave, if you please. You could not put it under an eldership, one of the elderships, for then the churches would not all sustain the same relationship to it. Brother Porter says that he thinks it will be all right for some twenty-five or thirty churches to combine their energies, but he doubts the wisdom of making it a brotherhood undertaking. Now, get it, please. He *doubts* the *wisdom* of it. It is not with him a matter of unscriptural procedure. He just doubts the wisdom of such a procedure. And, he stands before us tonight, advocating a position, the result of which is causing division in the church of our Lord over what he just *thinks* is a matter of wisdom. Brother Porter, you have asked me repeatedly tonight to explain the nature of the organization. When you get through explaining the kind of organization the churches of Memphis would have with this old folks home, I think we will be pretty close together on the type. Now you get busy on that, will you? When you get back up here, you tell us what kind of an organization that is. Remember now, it can't be any *human* organization. It just can't be!

I would much prefer, friends, to leave all such matters as that out, but what alternative do I have? He introduces it, and we will follow him on these matters point by point.

His questions: "What is the significance of the word 'corporation'?" Well, it means a body politic.

"What is the meaning of a body corporate and politic?" It is an organization chartered under the laws of the state.

"What organization of the church had brethren formed in the past to do the work that the church itself was designed to do that you opposed as unnecessary and sinful?" I was discussing at the particular time the Missionary Society and any organization that is on a par with it.

"What organization similar to Missionary Societies did brethren form for the purpose of caring for orphans in which you saw grave danger?" The brethren haven't organized any organizations similar to Missionary Societies among us. I have shown you in my previous speech the difference.

"Would you endorse a centralized Sunday school corporation, chartered under the laws of the state, placed under a board of directors, with a president, vice president, secretary and treasurer, to do the work of edification for the churches throughout the brotherhood?" That is a moot question. It would be impossible to arrange such today. There is no situation that could call for such, and so there is no point in asking such.

"If your answer to number five is, 'No,' then on what basis do you endorse a similar arrangement for the benevolent work of churches throughout the brotherhood?" I don't endorse such an arrangement as that. There is no similarity between the two.

"Do churches have a right to build and maintain missionary organizations, chartered under the laws of the state, with the same officers and arrangements that are characteristic of our benevolent organizations, through which to do their work of evangelism?" Such as you here describe would not be the same as that which we are doing, and therefore, is not pertinent to this question.

"What New Testament teaching causes you to oppose the

idea of supporting Christian colleges, but at the same time causes you to endorse the churches supporting our benevolent organizations?" If I were to take up that and discuss it as Brother Porter wishes I would, I would have no time to discuss the question of benevolence. The subject of the Christian colleges is not involved in this discussion; and hence, so far as I am concerned, has no place here. I could bring up the question of the religious papers and matters of that kind, but I do not at this point intend to introduce it and, therefore, I am going to leave that for the time being. If Brother Porter insists on it, we shall be glad to deal with it further.

Now, I believe in being as good to him as he is to me; so I have some questions for him, too! Would you hand them to him?

1. Do you affirm that any organization performing religious duties not essential to the existence of the church is sinful? If not, what makes such an organization sinful?

2. Would you consider an orphan home, such as Boles, scriptural if it accepted contributions from individuals only, if it merely rented its services to the churches?

3. May a preacher use money which the churches give him for the support of his aged parents or orphan brothers and sisters? Could he bring them from another state and take them into his own home for this purpose?

4. May a congregation send a needy Christian, requiring specialized medical or surgical care, to a hospital or a clinic in an area far removed from the vicinity where such a person lives and holds membership?

5. Do you agree with the premise that when the Lord commands a thing to be done, but does not specify the procedure in which it is to be done, the procedure is in the realm of expediency?

6. Can you give the details or the manner in which the church provided care for the homeless and destitute widows of 1 Tim. 5: 16? If not, how do you know it was not in a home for the aged, such as Gunter, and other homes for the aged among us today?

Now, those are questions which Brother Porter will, we feel sure, take care of in his next speech. He tells us that he believes in caring for the needy. Brother Porter is on record as saying that he endorses the idea of caring for the needy. Well, now, fine! Now, Brother Porter, *where is the chapter and verse in this book* that specifies the procedure by which such care is to be accomplished? How are you going to proceed? How are you going to get that which the needy stand in need of *to the needy,* and in what fashion are you going to see to it that the needy have the care that you believe the New Testament teaches? That is the point, friends; and I put on the screen a few moments ago a diagram showing what would be required in the care of the needy. And I asked Brother Porter, which he neglected to mention, but which doubtless he will in his next speech, to tell us how you can administer such aid without describing the orphan home. Now, listen. He will tell you in every speech that he believes in the care of the needy. He will tell you that. But I am going to make a prediction. I am going to predict that this man on my left (Brother Porter) will remain as silent as the stars above us from this night through Friday night as to how to go about it. Now, that is a prediction I am going to make. You wait and see if I am wrong. I hope I am. I would be glad if Brother Porter would come up here and say, "Now, here is the scriptural way; here it is set out in detail." But I am going to make a prediction that he will tell you he believes in it; but he will let you leave here, not only tonight, but every night of this debate, *and he will never tell you how it is to be done!* Now, you wait and see if that is not right. Brother Porter, you have a task cut out for you. If I am not right in that, you get up here and prove to this audience that I am not right. You have said the ways that I am defending are not right, but you say there is a way that is right. Now then, get up here and tell us how to do it. Will you? You will, won't you? Won't you? (Laughter.) He *will not,* friends. You wait and see.

He says it is not a matter of method, but a matter of organization. Brother Porter is in conflict with himself. That explains, friends, why it was necessary for me in the outset to spend the time that I did in telling you what I mean by organization. We have all used the word "organization" in the sense of the Missionary Society; but it has a dictionary meaning too; and the dictionary meaning of it is to proceed in a systematic manner. When I use the word "organization" as applied to the care of the needy, that is exactly what I mean. A systematic manner of procedure. Now, get it. Whenever you send a basket of food out to a needy family, you resort to an organization. You have a systematic method of procedure. It may not be a highly organized affair. It may be a very simple organization, but the simplicity of it does not enter into it. Whenever you proceed in a systematic manner, that makes an organization. He says that it not the kind of an organization you have when you defend Tipton and Boles. I have the same kind of organization under consideration that he has with this Memphis old folks home. If he can have the Memphis old folks home, I can have the Gunter Old Folks Home. If not, why not? Ah, Brother Porter, I am thinking you are going to wish you had stayed with the scriptures before this debate is over.

He says that we want to set up a human organization to do the work which God assigned the church to do. He argues on both sides of the question. At one time he takes the position that the organizations are no part of the church and, therefore, rivals of the church; and then on the other hand, he comes along and says that we have set up an organization that is performing the work of the church and, hence, makes it a church organization. Now, which one are you going to stay with? You have got to take one or the other. One time the orphan homes are wrong because they are apart from the church and no part of it; then, on the other hand, they are church organizations and performing work that God told the church to do. Now, Brother Porter, make up your mind which side you are on. He is taking two sides on us here tonight—already did it in his first speech. No, friends, in the sense in which he speaks of setting up a human organization, we are not doing this. I am simply maintaining that there must be some way for this church to get assistance to somebody out yonder in need. Now, then, how? It boils down to this position. I have had a number of debates with anti-Sunday-school people, and I have often stated in debate along that line that those people cannot conceive of the church functioning except in an organized capacity. Brother Porter's position tonight is exactly that; that the church cannot function except in its collective capacity. He can't conceive of the church functioning outside of its organized capacity; that is, its assembled capacity, except when he writes a letter about the Memphis churches establishing their old folks home!

There, friends, is the issue. He says, "Surely, the church has an obligation to care for the widows." Where is the passage of scripture that describes the method or manner? *Where* is it, Brother Porter? Now, you have stated repeatedly here that you believe it is right and that you believe the church has an obligation to do it. Now, how is the church going to carry it out? Friends, you will search this book in vain in trying to find *how* the church is to perform that duty. It's just not there. Brother Porter comes along and says you can't do it the way we are doing it. Well, then, if that is not right, he knows the way that is. Let him tell it. What is it? Again, I say this debate will close and Brother Porter will have remained as dumb as an oyster with reference to that question.

He read a statement from me with reference to the manner, or method, or procedure in the teaching of the great commission. He knows I was talking, or writing, there with reference to the manner of procedure in teaching. That was the point I was making. It had nothing to do whatsoever with the question of the public proclamation of the word, whether in an organization or otherwise.

But, now listen. Again, on this word "organize," Brother Porter believes that it is right for a part of the church to organize and conduct edification for itself and for others in the Bible school, in what is sometimes called the Sunday school. Now, is the Sunday school the church? It is not in the sense that it is organized exactly as the church is. It is in that sense *another* organization, because it is a separate procedure; and yet Brother Porter is on record as defending that. And I tell you, friends, his position with Waters in that debate will be a millstone around his neck in this discussion. I am unable to see how he ever found it in his heart to enter this discussion in the light of his statements in that debate. He says his position is the same as it was in the Waters debate. In that debate he contended that the Scriptures were silent with reference to methods of procedure. He maintained that there are many practices that are scriptural and that are not mentioned in the Bible. "Thousands" of things, he said. Therefore, Brother Porter believes that in the realm of matters not specified that we are at liberty to proceed as we might find best under the circumstances.

Then he says that the cups is not an organization. Well, now, isn't the administration of the Lord's supper an organization? We talk about the Lord's supper being instituted. We speak of the procedure that is characteristic of the service. Isn't there an organization in the sense of a systematic procedure in the administration of the elements of the Lord's supper to the congregation? He knows there is. Brother Porter, where is the passage of Scripture that specifies that six, or ten, or fifteen people are to stand here around the table and pass the emblems to the congregation in the manner that is characteristic of it? Where is the passage of Scripture that specifies that? Is that a part of the organizaion of the church? Is it? Now, there again, friends, is an illustration of it.

He wants to know if an orphan home uses means. Well, in the sense that all Christians use means. Christians are members who are a part of the church; and, of course, they use means in the carrying out of their Christian duties. That is certainly true. But now, here is the distinction. And I would like for Brother Osborne, (Roy Osborne who operated the opaque projector for the charts) from California, to give us that chart again. The chart on the Missionary Society.

Thank you. And I would like for Brother Porter to see a thing he did not answer in his other speech. In the first place, friends, the Missionary Society is a super organization composed of churches, individuals, and non-members. It operates in the field of missions, and hospitals, and schools, and papers, and homes for the aged and orphans. It is ridiculous to talk about a super organization like that being

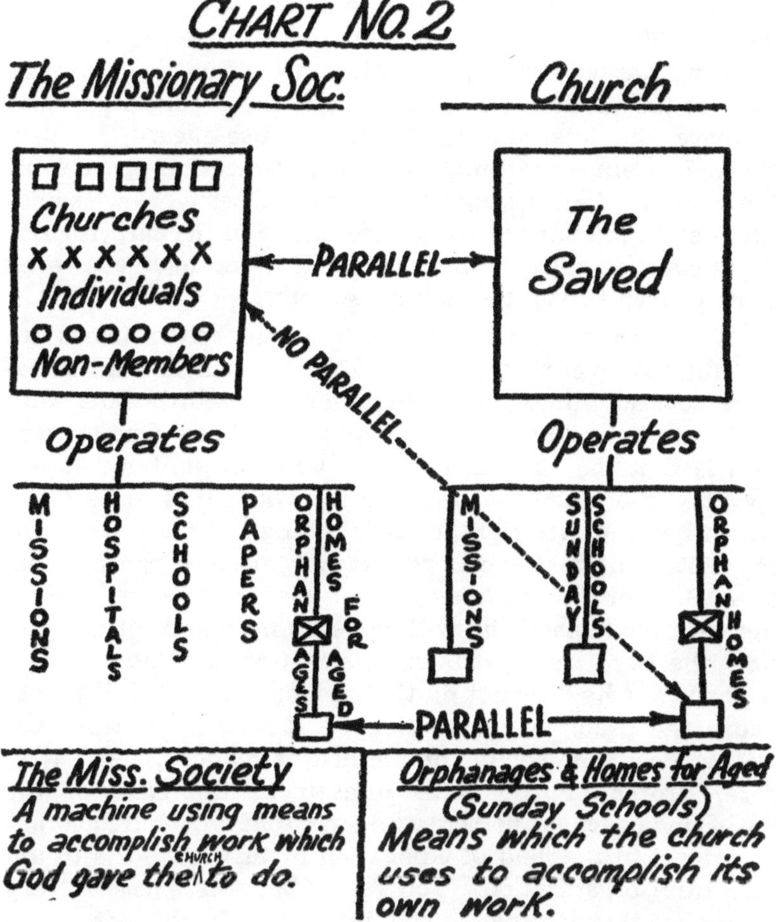

parallel to orphan homes. There isn't a parallel between the orphan home and the Missionary Society. There is a parallel between the orphan home that the Missionary Society operates, and one of the orphanages among us today, in the sense that they are on the same level, or same basis. There is a parallel between the church and the Missionary Society. That is the reason why the Missionary Society is wrong. *It is a machine using means to accomplish that which God ordained that the church should do, whereas the orphanages, the homes for the aged, the Sunday schools, and so on, are the means which the church uses to accomplish its own purpose.*

Now, I asked him this question in the matter of edification, in the matter of Sunday school, the organization that is there characteristic of it: Does it use means, Brother Porter? I am not asking: Is it an organization apart from the church? I am asking this question: Does what we sometimes style the Sunday school use means in the carrying out of its effort to edify or instruct? When you have answered that, you will have the picture exactly.

We do not maintain, friends, that the orphan homes are institutions rivaling the work of the church. I shall introduce several things along that line just a little later that will give you plenty of proof along that line. Our contention is that the Lord has told us what to do, but has not specified the method or manner by which it is to be done. Now, that is either right, or it is wrong. If I am wrong in my statement that the Lord has not specified the method, then Brother Porter knows what that method is; and in his very next speech he will come up here and set out just how the Lord said go about this matter of taking care of orphans. If he does not do that, friends, then it will be because the proof is not available. It will be because the Father does not specify the method or manner; and, therefore, Brother Porter finds himself in the class of the anti-Sunday-school person who says that the church is unscriptural in the field of edification in that it resorts to unscriptural organization. You remember this, please: Every argument that Brother Porter introduces in this debate tonight, or any night, against the idea of caring for the needy and orphan homes, such as Tipton and Boles, and homes for the aged, such as Gunter and others, has been made by the anti-Sunday-school people, with just as much force and effect, and just as pertinent to the matter, and just as scriptural; and both of them are wrong!

Now, that, friends, is the picture of this situation here tonight. I maintain that Brother Porter hasn't met the issue. He has sarted out on the assumption that our procedure is wrong because it is in conflict with the Bible. Now, then, let him tell wherein it is wrong and why it is in conflict with the Bible. (Time called.)

I thank you.

Porter's Second Negative

Brethren Moderators, Brother Woods, Ladies and Gentlemen:

I am thankful for the opportunity of returning to the stand again to make a reply to the things that Brother Woods has just said, and I want to call to your attention the chart I have over here on the stand on which I have printed "The Church and Human Organizations," and beneath that, "My Opponent's Position."

Porter's Roll
Chart No. 1.

THE CHURCH and HUMAN ORGANIZATIONS

MY OPPONENT'S POSITION

CHURCHES CAN SCRIPTURALLY DO THEIR WORK OF BENEVOLENCE THROUGH HUMAN ORGANIZATIONS KNOWN AS ORPHAN HOMES AND HOMES FOR THE AGED.	CHURCHES CANNOT SCRIPTURALLY DO THEIR WORK OF EVANGELISM THROUGH HUMAN ORGANIZATIONS KNOWN AS MISSIONARY SOCIETIES.

1. BOTH BENEVOLENCE AND EVANGELISM ARE WORKS OF THE CHURCH.
2. BOTH INSTITUTIONAL HOMES AND MISSIONARY SOCIETIES ARE HUMAN ORGANIZATIONS.

— — — — — — — — — — —

WHAT MAKES THE DIFFERENCE?

And here is the position occupied by my opponent: that "Churches *can* Scripturally do their Work of Benevolence through Human Organizations known as Orphan Homes and Homes for the Aged"; but "Churches *cannot* Scripturally do their Work of Evangelism through Human Organizations known as Missionary Societies." "First, Both Benevolence and Evangelism are Works of the Church." And, "Second, Both Institutional Homes and Missionary Societies are Human Organizations." "What makes the difference?"

Of course, he has tried to explain a little to us during

the speech he has just made; but we shall attend to that when I get to it. But I want you to keep that chart in mind now as we go along, meditating upon the position which Brother Woods occupies tonight, that the church or churches *can* scripturally do their work of benevolence through human organizations. It is more than a mere arrangement, more than a systematic approach, Brother Woods. It is more than that. But they *cannot* scripturally do their work of evangelism through human organizations known as Missionary Societies. Now, both *evangelism* and *benevolence* are *works of the church.* Why *can* they do one of them through human organizations but *cannot* do the other through human organizations under the same setup, and after the same arrangement?

Well, first, I will deal with the questions which he asked me.

First. "Do you affirm that any organization performing religious duties not essential to the existence of the church is sinful? If not, what makes such an organization sinful?" Well, to the first part of it, I would say, "No," just as the same thing is true with you, Brother Woods. And there are some duties that run parallel. You remember you had a debate one time with Leroy Garrett out in California. You were discussing the Bible college question—and you did a masterful job in it, Brother Woods. But at the same time, you made an argument that duties oftentimes run parallel; that there are duties which belong to the church, and there are duties which belong to individuals; and that a distinction must be made between the individual and the congregation as such. Upon that basis you justified the Bible college, an organization that can do a similar work that the church was doing, and yet the church not be involved in it, all because you did not endorse the churches supporting those Bible colleges. All right.

Second. "Would you consider an orphan home, such as Boles, scriptural if it accepted contributions from individuals only?" Well, if I did or didn't, it still would not touch the question before us tonight. After all, we are discussing whether or not *churches* have the right, not whether *indi-*

viduals have the right. That isn't even involved in it, Brother Woods, as far as that goes. The question is: Do churches have the scriptural right to build and maintain human organizations or benevolent organizations? It isn't a matter of what an individual may build, an individual enterprise. That isn't even involved in it. And "if it merely rented its services to the churches?" But if Boles Home was set up simply as an individual enterprise, just as a hospital might be, and things of that kind, and somebody wanted to help it, I suppose he would have as much right to help it as he would the Bible college which you agree that he has the right to help.

Third. "May a preacher use money which churches give him in the support of his aged parents and orphaned brothers and sisters?" Yes. "Could he bring them from another state and take them into his own house for this purpose?" Yes, they are still his obligation, Brother Woods.

Fourth. "May a congregation send a needy Christian, requiring specialized medical and surgical care, to a hospital or clinic in an area far removed from the vicinity where such a person lives and holds membership?" Yes. But, Brother Woods, do you think that is parallel to its making a contribution to a hospital or clinic? Turning its work over to them to do for it? Do you think that is parallel? Brother Woods, you tell us this: May a congregation make a contribution to a hospital or a clinic in an area far removed from its vicinity and tell them to go ahead and take care of those that are afflicted? Does a congregation have that right to do that? Now, we will see what distinction you make between duties that run parallel.

Number five. "Do you agree with the premise that when the Lord commands a thing to be done, but does not specify the procedure in which it is to be done, the procedure is in the realm of expediency?" Well, that depends upon what you mean by *procedure*, Brother Woods. If you mean only a method, or a means, or a mode, or a manner in which it is done, yes. If by the word "procedure" you mean he has a right to set up a human organization with a president, and a vice-president, and a secretary, and a treasurer, chartered under the laws of the state—and operating in a realm like that, I would say, "No."

Number six. "Can you give the details of the manner in which the church provided care for the homeless and destitute widows of 1 Tim. 5: 16? If not, how do you know that it was not a home for the aged, such as Gunter, and other homes for the aged among us?" Well, I might answer that by asking him one. Brother Woods, can you give the details of the manner in which the church preached the gospel to the lost, according to Matt. 28: 19? If not, then how do you know that the means which they followed were not the same thing as the Missionary Society today? How do you know, if the details are not given, how do you know that it was not? So that gets you right back where you started, and that takes care of your questions.

Now, then, to his answers to my questions. I want to notice the things he said also in his speech. First, I want to call attention to this. He said, "Brother Porter did not do as I had hoped he would. He did not take up the matter from a scriptural standpoint and discuss it, but he read statements that I made sometime in the past that do not prove the proposition one way or the other. So he has introduced that into it and it has nothing to do with it." Well, Brother Woods, why didn't you think of that when you were reading the *Porter-Waters Debate*? About cups and classes? (Laughter.) Why didn't you think about that? Do cups and classes have anything to do with the debate? Why, you're the man who introduced that, Brother Woods. It wasn't Porter. Porter was just following along in your tracks. You read from the *Porter-Waters Debate* before Porter ever said a word in this discussion—regarding cups, and plates, and baptistries, and things of that kind. Do they have anything to do with this issue today? And because I read something *you* said, why, that is altogether foreign to the matter and should never have *even been mentioned*. But, of course, that did not apply to Brother Woods when he came up and read from the *Porter-Waters Debate*, you see. He has special privileges along that line, I suppose.

Then he brought up a letter, written in January, 1955,

in which Brother Porter said that if the churches in Memphis have enough old folks that need to be cared for, that have no relatives that can care for them, that I supposed they could maintain a home for them if the churches sustained the same relation to it and did not organize or form a brotherhood project. And he came up with that, trying to make it parallel with what he is defending tonight. He had a number of things to say about it along during his speech, and I will get to some others as we go along. But, Brother Woods, did Porter say in that statement that they had a right to maintain or build a human organization with a president, and a vice-president, and a secretary, and a treasurer, and get it chartered under the laws of the state as a human corporation? Did Porter say that in that letter? I just challenge you to find anything like that in the letter. Not only that, Brother Woods, I am going beyond that. I am going to challenge you, Brother Woods, to find in the orphan homes and the homes for the aged *among us today* one that is conducted after that manner. Can you? Can you? You are trying to get me to endorse what you are contending for tonight by that letter, and that letter gave no endorsement to the setting up of a human organization. Don't the churches in Memphis provide and maintain homes for the preachers over there? Do they set up a human organization and charter under the laws of the state with a president, a vice-president, a secretary, and a treasurer over it, in order to have a home for the preacher? Couldn't they do the same thing for old folks? If not, why?

Now, to his answers to my questions. I asked, "What is the significance of the word 'corporation'?" He said it is a body politic. Do you mean it is a body? Are you going to stay with that, Brother Woods? That a corporation *is a body*? Is it? If it is, now, you have two bodies in spite of everything you can do, because the church is one body, and Paul said, "There is one body." The church is one body; and you get another corporation set up with a president, and a vice-president, and a secretary, and treasurer, and have *another* body. And he says it is a body. Also he has an extra body, an additional body to the church, doing the work of the church. He said it is a *body politic*. That is what it is. Well, that is what the orphan homes are. They are corporations. I have in my brief case over there some fifteen or sixteen charters under which the homes for the aged and the orphan homes we have in the United States today are incorporated. And he says they are bodies. Bodies, bodies. Brother Woods, let me ask you this question: Is the orphan home the church? I challenge you to say yes or no. Is the orphan home the church? You say it is a body. Now, I want to know if it is the church.

Second. "What is the meaning of 'a body corporate and politic'?" And he said, "Well, it's a group that has obtained a charter under the laws." All right.

And third. "What 'organizations in the church' have brethren 'formed' in the past 'to do the work the church itself was designed to do' which you opposed as 'unnecessary and sinful'?" He said Missionary Societies. All right.

Fourth. "What organizations 'similar' to 'Missionary Societies' did brethren form 'for the purpose of caring for orphans' in which you saw 'grave danger'?" And he said they have not organized anything similar to it. They haven't? Are you right sure, Brother Woods? They have not organized anything that is similar to it? Now, listen to this. This is taken from the Abilene Christian College Lectures in 1939, pages 53 and 54, and Brother Woods said: "This writer has ever been unable to appreciate the logic of those who affect to see grave danger in Missionary Societies, but scruple not to form a similar organization for the purpose of caring for orphans and teaching young men to be gospel preachers. Of course, it is right for the church to care for the fatherless," and so on, and he went on to endorse the Tipton Orphan Home in that connection. Now, he said brethren have not scrupled to form such organizations. What were they, Brother Woods? You said they formed some. You say now they didn't. Back in 1939 you said they had formed some like that. Right back up here you made the same statement: "We are unable to view the future with that unalloyed optimism which seems so characteristic of some. That God's people will ultimately triumph, we have not the slightest doubt; yet we think we see on the horizon signs which augur ill for the cause of primitive New Testament Christianity." And then he said, "The ship of Zion has floundered more than once on the sandbar of institutionalism." It *has* done it *more than once.* "The tendency to organize is a characteristic of the age. On the theory that the end justifies the means, brethren have not scrupled to form *organizations in the church* to do the work the church itself was designed to do. *All such organizations usurp* the work of the church, and are unnecessary and sinful." Now, he said the Missionary Society is one of them. Then he said there were others. *"All such organizations."* What are some of the others? Tell me some of the other organizations brethren formed back in that day that you opposed. I want to know what they look like. Will you tell me what those organizations were? And among them he mentioned organizations to care for the orphans. Yet he says now they hadn't done any such thing. But in 1939 they had. Now, I want to know the name of some of those organizations that Brother Woods opposed in that day.

Number five. "Would you endorse a centralized Sunday School Corporation, chartered under the laws of the state, placed under a Board of Directors, with a president, vice-president, secretary and treasurer, to do the work of edification for churches throughout the brotherhood?" And he said it is impossible to arrange such a thing. It would be impossible for brethren to form any such organization. Well, it was possible for them to form one like this over here. They could set up an organization through which the church could do its benevolent work—churches all over the brotherhood. Get it chartered under the laws of the state, have a centralized effect out of it, have a Board of Directors, and the Board of Directors contain President, Vice-President, Secretary, and Treasurer; and the most of them have just that, as their charters show definitely. He says you could not set up a thing like that for the Sunday school, for the Bible teaching, but you can set it up for a benevolent organization. One of them is impossible, and the other is possible and a reality. Now, Brother Woods, I want you to tell me why it is impossible. Why would it be impossible for brethren to set up a human organization like that to do the work of edification? Will you tell us?

How much time do I have?

BROTHER DOUTHITT: "You have five minutes."

Five minutes—thank you. Well, then, here is one more, I believe, maybe two.

Number seven. No, number six. "If your answer to question number five is "No," then upon what basis do you endorse a similar arrangement for the benevolent work of churches throughout the brotherhood?" He says, "I don't." Well, then, let us just shake hands and quit the debate. That is exactly the same arrangement you have in the Benevolent Organization today; and if you don't endorse that, what are you doing over here, Brother Woods? Why did you come here? Why did you come to Indianapolis? *Why did you come here if you don't endorse that?* That is the kind of arrangement that you have in the benevolent organizations. The very things that I described there for a Sunday School Organization are the things that are characteristic of the benevolent organizations that you are defending; and yet you say, "I don't endorse it." You don't, but you do.

Number seven. "Do churches have a right to build and maintain missionary organizations, chartered under the laws of the state, with the same officers and arrangements that are characteristic of our benevolent organizations, through which to do their work of evangelism?" He said, "They are not the same." They are not the same. Well, I didn't say they were. I said, "Could they build one like it?" That's what I am asking you. I am not asking you whether the Missionary Societies, as the Christian Church has today, are the same. I am not asking you that. I asked you: "Do churches have the right to build and maintain Missionary organizations, chartered under the laws of the state, with the *same officers* and *arrangements* that are characteristic of our benevolent organizations, through which to do their work of evangelism?" Do brethren have *the right* to do it? That is what I am asking you. I am not asking you whether it is exactly the same as the Christian Church Missionary Society or not. I want to know if churches have a right to build and maintain such missionary organizations, with the very same methods, the same arrangements, the same officers, the same board that we have in the benevolent organizations today. Can they do it? If not, why?

Number eight. "What New Testament teaching causes you to oppose the idea of churches supporting our Christian colleges, but at the same time, causes you to endorse the idea of churches supporting our benevolent organizations?" And he said, "Well, that would just take me too much time, and that is irrelevant anyway; that doesn't have anything to do with the proposition; and so I just dismiss it." And on the same basis you better dismiss the cups and plates and the baptistries that you brought up in the *Porter-Waters Debate*, because they have just as much relation to it as the other, and the other just as much as they have.

He wants to know about some matters here. He says Porter believes we can do it, and if he believes that we can take care of the needy, he said then you can't describe it without describing our human organizations, or our benevolent organizations. Brother Woods, are you saying that orphans can't be taken care of, and the widows can't be taken care of, except through the method that you are defending tonight? You say I couldn't describe a method that wouldn't be that. You say I couldn't describe a method by which the churches care for the widows and orphans without describing our benevolent organizations. Then, do you mean, Brother Woods, that the church cannot take care of the widows and orphans except through benevolent organizations like we have? That is the only way? That is what your question implies. That is what your statement means. Tell us about it when you take the floor again.

He wants to know, then, on 1 Tim. 5: 16 again, where is the method of caring for the needy that the New Testament specifies, and became a prophet about the matter of "how," *how* they can be taken care of, and predicts that Porter will never say *how*. He'll be as dumb as an oyster. That may be so. We will see. The debate isn't over yet, Brother Woods. But he will be as dumb as an oyster, he says, about the "how." But just at the present time I want to ask you a question in that connection and see how dumb you are. (Laughter.) Listen, Brother Woods, will you tell me what method is specified by which to carry out the proclamation of the gospel in Matt. 28: 19? Does it specify the *how?* You tell me *how* it is to be done; and when you tell me *how,* will you describe a Missionary organization? If not, why not? If I have to describe a benevolent organization in order to tell you *how* to care for orphans, since the *how* is not specified or detailed, you will have to describe a Missionary organization of some kind in describing *how* the gospel is to be preached, since the Bible does not detail the *how.* Now, let us have some more on your "how."

He said it *is* a matter of methods, and *not* simply organization; that Porter is confusing the dictionary meaning of an organization; that the dictionary meaning is just a systematic method. Is that the only definition the dictionary has? Is it? Do you mean that is all the dictionary says about it? I don't believe you will take your stand on that, Brother Woods, and say that.

Now, he said, Brother Porter has in mind some kind of organization in Memphis, and he wants to know what kind of an organization did I have in mind in Memphis. I did not have any organization in mind *at all.* Is there an organization in Memphis that provides homes for the preachers over there? Do you have something set up over there and chartered under the laws of the state of Tennessee? Do you have a president, and a vice-president, and a secretary and treasurer overseeing those things in Memphis? Do you?

(Time Called)

Thank you very kindly.

Woods' Third Affirmative

Gentlemen Moderators, Brother Porter, Ladies and Gentlemen:

My prophecy holds good up to now, doesn't it? Brother Porter hasn't told us yet *how* the Bible teaches we ought to take care of the needy. He tells us that he is going to; but up to right now, when I have no further reply tonight, Brother Porter hasn't told us. Now, it is one thing to promise to do a thing, and it is another thing to do it. I still say that I am a good prophet, and I am going to continue to predict that Brother W. Curtis Porter will let this debate close, saying he believes in doing a thing, but won't tell us how to do it. You wait and see if that's not right. He knows a lot of things *against* it. He knows that the Bible teaches that the way we are doing it *is wrong*. He hasn't told us how to do it the right way, has he? Now, friends, a man is ethically obligated, particularly when Christian people have met for the purpose of testing the scripturalness of procedure, a man is obligated, especially when he says you are doing it the wrong way, to turn around and tell us the right way, isn't he? That seems to me to be an ethical obligation. And yet, Brother Porter has made two speeches tonight, and has spent his entire time telling you how not to do it.

Porter's Roll
Chart No. 1.

THE CHURCH and HUMAN ORGANIZATIONS

MY OPPONENT'S POSITION

CHURCHES CAN SCRIPTURALLY DO THEIR WORK OF BENEVOLENCE THROUGH HUMAN ORGANIZATIONS KNOWN AS ORPHAN HOMES AND HOMES FOR THE AGED.	CHURCHES CANNOT SCRIPTURALLY DO THEIR WORK OF EVANGELISM THROUGH HUMAN ORGANIZATIONS KNOWN AS MISSIONARY SOCIETIES.

1. BOTH BENEVOLENCE AND EVANGELISM ARE WORKS OF THE CHURCH.
2. BOTH INSTITUTIONAL HOMES AND MISSIONARY SOCIETIES ARE HUMAN ORGANIZATIONS.

— — — — — — — — — — — —

WHAT MAKES THE DIFFERENCE?

Now, he says here on the chart churches can scripturally do their work of benevolence through human organizations known as orphan homes and homes for the aged. He says I say that is all right. Yes. Churches cannot scripturally do their work of evangelism through the human organizations known as Missionary Societies. He says I say that's wrong. Yes. He is right. That's wrong. But, now get it: The difference here is in the fact that he shifts gears on me from one side of the chart to the other. He is using the word "human organization" in one sense here; (pointing to the chart) but when he gets on this side here, it is in another sense. Now, that is what I have tried to tell him all along tonight; when he speaks of the word "organization" as used on this side of the chart here, I simply mean the procedure with which you are carrying out the obligation which he says exists. When we get over on this side and apply it to the Missionary Society, he is talking about a machine that usurps the church and thus puts itself in the position of the church. Now, that is the difference. You watch it, friends. Neither Brother Porter, nor any other man on the top side of God's earth, can debate this question without using the word "organization" in two different senses. He talks about it in one sense for a while, and then he turns right around and he is talking about it in another sense. I will show that as we go along.

He said I did a masterful job in my debate with Brother Garrett. On the orphan home question? Brother Porter?

BROTHER PORTER: "Did I say that?"

No, you didn't. That was very significant. I debated the same question with Leroy Garrett that I am debating with Brother Porter. Do you know who Leroy Garrett is? Brother Leroy Garrett is a man who opposes the orphan homes in exactly the same fashion that Brother Porter does. And up to now, I will have to say that he did a better job in trying to explain his position than Brother Porter has done here tonight. Yes, Brother Porter, you have some things in common with Brother Leroy Garrett, and maybe with some other people about whom we may have to speak later.

He says that I introduced the *Porter-Waters Debate,* and yet I complained at him about introducing other matters. Now, Brother Porter, the difference there is this: I agree one hundred per cent with what you said in the Waters debate. That is the reason I introduced it, because I approved of the statement. But you don't agree with my position with reference to Tipton Orphan Home in the speech that I made at Abilene Christian College. There is the difference. I asserted that this is simply a splendid statement of the matter without the necessity of making the statement myself. But Brother Porter reads a statement from me with which he disagrees, and comes up here and says that they are both parallel. Just exactly the same. Ah, no, they are not the same.

Now, let me make this statement, friends. Back in 1939 I made a speech in Abilene Christian College on their annual lectureship program. Leroy Garrett, in my debates with him, read from that speech to prove that I do not believe in located preachers; *but I was a located preacher at the time the speech was made.* He read from this statement to prove that I do not believe in Christian colleges, *but I made the speech in Abilene Christian College.* He read from the statement to show that I did not believe in orphan homes, when at the time the statement was made the congregation for which I was preaching *was contributing to Boles Orphan Home!* Now, what was I doing in that speech back yonder ten years before anybody in the South ever thought of opposing the Christian colleges? I was doing what Porter and all the rest of us have done. I was preaching against any sort of an organization that usurps the function of the church. That is what I was doing. That is what a lot of us were doing. And, I could take such statements from the writings of all of us, because we were using the word "organization" in the sense of an organization rivaling the church.

Now, I want Brother Osborne to put on the screen our chart number one. It is just as good a time as any to discuss this. I shall show you that an organization can exist and yet not be objectionable.

Down just a little bit more if we can get it. We may not be able to get all of this on the screen here. But at any rate, the top of it says, "Organizations in Different Categories," or something of that nature. Now, here the Federal Government is an organization. The Post Office Department is another organization in the sense in which I am speaking of it here. But the Post Office Department does not usurp the functions of the Federal Government. It is merely a means by which the Federal Government carries

Chart No. 1
Organizations in Different Categories

Fed. Gov't.----Post Office Dept.
State Gov't.---Highway Dept.
Masonic Lodge---Homes for Aged.
Catholic Church---Orphanages.
Church of Christ---Orphanages & Homes for Aged

Rival These?
Do These

out that particular function. The State Government is an organization. The State Government has a Highway Department. The Highway Department is an organization; and, if you please, it is an organization that develops from the State Government. The Masonic Lodge is an organization. The homes for the aged that the Masonic Lodge operates are organizations apart from the Masonic Lodge in some sense, but they do not detract from the Masonic Lodge. They are simply means through which the Masonic Lodge acts. Anybody can see that. Then the Catholic Church has orphanages. Are these Catholic orphanages in conflict with the Catholic Church? Of course they are not. They are means by which the Catholic Church operates. Do they rival the Catholic Church? Of course not. Then the church of Christ operates orphanages and homes for the aged; and, while they are organizations that differ from the organizational setup of the church, at the same time they are merely means by which the church carries out its functions, just like the Catholic orphanages carry out the functions of the Catholic Church. The homes for the aged, the Masonic Lodge; the Highway Department, the State Government; and the Post Office Department, the Federal Government. Now, that, friends, is the sense in which I am talking about organizations. That is sufficient. Now, Brother Porter, instead of quibbling around, get up here and answer that! That will be more on the point.

And he says he believes in the Memphis old folks home. Yes. But then the reason that he thinks that is right, and something else wrong is, he did not have in mind any president, any secretary, any treasurer, or any human organization. It would be interesting to know, very interesting to know, how twenty-eight churches could combine their resources and operate an old folks home for all the needy destitute old folks in that area and not have *any kind of organization at all!* But he believes that that's possible. Now, Brother Porter, you have a second task assigned you. Get up here and tell us what kind of procedure that would be without *any kind* of organization. You say it isn't the organization necessarily, or it is not the fact that a home operates; it is just the fact that it has a president, a secretary, and treasurer, and so on. That is what makes it wrong, according to Brother Porter. It isn't the benevolent work that the homes do. That is not what is wrong with it. It isn't the fact that the homes exist. It is not even the fact that they are organizations apart from the church, in that sense. He says it is because they have presidents, secretaries, and treasurers, and so on!

Out in California a church can't exist unless it is incorporated under the laws of the state, and they have to have what is comparable to a president; at least it has to have a board of directors and a man who officiates over that board of directors in order for a church of Christ to exist in California. According to this man, every church of Christ in the state of California is unscriptural for they have all got presidents, and secretaries, and so on. Every one of them, Brother Porter. Every one of them. What about those churches out there? When you get back up here you tell us if those churches are right. Don't forget that, Brother Porter. I will remind you of it again tomorrow night.

Friends, I was disappointed. I do not hesitate to tell you that I was disappointed in the next thing that Brother Porter did. It is unfortunate that a fellow will resort to plain, straight-out quibbling rather than to admit that he is wrong. That is unfortunate. Brother Porter says now the matter that he had in mind for the churches in Memphis is just like the homes for the preachers. Every one of those churches down there, at least most of them, have homes for the preachers. He said that old folks home would be just like that. Is there a preacher in this audience tonight who remotely thinks there would be any parallel at all between the church buying a place for the preacher to live in, one congregation doing that for its own preacher, and *all the churches going together,* establishing a central place, and putting all the old folks in it? He said that was all right. Yet, he came up here and said it is just like each church buying its own preacher's home. Brother Porter, I'd be ashamed of that. I do not hesitate to say that is below the calibre of debating that is characteristic of a man like you. But, friends, when you haven't got anything to defend, you have to do something along that line.

He says the church is one body; the orphan home is another body. That is something he learned from Leroy Garrett. That is the only argument Leroy Garrett made. He made it every time he got up. He did just as well as Brother Porter did with it. He says that the church is one body; and the orphan home is another body; therefore, the orphan home is wrong. Well, the private home is *another* body too, isn't it? He believes that you can take an orphan into the private home. But any time you are doing the work of benevolence in another body, another organization, that makes it wrong; so then, the private home is in conflict with the church! Now then, he does not believe it is right to take care of the orphans in an orphan home; and if you take an orphan into a private home, you have another organization besides the church; therefore, that would make that wrong. I wonder how on earth he thinks it *is right* to do it. Now, suppose I should come up here and say that the right way to do it is to take them into your home. Remember now, the home is another body; and, therefore, you can't do it that way, because you have two bodies doing the same thing. And besides that, he has already said it is the church's obligation to do it; and if it is the church's obligation to do it, can the church work through your home? That is another one to put down, Brother Porter. Can the church work through your home?

He wants to know why it is that it is impossible to set up an edification society. Simply because you can't get all the students in all our Bible schools all over the world, all over the United States, or even all over this state, into one community. That is a moot question. The very idea of bringing up something along that line!

He asks, "Is the orphan home the church?" No. That is the reason why it is right, because it is not the church. That is the very thing that I am arguing here. He just dares me to answer yes or no. Well, I answered. I said, "No," it is not. That is the reason it is right. If it were the church, it would be wrong, because it would be a home trying to do the work of the church.

Now, what is the orphan home, friends? Basically, the orphan home is simply that which results when the church restores that which no longer exists. God has ordained two divine institutions; the church and the home. Now, get it: It is God's intention that all normal people, all people, have normal homes. But, sometimes, through misfortune, or for one cause or another, a home is gone. Now then, it is simply the effort on the part of the church to restore that which the child no longer has. So the home is not the church. It is not in conflict with the church. It is another organization in the sense in which the Post Office is another organization from the Federal Government, but it does not rival it. Now, that, ladies and gentlemen, is the truth on it!

He wants to know what organizations were organized in the past. Well, for example, the Woman's Board of Missions is one. I could mention a number of them. Get John T. Brown's history and there is a whole list of them in there. It will give you a lot of them.

He says, "I am going to answer your question by asking you another one." I never did like that way of answering my questions. Now, it might be all right to ask other questions; and I do not object to his doing that; but it doesn't answer one question to ask another. I never did learn anything by somebody asking me a question! I asked him a plain, straight-out question. Here is the question, and here is the reason he did not answer it: I said, "Brother Porter, what was the procedure by which the church in 1 Tim. 5: 16 took care of those widows?" He said, "I will answer that by asking you one." Well, I got a lot of information (?) out of that matter! Brother Porter, again I ask you the question: *How* did the church take care of those widows? You get busy on that. You haven't told this congregation. Well, he says, "Now, I will just ask you this: How did the church carry out the command to preach the gospel?" By doing what the Lord said to do. That's right. By just doing what he said to do. Well, how do you carry out the command to care for an orphan and the widow? Just do what the Lord said do. But did he say how to do it? There, friends, is where we get into this realm of expediency. It isn't a matter of what is said. It is the question of the matter of carrying out what he said. And remember this fundamental principle (you know Brother Porter dodged my question on that), but I will get to that in just a moment. At any rate, it is back to this principle that, when the Lord tells us to do a thing, but does not tell us how to do it, it is up to us to follow the best method outlined at the time.

Do you affirm that any organization performing religious duties not essential to the existence of the church is sinful? Well, he says, "No," he doesn't. Well, all right, then. He says it is not wrong for an organization—he even referred to me here—to exist. Brother Porter thinks it is all right for organizations to exist, performing religious duties, just so they are not supported by the church.

He has said that the Missionary Society and the orphan home are parallel. He has also said that you can form an organization, provided you support it individually. Now, get it! I asked him this question: Would you consider an orphan home, such as Boles, scriptural if it accepted contributions from individuals only, if it merely rented its services? He said, "I would consider that to be right." Now, look: He believes it is parallel to a Missionary Society; therefore, it is wrong for the church to support it. But he says an individual can support it; therefore, *he believes an individual can support a Missionary Society, as long as the church doesn't do it!* Now, if not, why not, Brother Porter? One of two things is true. Either the Missionary Society and the orphan home are not parallel, in which case your argument breaks down, and you try to make it appear that they are; or else you believe an individual can support a Missionary Society. Now, put it down in black and white and answer that question: Can an individual support a Missionary Society?

BROTHER WATSON: "You have five minutes."

Thank you. May a congregation send a needy Christian, requiring specialized medical and surgical care, to a hospital or clinic in an area far removed? Well, "Yes," he says. He wants to know if a church can make a contribution to it. Well, if it were purely a procedure set up for caring for those who were of the church alone, of course, it could, because it would be the church doing it. I am not talking about a secular institution set up to make money. I am talking about one in the field of benevolence. That is what I am talking about.

Do you agree with the principle that when the Lord commands a thing to be done, but does not specify the procedure in which it is to be done, that the procedure is in the realm of expediency? "Yes." But he says, "I don't agree that you can have a president, and a secretary," and so on. So then, it isn't the fact that we proceed systematically; it is the fact that the orphan homes have a president and a secretary. Now, let him tell us how the orphan homes can operate *without* a president and a secretary; and we will be glad, I think, to get rid of our presidents and secretaries, if that is what is wrong with it.

Can you give the details of the manner in which the church provided for the homeless and destitute? He said, "I will answer that by asking you a question." Well, we found out all about it, didn't we? ? ? Surely did! Now, friends, that suffices for his speech.

I want to introduce another argument here, and I have a whole bunch of them, but I will have time but for one more. There are two divine institutions in the world: the family and the church. The establishment of the family is recorded in Gen. 1: 3; and, of course, we have the establishment of the church in Acts 2. These institutions, though their work overlaps occasionally, are not rivals, nor are they in competition with each other. The orphan home is not in competition with the church, because it is not performing the functions of the church, as such. The orphan home is not in competition with the child's natural home, because it hasn't any natural home. The orphan home is simply the result of an effort on the part of the church to supply for the child that which God ordained it should have, but lost. Now, whether this home is a small one with one child and directed by Christian parents, or whether it is managed by a group of brethren in its care of children is simply a matter of judgment and in the realm of expediency. That's all. It doesn't change the matter one bit, whether there is one or four hundred children. That hasn't a thing on earth to do with it. It is simply the church giving a home back to the child as far as it is possible.

Let's have chart number seven, please. It is admitted by all that it is right for a congregation to build a house in order to carry out its obligation to worship God; yet, there is no precedent for such in the New Testament, nor do we have a direct injunction from God to erect such. We believe that the authority for such a building is inherent in the

CHART NO. 7

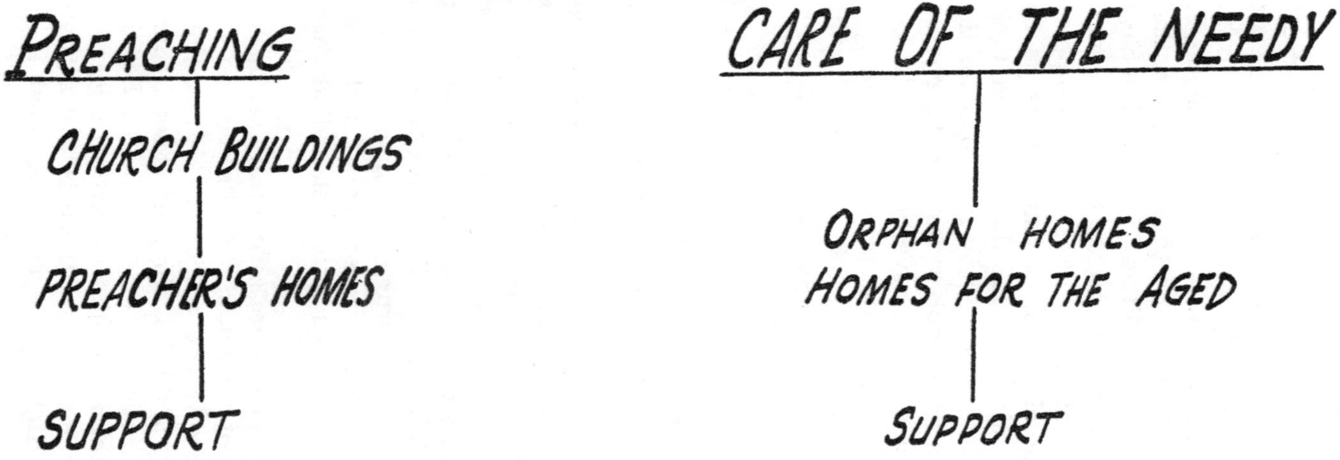

PREACHING	CARE OF THE NEEDY
CHURCH BUILDINGS	ORPHAN HOMES
PREACHER'S HOMES	HOMES FOR THE AGED
SUPPORT	SUPPORT

Cite Scripture for:

1. CHURCH BUILDINGS ______
2. BUILDING COMMITTEES, FINANCE COMMITTEES ______
3. Church-OWNED PREACHER'S HOMES ______
4. INCORPORATED CHURCHES ______
5. CHURCH TRUSTEES ______

command to worship and the example of the New Testament church in meeting on the first day of the week. The size, type, location, are all matters of expediency and in the realm of judgment. Now, friends, in the realm of preaching, it is right to have church buildings; and there is no mention of church buildings, as such, in the Bible. It is right to have preachers' homes. There is no mention of preachers' homes, as we have today, in the Bible; yet, it is right to support such. In like fashion, the obligation to care for the needy requires orphan homes and homes for the aged and their support. We have preachers who believe it is right for the church to furnish them a home, but wrong for the church to furnish the orphan a home. We have brethren who believe that the church can supply the preacher a place in which to live, to take care of himself; but it is wrong for the church to supply a home for the aged to live in. We have brethren who do that. (Time called.)

Thank you very much.

Porter's Third Negative

Brethren Moderators, Brother Woods, Ladies and Gentlemen:

This, now, is to be the concluding speech of this session of the debate. It will be just twenty minutes long. And I want, during that twenty minutes, to deal with the things which Brother Woods said in the speech that just preceded. The first thing I would like to have, brethren, is that chart used a while ago in which he had the Catholic Church with its orphanages, and the State Government, and so on—with its Highway Department. Chart number one? Chart number one, please. We want to take a little peek at that chart just here.

He is arguing that the homes are scripturally set up because they are *not rivals* of *the church.* And so he uses this chart on organizations in different categories. He said there is a Federal Government, and it has the Post Office Department, and that is also an organization—within the Federal Government. But that the Post Office Department *does not rival* the Federal Government. And there is also a State Government. It has a Highway Department. That is an

Chart No. 1
Organizations in Different Categories

Fed. Gov't.----Post Office Dept.
State Gov't.---Highway Dept.
Masonic Lodge---Homes for Aged.
Catholic Church---Orphanages.
Church of Christ---Orphanages & Homes for Aged

Rival These? Do These

organization—an organization within an organization, and so *it does not rival* at all. And the Masonic Lodge has its home for the aged on the same basis. And the Catholic Church has its orphanages. And they *do not rival* the Masonic Lodge and the Catholic Church. And so *our orphanages* and *homes for the aged* do *not rival* the church of Christ. "Do these rival these?" he said. That is the question down at the bottom (pointing to the chart). Now, then, it just happens that the Federal Government makes its own laws, and, therefore, can make its laws so as to include an organization within an organization. And the State

Government makes its own laws, and it can include a Highway Department as an organization within an organization. And the Masonic Lodge is a human organization that can make its own rules and regulations, and, therefore, can put its home within the realm of the organization, or the Masonic Lodge itself. And the Catholic Church operates upon its own authority, the authority of the pope as the head of it; and whatever it may see fit to organize as organizations within the church, from the standpoint of the Catholic Church, it has the right to do it. But when we come to the church of the Lord Jesus Christ, *who has the right* to set up an organization *within the organization?* Since *God himself did not set up* an organization within the organization, how are you going to make it parallel with these? You must have somebody in the church that has the right to *legislate.* That's what you have in all of these. In the Federal Government there is the power to legislate that can give them that. In the State Government there is the power of legislature, the legislative branch of the Government, that can make a law concerning the Highway Department. And so with the Masonic Lodge and the Catholic Church. But is there any such legislative power in the church of Christ today? Brother Woods, will you tell us? Will you tell us? Who has the right to make the laws that are comparable to the laws of these other organizations to put an organization *within the church?* Besides, you haven't forgotten, have you, that you said in that statement I quoted a while ago that when brethren formed "organizations *in the church,*" that such organizations became "unnecessary and sinful." *If they are in the church.* Now, since these do not rival these (pointing to the chart), and whatever these organizations have that do not rival these, upon the basis of Brother Woods' argument, you have the right to put into the church of Christ today. Well, the Catholic Church not only has orphanages which are organizations within the organization, but the Catholic Church, Brother Woods, has Missionary Societies—even Foreign Missionary Societies that do not rival the Catholic Church. Upon your argument, then, we can have Missionary Societies here today in the church, just as the Catholics do. So you have opened the gate wide for the introduction of Missionary Societies in the church today, Brother Woods. Talking about being ashamed of something, I'd take that home and hide it if I were you. (Laughter.)

Now, then, I lacked just two or three points finishing the other speech when my time was called, and I want to notice that as we go along. He said that "Porter is confused on this matter." "He has these organizations. One time he says they are human—they are human organizations." Then he says, "But later he turns around and says they are doing the work of the church; therefore, they are church organizations. He is all confused about it." Are you that badly confused on the Missionary Societies, Brother Woods? Are you? Are you as badly confused on the Missionary Societies as Brother Porter is on the benevolent organizations? Huh? One time you say the Missionary Societies are human organizations, and then you turn right around and say they are doing the work of the church—the work that God designed the church to do; and so they are church organizations. One time they are human organizations, and another time they are church organizations. Therefore, Porter is confused and contradicts himself; and I suppose Brother Woods is in the same position. We will just have a big time together, won't we, Guy? (Laughter.) And besides, Brother Woods, I want to ask you this. The contrast which I was making was not between *human* and *church,* but between *human* and *divine.* Do you know the difference between human organizations and divine organizations? The contrast is not merely between *human* and *church* but between *human* and *divine.* You won't say that all church organizations are *divine* organizations, will you? Will you? You'll have to, or else you will have to admit they are human; and if you admit they are human, then you have *church organizations* and *human organizations* which are the same thing. Yet that was the fault he tried to find with the argument Porter made regarding human organizations and divine organizations. Well, that's a little bit disappointing to a number of us, Brother Woods.

"Brother Porter," he said, "can't conceive of the church

operating outside of an assembly." I wonder where he got that idea.

On the Sunday School and the *Porter-Waters Debate*, he comes back to those things; but he brought them up in his next speech, however; and so I will get to them presently in that.

His chart on the Missionary Societies—and I want that now. That was chart number—? What was it where you had the Missionary Society and the church contrasted; what the Missionary Society does and what the church does; they are not parallel? One operates as a machine and the

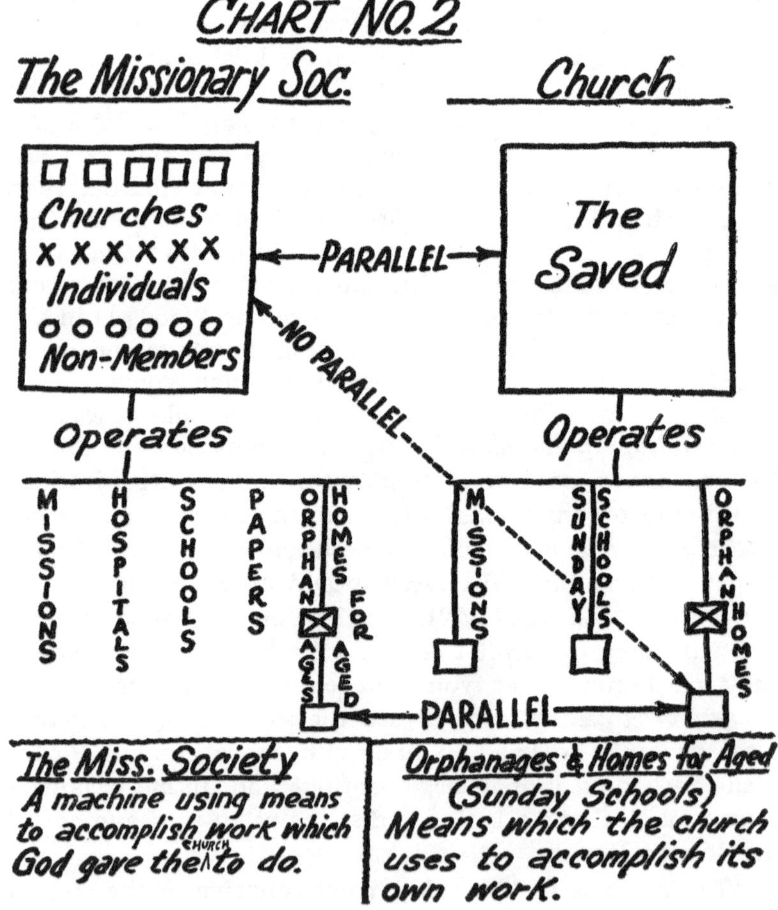

other simply as a means? We would like to take a little peek at that just here. (Someone answered, "Number two.") Number two. All right.

He has the churches under the control of the Missionary Societies, over here. And over there is the church or the saved. And this, he says, is just a "machine that uses means to accomplish the work God gave the church to do." The word "church"—he said he left out a word here (pointing to chart). It is the word "church." I did not discover just what it was until I started to read it. But the word "church" is left out. "The Missionary Society is a machine using means to accomplish the work which God gave the church to do." Well, is it a church organization then? And if it is a church organization, then I want to know, Is it a *human* organization, or a *divine* organization, Brother Woods? You have a mighty good "forgettery." I asked you a number of things a while ago, and you did not even refer to them. And I predict that you will not tell us about that. You may be "as dumb as an oyster" before this thing is over about (laughter) whether a church organization is a divine organization. Or can there be human organizations and church organizations—all the same thing? Are all church organizations divine? I wonder if he will tell us about it. So we have here the Missionary Society on one hand, the orphanages and homes for the aged on the other. And he puts Sunday Schools there, and these are *means* which the church uses to accomplish its own work. But I am asking about—and I did ask about—whether you believe in a Sunday School Organization, chartered under the laws of the state on exactly the same basis, with the same officers and the same arrangements we have in our benevolent organizations. He said it would be *impossible* to have a thing like that, because you just couldn't get *everybody everywhere* into one place. Well, you don't in our benevolent organizations, do you? No. I did not say you had to get everybody all over the world in one particular place. Take in just as much as we have in the orphan homes today. How many do we have? I don't know. Let's say fifteen or twenty in the United States. So we can have fifteen or twenty places for them. Would you endorse, Brother Woods, a Sunday

School Organization, chartered under the laws of the state, with the same officers and the same arrangements that characterize our benevolent organizations, and have them in twenty different parts of the states? Now, tell me about that. Would it be possible to get one like that?

And Brother Woods' "prophecy holds good until now." Porter hasn't told us *how*. And so his prophecy holds good *until now*. He said, "He tells us *how not to do it*." Yes, "He tells us *how not to do it*." Well, actually that is what my duty is tonight, Brother Woods. I am in the negative of this telling you *how not to do it*. That is what I am signed up to do. Exactly that's what the proposition requires of me. And so "he tells us *how not to do it*, but he doesn't tell us *how to do it*." And that will come up again just a little bit later, because he kept coming back to it.

Then he came to the matter on this chart over here, and he said, yes, *he agrees with this*.

Porter's Roll
Chart No. 1.

THE CHURCH and HUMAN ORGANIZATIONS

MY OPPONENT'S POSITION

CHURCHES CAN SCRIPTURALLY DO THEIR WORK OF BENEVOLENCE THROUGH HUMAN ORGANIZATIONS KNOWN AS ORPHAN HOMES AND HOMES FOR THE AGED.	CHURCHES CANNOT SCRIPTURALLY DO THEIR WORK OF EVANGELISM THROUGH HUMAN ORGANIZATIONS KNOWN AS MISSIONARY SOCIETIES.

1. BOTH BENEVOLENCE AND EVANGELISM ARE WORKS OF THE CHURCH.
2. BOTH INSTITUTIONAL HOMES AND MISSIONARY SOCIETIES ARE HUMAN ORGANIZATIONS.

WHAT MAKES THE DIFFERENCE?

He believes that "Churches *can* Scripturally do their Work of Benevolence through Human Organizations known as Orphan Homes and Homes for the Aged." He believes "they *cannot* Scripturally do their Work of Evangelism through a Human Organization known as a Missionary Society." But he said the difference is that Porter uses the word "organization" in two different senses. No, it is Guy that does that. I used it in the same sense. You are the fellow who is making two different senses out of it, Guy. It is not Curtis; it is Guy. You are making "organization" over here (pointing to chart) mean one thing, and over here you are making it mean something else. I used them in the same sense. Brother Woods is the man who is confused about it. It is not Brother Porter at all. He's the man who has made two senses out of it there. He says it means one thing over there, and I endorse it. And he says it means something else over here. "Porter confuses it by making it mean one thing here, another thing over here." No, Porter did not make it that at all. That is what Brother Woods made. It is not what Porter made. So it is Brother Woods that is confused on that point instead of Brother Porter.

He was talking then about the procedure and about the machine that rivals the church. That chart we had just a moment ago—rivaling the church. It doesn't rival the church, he says; and, therefore, it is perfectly all right. Well, I am still asking—I asked you a while ago, and you haven't answered it. You talk about a man dodging questions. You did not answer it, Brother Woods. *Do churches have a right to build and maintain Missionary organizations?* I am not talking about the Christian Church Missionary Society. I am just asking you: Do churches have a right to build and maintain Missionary organizations, chartered under the laws of the state, with a president, vice-president, secretary and treasurer, the same officers and the same arrangement we have in our benevolent organizations today, through which to do our work of evangelism? Did you ever tell us? No, you didn't tell us, Brother Woods. And I am predicting you are not going to tell us. Now, you just tell us something about that. Do you believe they can do it? Forget about the Christian Church Missionary Society. I said Missionary organizations upon the very same style or arrangement that is characteristic of our orphan homes, our benevolent organizations. Would you endorse churches building and maintaining organizations like that, Brother Woods, for evangelism? We are wanting to know. So far, we don't. So let us know.

I said that Brother Woods did a masterful job in his debate with Brother Leroy Garrett. And he said, "Did you say on orphan homes?" I said, "Brother Woods, did I say that?" And he said, "No, you did not say that." No, I said on Bible colleges. I mentioned it, didn't I, Brother Woods? Didn't I mention Bible colleges? I think if you will go home and play the record, you will find that I said on the Bible college question you did a masterful job. Certainly. And I believe you did, Brother Woods.

You made an argument there on parallel duties, showing the difference between *individual* duties and *church* duties. You did do a masterful job on that. But then he turns right around and tries to connect me up with Leroy Garrett, and says they have a lot of things in common. Brother Woods, do you have anything in common with Leroy?

BROTHER WOODS: "I don't know what it is."

You don't? He opposes the Missionary Society. You don't? Huh? (Laughter.) Brother Woods, he opposes the Missionary Society. *Do you?* Brother Woods says he *doesn't know of anything he has in common* with Leroy Garrett. Leroy Garrett opposes Missionary Societies through which the work of evangelism is to be done. Brother Woods doesn't oppose it. I guess that is the reason he hasn't answered the question. (Porter laughs.) You want to take it back? (Laughter.) You would like to, wouldn't you, Guy? You would like to take that back and say, "I believe I do have some things in common with him." You do, don't you, Brother Woods? Huh? You do have some things in common with Leroy, don't you?

BROTHER WOODS: "Not as much as you do."

You have some things in common, don't you? (Laughter.) You have some things in common with him, don't you?

BROTHER WOODS: "I don't have as much as you do."

That's all right, whether you have as much as I do or not, you have things in common with him. A while ago you said you didn't, and now you do. So one time you do, and the next time you don't; and then you don't, and then you do.

He quoted from the *Porter-Waters Debate,* he said, because he agreed with what Porter said. And I agreed with what Woods said in the quotation I made from him. I did not agree with everything Woods said in the speech, but I certainly agreed with what Brother Woods said in the quotation I made. The thing that I quoted from, I endorse one hundred per cent—that those things, those organizations, established, which brethren formed or established *to care for orphans* had in them *grave danger,* which Brother Woods saw. And I asked him to name some of the other organizations; and he said, "Well, the Woman's Home Mission." That is not an organization set up to care for the orphans, is it? You mentioned the ones to care for the orphans. You were talking about organizations that brethren had formed *to care for the orphans.* I want to know *what organizations* brethren had formed *to care for orphans* that you opposed. That is what I am wanting to know. Not these others. You did not name the ones I am talking about. I am still asking. He is just "as dumb as an oyster" yet. Maybe he will come to life tomorrow night and tell us about it.

And another thing in that connection. He referred, of course, in that to his endorsement of the Tipton Orphan Home. Brother Woods, did you endorse—you came right on and mentioned endorsing Boles Home in that connection —did you endorse Boles Home in 1939? Did you? You mentioned it in your speech. I thought maybe you intended to say Tipton Home, but you said Boles Home. In 1939? Did you endorse Boles Orphan Home as it was in 1939? Did you? Now, don't be "as dumb as an oyster" about it. Tell us.

Then back to his chart on organizations in different categories. But I dealt with that.

Next he calls our attention to the Memphis home for the aged. And he has a number of things more to say about that. He is wondering how it can be set up without its being a human organization. And then before he got through, he came up with the idea of another chart, and we will get that right in this connection, which was chart number seven. I think we can remember well enough without having to flash it on.

Building a house to care for the preacher, or to have a home for the preacher, and he said we have no example or command to build a house; it is *inherent in the command.* And we have also preachers' homes, and we have no example of that. And orphan homes the same way. He said there are many preachers who believe it is right for *preachers* to have homes, but believe it is wrong for *orphans* to have homes. I wonder who they are. I just wonder who they are. I have never said it was wrong for orphans to have homes, and I don't know of anybody else who ever did. I wonder if that is a misrepresentation. Brother Woods, do you believe it is right to have preachers' homes, chartered under the laws of the state, set up as human organizations, with officers and arrangements such as we have in our benevolent organizations today to house the preachers? Do you? That isn't what we have. Do you believe it is right to have one like that? Tell us about it. So his little effort along that line is wasted energy:

"Orphan homes are not in competition with the church or the home," he said. They are not in competition with the church or the home. Well, what about those organizations that *brethren had formed* in the past for the *care of the orphans* that *were in competition* with it—that were doing the work of the church in which you saw *grave danger?* We are still wanting to know; and so far, we haven't been able to find out. But we want to find out more about that. How much time do I have?

BROTHER DOUTHITT: "You have about a minute and a half."

About a minute and a half. Well, that won't be time to introduce anything more in this connection, except as I glance back here—let me see—"The only thing that's wrong," he says, "is the fact that it has a president or a vice-president." Well, you argued back yonder some time ago that in a Sunday School like that it would be wrong. You argued against a denominational Sunday School, because they had a president and vice-president. You won't deny it, will you? If you do, I will read it for you tomorrow night. Certainly, you won't deny that. But that isn't *the only thing.* He said that's "the only thing." No, *that is just one of the things.* Now, I am pointing out to you some of these matters.

Now then, on that question of *how,* Matt. 28: 19 says "go into all the world and preach the gospel." How are you to do it? He said, "Well, I'll tell you how. We'll do it just like the Lord said do it." Well, why not do the other like the Lord said do it? Now, if you can find any methods in one, I will find the same methods in the other. The fact is, if by the *how* you mean only *means,* or *methods,* or *modes,* or *manners,* things that come within the realm of *incidentals* —why, certainly we would agree upon that. But those things do not authorize organizations. You know what I mean by "organizations." It is more than just a systematic arrangement. You had more than that in mind in these statements you made when you opposed *human institutions* and *human organizations.* You were not opposing arrangements, were you? You were not opposing a systematic approach to something, were you, when you were opposing those things? And you know that "organization" means more than you are letting it mean tonight. You know it does, and you are not willing to endorse "organizations" after that fashion.

(Time Called)

So I thank you very kindly.

Woods' Fourth Affirmative

Brethren and Sisters and Friends:

I am indeed thankful that in the providence of God we have been brought safely through another day and now have this privilege of engaging in this religious discussion. I regret the occasion for such in the church of our Lord today; but, in view of the fact that these differences obtain, it is our duty to contend earnestly for the truth as we believe it to be recorded upon the pages of God's word.

The proposition that I am affirming reads as follows: "It is in harmony with the scriptures for churches to build and maintain benevolent organizations for the care of the needy, such as the Boles Home, the Tipton Home, and other orphan homes and homes for the aged that are among us." On last evening I gave a somewhat detailed definition of terms; and I shall, therefore, waive that formality this evening. It seems to me that the issue is crystal clear and that there isn't any difficulty in recognizing what the issue is. It is mine simply to sustain the practice that is characteristic of the churches generally of supporting the homes mentioned in the proposition and others of similar nature, such as Boles, and Tipton, and Maude Carpenter, and others that might be mentioned.

On last evening I urged Brother Porter to confine his discussion to matters pertaining to the scriptures; but that he did not see fit to do. And, I should like to say that at any time he wishes to leave these irrelevant matters and discuss this question from a scriptural standpoint I shall be happy so to do. I cannot see how any effort to prove inconsistency on my part has anything to do with whether or not the proposition is true or false. As a matter of fact, it is an evident token of a weakness on Brother Porter's part that he resorts to that type of debating; and I think the congregation can recognize that fact.

I propose this evening again to affirm the matter from the standpoint stated on last evening. The New Testament obligates us to visit the fatherless and the widows. In James 1: 27, we are told that, "Pure religion and undefiled before God and the Father is this, To visit the fatherless and widows in their affliction, and to keep himself unspotted from the world." To visit is to offer help after inspection. Now, this is a responsibility of the church such as is affirmed in 1 Tim. 5 and 16 where the apostle said that the church is to care for the widows indeed. It isn't necessary for me to prove that, because Brother Porter, on last evening, conceded the responsibility of the church to care for orphans and the destitute widows. And, in a letter dated January 27, 1955, he said this: *"Of course Paul's instruction to Timothy regarding widows that should be taken care of by the church is pretty definite. If, however, there are enough old folks in Memphis to justify a home, old folks, I mean, who have no relatives to care for them, I suppose the Memphis churches could maintain a home for such if they sustained the same relationship to the home. But if a brotherhood project is to be set up to take care of old folks from all over the nation, I doubt the wisdom of such an undertaking."* That's the end of the quotation. Now, I would like for you to note some concessions that are in this statement. In the first place, Brother Porter admits that the church has an obligation to some old people. I call upon him, inasmuch as he has said that the method which my proposition states is unscriptural, to tell us *what* method or *what* procedure *is* scriptural. He said on last evening that he would do that, and it remains yet for him to do so. He believes that the Memphis churches may cooperate in the establishment and support of a home for old folks on two conditions: First, the old folks must be without relatives to care for them; and secondly, the church or the churches participating must sustain the same relationship to the home. Now, get it, please. That could be so only if the home were under a board of directors and not under one of the elderships. Brother Porter here admits that the establishment of such a home, and the extent to which it is to serve is in the realm of human judgment and is a simple matter of expediency. He questioned a brotherhood project to take care of old folks all over the nation, not because such would be unscriptural, mind you, but because he, that is, Brother Porter, *doubts* the *wisdom* of such an undertaking. With him it is a matter of *wisdom* and not of *scripture;* and yet he is identified with a group, some of whom are dividing the body of Christ over what Brother Porter admits is simply a matter of human judgment.

I would like to have chart number six, Brother Osborne, and we shall see some things suggested there. While Brother Osborne is getting that, let me call attention to the fact that James 1: 27, in addition to mentioning widows, also designates the fatherless.

Now, we have here a "deadly parallel," and I want you to see what Brother Porter has conceded already in this debate. On this side (pointing to the chart) we have the anti-class groups. And may I say that I have had numerous debates, twenty debates, with the anti-class groups, and two or three debates with Brother Leroy Garrett, and now this one with Brother W. Curtis Porter. When we are debating the anti-class groups they say we misrepresent them when we charge that they do not believe in dividing the assembly. They say they do believe in dividing the assembly. They

CHART NO. 6—"A DEADLY PARALLEL"

Anti-Class Groups	Garrett, Ketcherside, et al	W. Curtis Porter
1. May Divide Assembly.	1. Preacher May Locate.	1. Care for the Needy.
2. Teach Classes.	2. Receive Support	2. Churches may care for the needy.
3. Use Women Teachers	3. Work with Elders.	3. Churches may cooperate in such care.
	4. Stay "50 years"	4. Churches may establish a home for such care.
"Modern Sunday School"	"The Pastor System"	"INSTITUTIONALISM"

further say it is a misrepresentation of their position to say that they do not believe in classes; they do; they also believe it is right (so they say) to use women teachers. But, notwithstanding the fact, when you put all of these together, they say it all adds up to the modern Sunday school. They admit each item, and then maintain that all of it together is the modern Sunday school. But more than that. In debates with Brother Garrett he has said that a preacher may locate; that it is a misrepresentation of his position to say that a preacher cannot locate. He believes that a preacher may locate. Secondly, he agrees that a preacher may receive support. He concedes that a preacher may work with elders, and he says they may stay with such work fifty years; yet, when you put it all together, Garrett says it is the pastor system. Further, Brother Curtis Porter has admitted that it is right for churches to care for the needy. He says that *churches* are obligated to care for the needy. Thirdly, that churches, the Memphis churches, may *cooperate* in such care. And, fourthly, that the Memphis churches may establish a home for such care. But, when we put all those concessions together, he says it adds up to *institutionalism!* Now, friends, there is the parallel. I urge him to get himself out of the company in which he finds himself tonight. Now then, that is sufficient for that.

Here, if you please, is an argument *ex concessis,* an argument from things admitted. He has admitted (1) a home may be maintained in Memphis for destitute old folks; (2) this home may be supported by Memphis churches; (3) this home may be maintained, though not under an eldership of some Memphis church. But (1) to operate such a home, some sort of an organization is necessary; (2) whatever organization that is necessary to operate such a home, Brother Porter endorses; (3) therefore, Brother Porter believes that it is scriptural for an old folks home to operate with an organization other than that of the elders of the church.

Now, look: In an orphan home, such as Tipton, the elders have necessarily delegated direction of the home to a superintendent who, in turn, employs matrons, teachers, helpers, etc. This organization is other than the church in Tipton; but whatever organization is essential to the discharge of the work of the church is scriptural. Such an organization is necessary in the care of orphans. *Some such* organization; maybe not exactly that, but an organization of some sort; therefore, such an organization, that is, whatever organization it takes to carry out this obligation, is scriptural.

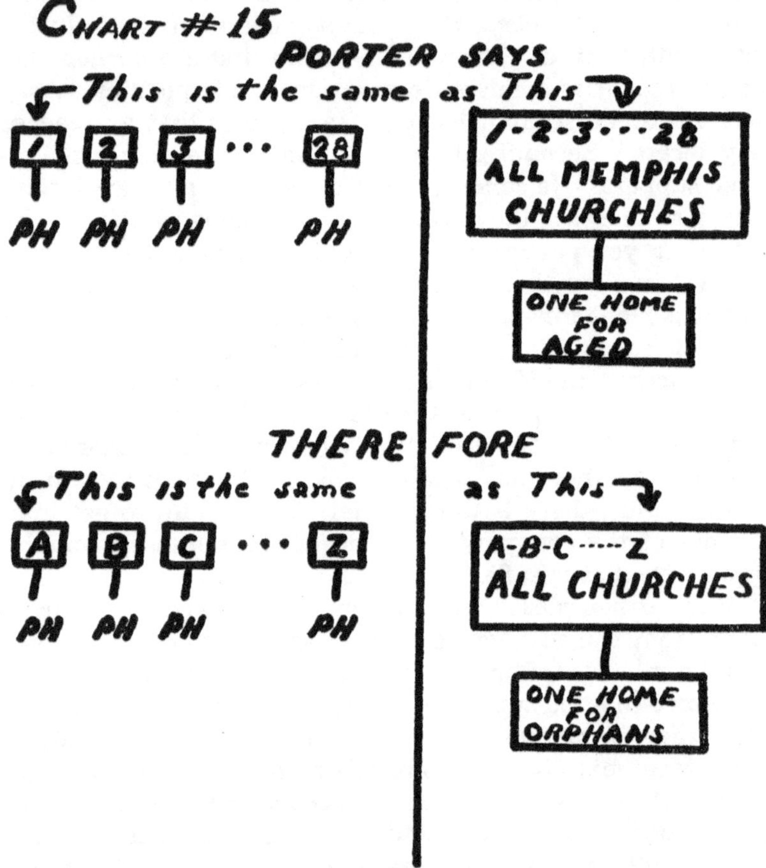

Now, let me have, please, chart number fifteen. In his effort to answer this last night Brother Porter told us that the Memphis home that he endorsed was on a par with the preachers' homes of that same city. Now, on this side (pointing to the chart) we have Brother Porter saying that this is the same as that. There are about twenty-eight churches in the Memphis area. Now, Brother Porter said for all twenty-eight churches to combine their efforts and cooperate in the establishment of one home, or a home for the aged, is exactly parallel with each congregation building a preacher's home for each preacher! I charged that was pure quibbling last night to say that, and I think you can see that. But now, look, friends, if that is parallel to this, now watch down here: Let this represent all the preachers and the preachers' homes in the brotherhood; therefore, if because each preacher in Memphis and each church in Memphis has a preacher's home for its preacher, and that is parallel to all the churches in Memphis combining their efforts in one home for the aged, then, since it is right for all the preachers in the world to have preachers' homes and all the churches to establish them, it would then be right for all the churches in the world to build *one home* for orphans. And so you have the church universal activated, about which they talk so much; and in which right here he finds himself in the situation of endorsing. Now, Brother Porter, get out of that difficulty if you can. That is sufficient on that.

Now, friends, I submit that he has his work cut out for him. All of the talk about what somebody said or didn't say, all the discussion of matters in the past will not eliminate the question of whether these things are scriptural. I may be as inconsistent as it is possible for a man to be. I may be in conflict with myself. All of that may be true. It doubtless is true on many subjects. But that hasn't a thing on earth to do with whether or not my position on this is right tonight. What we are interested in, Brother Porter, is the truth; not whether you can prove me inconsistent or not. We want the truth on *this*. That's what we have met here for. What do these folks out here care whether I have contradicted myself one time or another? That is not the issue. You get busy on it and let us hear something with reference to this matter.

Let us have chart number eleven. Here is another argument; and I consider this, friends, one of the finest arguments that I have seen in twenty-five years of controversy and a hundred debates. Brother Thomas Warren arranged this—not the particular argument that I have, but basically it is his idea—and I adapted it to this particular subject. He worked it out on another matter, but I have adapted it to this particular subject, and he is entitled to the credit on the argument. I consider it absolutely unanswerable and irresistible. I do hope that Brother Porter will come with something better than the pitiful effort that was made four or five weeks ago in answering a similar argument along this line.

CHART NO. 11

AXIOM: "The WHOLE of anything is the SUM of its parts"

•

PROOF MY PROP. REQUIRES:
- Care Of Orph. & Aged
- Ch. Support " " " "
- Ch. Cooperation in the Support of " " "

(a) This we have already done.
(b) Porter concedes foregoing anyway.

•

Syllogism:
(1.) All situations, the component parts of which are scriptural, are scriptural situations.
(2.) The component parts of the whole work involved in my prop. are scriptural.
(3.) ∴ the whole work involved in prop. is scriptural.

•

PORTER'S ALTERNATIVE:
(a) Deny the major premise.
(b) Repudiate Public Statements.

Now, first, the axiom at the top here: The *whole* of anything is the *sum* of its parts. That is so obvious as not to need any proof; in fact, it is not susceptible of proof; it is a demonstration. That, if you please, is axiomatic. Now, here is the kind of proof my proposition requires. I am in the affirmative in this debate. I have an obligation to prove certain matters. My proposition obligates me to prove at least three things: First, it is my obligation to prove that there is an obligation to care for orphans and the aged. That is point number one. That is an obligation that is mine. Secondly, I must prove, if I sustain my proposition, that the church must support or contribute to the support of orphans and aged. And, thirdly, I must prove that there is church cooperation in the support of orphans and aged, and that the scriptures so teach. Now then, those are the three things essential to the establishment of my proposition. If I were to fail in any one of them, my proposition goes down. I must prove the care of the orphans, church support of such orphans, and church cooperation in the support of such.

Just a moment or two while I am on that. In Acts 11: 29, 30, we have an account of churches contributing to the needy. In 2 Cor. 8 and 9, we have an example of churches contributing of their means to the support of the needy in the Jerusalem area. And thus far these matters have not been introduced, and I merely mention that for the purpose of showing that there is such church cooperation, and Brother Porter doesn't deny it. In the first place, we have already proved these matters; and in the second place, he concedes them anyway. Why prove something then, more than merely to state it, that is already conceded?

Now then, here is the syllogism. Can we get that up to where we can see it? All right, number one. Here is the major premise: (1) All situations, the component parts of which are scriptural, are scriptural situations. Now, ponder that for a moment, friends. All situations, the component parts of which are scriptural, are scriptural situations. That is the major premise. The minor premise is: (2) The component parts of the whole work involved in my proposition are scriptural. That is the minor premise. Now then, the conclusion is this: (3) Therefore, the whole work involved in my proposition is scriptural. Now, Brother Porter must do one of two things. Here is his alternative. He must either deny the major premise, which is like denying the multiplication table, or that two plus two equal four; or he must repudiate his public statements along this line already made in this debate. If he concedes the major and the minor premise, then the conclusion is irresistible. What is the major premise? All situations, the component parts of which are scriptural, are scriptural situations. That, friends, has all the force of a mathematical demonstration. Another premise is that the component parts of the whole work involved in the proposition are scriptural. Brother Porter admits that; that it is right to care for the needy; that it is right for the church to care for the needy; that the churches of Memphis could combine their energies in such care. He concedes the matter, my friends. The major premise is unassailable; the minor premise is admitted; therefore, the conclusion is irresistible; and the conclusion is that the whole work involved in my proposition is scriptural. What is the work involved in my proposition? Here it is: "It is in harmony with the scriptures for the churches to build and maintain benevolent organizations for the care of the needy, such as Boles and the Tipton Home and other orphan homes among us."

BROTHER WATSON: "Three minutes."

That, ladies and gentlemen, will stand, and this debate will end and Brother Porter will never touch top, side, edge, nor bottom of that argument. Now then, that is sufficient for that chart.

Let us note another. What is the issue in this debate? It is not over whether it is right for the church to take care of the orphans and aged. Brother Porter admits it. It is not over the number to be cared for. Both of us agree, I think, that the number is not essential. It is not a question of place. Surely it is not. It wouldn't be scriptural in one place, but unscriptural in another, surely. The issue, he says, is not a matter of denying the responsibility of it. The issue is simply over *how* the work is to be done.

Now, on last evening, friends, I gave you a chart, and we will not present it tonight. I will just remind you of it, showing what is involved in the care of the orphans. It requires a place; it requires food; it requires clothing; it requires supervision; it requires care and so on. Now, when you put those elements together and supply them you have *a home.* It doesn't make any difference what you call it, you have *a home of some sort!* Now then, let Brother Porter tell us just how it is possible for the church to discharge what he says is its obligation and yet not have what my proposition calls for. On other matters where the *how* is not revealed Brother Porter reasons correctly. Where is the *how* for caring for the preacher? Where is the New Testament procedure as to the time, place, and circumstances for the observance of the Lord's supper on the first day of the week? What are the details as to baptism, or where are the details of the baptismal service set up? Here are some pertinent questions for him. Where is the authority, in a detailed, specific statement, for a meetinghouse, a board of trustees, a bass singer, four parts of a song, a song leader, a table to observe the Lord's supper, plates on the table, cups to hold the fruit of the vine? Where is specific authority for this debate? Now, these are matters that all of us believe to be right. The command to assemble implies a place and necessary details. The command to visit the fatherless necessitates the place and the equipment. The argument is thus over methods. My opponent has entered the realm of the expedient and made it a matter of faith, and the issue bids fair to divide the body of Christ. It is the anti-Sunday school position applied to benevolence. He is simply making the same objections that I have listened to in twenty debates with the anti-Sunday school people, and it bids fair to become another faction that withdraws fellowship from the rest of us on the same ground as that of the anti-Sunday school position. (Time called.)

I thank you.

Porter's Fourth Negative

Brethren Moderators, Brother Woods, Ladies and Gentlemen:

I appreciate again the privilege of appearing before you to enter into a further discussion of the issue involved in this debate and to pay my attention to the speech that has just been made by Brother Woods. Along with him, of course, as he said a while ago, I regret that a debate like this is necessary; and certainly it would never have been necessary if brethren had not introduced and organized human institutions to do the work of the church, just as debates over the Missionary Society a hundred years ago would have been unnecessary if those who led in the development of the Christian Church had never introduced or organized Missionary Societies for the work of evangelism. Those things are the things that made debates necessary then, and they are the things that make debates like this necessary now.

I want to notice just a few things. Last night in my closing speech I turned two pages of my notes at once and failed to discover it, and I thought that I had missed something, and I tried to glance back through and locate it, but failed. But there were some three or four or five things on that page that I want to call attention to, as I desire to get to everything, before I go into the speech to which you have just listened. And one thing Brother Woods asked was: "Where does the New Testament specify sixteen men to administer the Lord's supper?" Well, no one claims that the New Testament specifies how many men are to administer the Lord's supper. But, suppose, Brother Woods, that somebody would take those sixteen men, form a body corporate and politic out of them, and get a state charter for them to operate, and then as an operation of that kind, or as a corporation of that kind, administer the Lord's supper. Would you accept that? That is what you have done in this other matter.

Then, he said, and he repeated a while ago, that Porter's arguments are the same as those made by the anti-Sunday school brethren that he has met all these years, which, of course, is not true, as I shall show before this debate is over. The time is not here when I shall deal with that elaborately. But I may also remind *him* that the arguments made by Brother Woods are the same arguments that have been made *through all these years* by the *digressive Christian Church preachers* in support of *their human institutions* to carry on their *work of evangelism.* And we will have some more on that right in this connection.

Regarding the matter of *how*—he said a great number of things about that last night, concerning the matter of *how,* and I called attention to some of the statements he made on the same line which he has not mentioned. And, incidentally, I may throw this in right here, though it came in his speech a while ago, that he had urged Brother Porter to come to a discussion of the scriptures, what the scriptures teach, and not deal with anything he had said that might be inconsistent with the position that he now occupies, because if I were to prove him inconsistent, that wouldn't establish the issue one way or another. That works fine when it works against Brother Porter, but is *altogether otherwise* when Brother Woods has hold of it, for he turned right around on the heels of that statement in which he said to follow a course of that kind is a token, an evident token of weakness on the part of the man who does so. He turned right around and spent perhaps five minutes dealing with a letter that I wrote Brother Bill Rogers over at Memphis last January, trying to prove me inconsistent. Brother Woods, was that an evident token of weakness on your part? It was, according to what you have been saying about it. That is an evident token of weakness on the part of Brother Woods. And I shall say more about that as I come to it in the notes.

Porter's Projector
Chart No. 3

THE "HOW" VERSUS "ORGANIZATION"

MAT. 28:19 - TEACH - HOW - ORGANIZATION { CHURCH / MISSIONARY SOCIETY }

1 TIM. 5:16 - RELIEVE - HOW - ORGANIZATION { CHURCH / BENEVOLENT ORGANIZATION }

Now, then, on this matter of *how,* we have a commandment given. I am sorry that everybody in this auditorium can't see this blackboard, but in Matt. 28: 19 the Lord gave a commandment to "go ye therefore and teach all nations." There is a duty; there is a responsibility for teaching, or preaching, the gospel. The *how* to preach the gospel is *not detailed* in *all of its parts.* We are told to preach the gospel; and anything pertaining to the *how,* or the method, the manner, or the mode, is *not detailed.* Therefore, digressive Christian Church preachers came up with the idea that since the *how* is not detailed, then we are privileged to organize any kind of organizations that we might want by way of Missionary Societies in order to do that work; and so they proceeded upon that basis. We called to their attention through the years that, while God had not designated in *all the details* the *how* of it, He *had designated organization,* and the organization that God had designated is that *divine organization* known as the *church;* and that, since the church is an all-sufficient institution, then it is to be done by the church, and not through human organizations. Now, then, Brother Woods comes along with 1 Tim. 5: 16; and he finds a command there to care for the widows and says, since the *how* is *not detailed* in all its parts, then we have the right to establish organizations, just as the digressive Christian Church did. And when we are opposing them, we make the same contention that was made by brethren who opposed those things in the past—that the work is done by the church. The Lord did not designate everything pertaining to the *how* in gospel preaching. He *did designate* the *organization* through which it was to be done, and that eliminated the human organization known as the Missionary Society. In the matter of caring for widows God *did not detail all the how*—the methods, the means, or the modes, or the manners; but God did detail the organization and gives no right to set up a human organization, such as he is contending for tonight, any more than He gave the digressive Christian Church preacher the right to set up an organization that was human in its origin to do the work of evangelism. Now, we are going to have him tell us something about *how* as we go along.

And, incidentally, while I am here, I have, I think, just a few questions I want to hand to him. Will someone pass these on to him, please. Let me see. I believe that is right.

1st. Since you stated last night that I could not tell *how* the church could care for the needy without describing our benevolent organizations, did you mean to say that the only possible way to care for the needy is through such organizations?

2nd. If you did not mean this, what are some of the other ways that you consider to be scriptural?

3rd. If our benevolent corporations, while retaining their present organizational setup, without any other change whatsoever, should decide to discontinue their work of benevolence and engage in the work of evangelism, would you endorse it as a scriptural arrangement?

4th. If "The Society for the Propagation of the Faith (a Catholic Foreign Missionary Society), is not a rival to the Catholic Church, would we be justified in organizing a similar Society for Churches of Christ?

5th. As the Federal Government has a legislative branch that can pass laws to authorize the Post Office Department through which to work, and the State Government has a legislative branch that can pass laws to authorize a Highway Department through which to operate, what group do we have in the church, comparable to such, that can pass laws to authorize benevolent organizations through which the church may function?

6th. Since you oppose church support of Christian schools, how can you endorse church support of benevolent organizations to build and maintain their own Christian schools?

7th. Would you endorse a Sunday School Corporation, chartered under the laws of the state, with the same organizational setup that characterizes our benevolent organizations, for church edification?

He referred to the matter of the California churches being chartered, or incorporated. He asked about that. I don't know the details of the requirements of the state of California. I am sure if they require something that is contrary to the scriptures, that such could be arranged in a scriptural way. But, if a congregation or church is incorporated, you have an incorporated congregation or church. Before it was incorporated, it was an unincorporated one. You still have just *the one body,* Brother Woods. But when you get another corporation, or another group incorporated and chartered, you have an *extra body* besides the *one body,* the church of the Lord Jesus Christ. And suppose that the laws of the state of California, or some other state, should require, in order for you to do the work of evangelism in the state, that you would have to charter a Missionary Organization. Would you do it, Brother Woods, and go along and say it would be scripturally done because they required it of you? Please tell us about that. Concerning the one body he said, "Well, what if it is?" He said, "The private home is another body, too." So he admits that the orphan homes are *bodies.* Then he turned around and said the orphan home is *not the church.* All right, if the orphan home is a body, and it is not the church, then it is an additional body, isn't it? And you have the church building and sustaining an additional body to the church which God authorized, and the church doing its own work through that additional body. Now, the home as God authorized, and the church as God authorized, he said a while ago, are divine institutions, or divine bodies. And in his debate with Brother Leroy Garrett he said, "I don't defend two bodies; I just defend one; but I am insisting that the church is doing its work through *the only God-ordained body* for this purpose, the church of the Lord Jesus Christ." He said that the orphan home is not the church, but another body; but if it were the church, it would be wrong. I just wonder what you meant by that, Brother Woods. You said if the orphan home were the church, it would be wrong. Brother Woods, do you mean to say it would be wrong for the church to care for its needy if you did not have the orphan home outside to care for them through that? Just what do you mean by that, anyhow?

And then he said he would endorse the churches contributing to a hospital if the hospital were set up for the church alone. Well, Brother Woods, is the orphan home set up for the church alone? You are endorsing it. Are you taking only the children of Christian parents? Are you? Are you, Brother Woods? Set up for the church alone? Is that the way the orphan homes are operating? You say you would contribute to a hospital, the churches could, if it were set up for the church alone. Well, what about a grocery store? Suppose somebody sets up a grocery store and sells only to church members. Would you endorse the church contributing to that? Or a garage? Or any other kind of mercantile establishment?

Now, then, we go on into the other things just here. He

came back to James 1: 27 and 1 Tim. 5: 16—the church duty; and I have dealt with that already.

Then to the letter that I wrote to Brother Bill Rogers. And he said that Porter admits that the churches are obligated to relieve the aged and that they may cooperate under two conditions: that there are no relatives to take care of them, and they sustain the same relation. He said the only way in which they could sustain the same relation is to be placed under a board of men of some kind, a *board of directors.* In other words, if there is a mission place out here that needs a meeting, and two of these churches in Indianapolis would decide to conduct a meeting out there, they could not sustain the same relation to that meeting unless they organized a board, and set it up under a board. If they did that, then they could have this meeting; otherwise they couldn't. Now, that's the same thing exactly.

Then he said, "Brother Porter doubts the *wisdom* of it; not that it is unscriptural; but he merely doubts the *wisdom* of it, and the church is being divided over a matter of human wisdom." I doubted the wisdom of it because of what the scriptures said about it, Brother Woods. And, certainly, I doubt the wisdom of any man's going contrary to the scriptures. Don't you?

Now to chart number six. We want to take a look at this, as Brother Woods introduced it a while ago, in which he endeavors to place me in the same position with the anti-class, with Brother Garrett and Brother Ketcherside, and so on.

We take a look at chart number six—A Deadly Parallel. The anti-class group over here said we may divide the assembly, and secondly, we may teach classes; and thirdly, may use women teachers; and that adds up to a modern Sunday school—that is, that's the contention they make against us. If we say we may divide the assembly, we may teach classes, we may use women teachers, then that adds up to a modern Sunday school. Well, it happens that a *modern Sunday school*—and Brother Woods has defined it in some of his writings—is one set up under a board, with a president and a vice-president, and all the things like that,

CHART NO. 6—"A DEADLY PARALLEL"

Anti-Class Groups	Garrett, Ketcherside, et al	W. Curtis Porter
1. May Divide Assembly.	1. Preacher May Locate.	1. Care for the Needy.
2. Teach Classes.	2. Receive Support	2. Churches may care for the needy.
3. Use Women Teachers	3. Work with Elders.	3. Churches may cooperate in such care.
	4. Stay "50 years"	4. Churches may establish a home for such care.
"Modern Sunday School"	"The Pastor System"	"INSTITUTIONALISM"

concomitants that are conspicuously *absent from Bible classes* as taught by us. You remember writing that, don't you, Guy? Well, I have it; if you don't remember it, I can read it to you before we get through.

Now, then, Brother Garrett and Brother Ketcherside and so on say that a preacher may locate, may receive support, may work under elders and stay fifty years; but if we do that, it adds up to the Pastor System. And W. Curtis Porter says we may care for the needy, churches may care for the needy, and churches may cooperate in such care, and churches may establish homes for such care; and that that adds up to Institutionalism. Now, then, the thing wrong with the whole setup here is that churches may care for the needy, and that the needy may be cared for, and that churches may cooperate in such care, and churches may care for them in a home—but not in a human organization set up under a board, chartered by the state, as a body politic and corporate, such as our orphan homes are. And his addition is just as wrong as his position on all of this thing all the way through. And this modern Sunday school that they claim it adds up to is just simply not true, of course, and his whole claim along that line does not prove a thing on earth for his proposition.

Now, then, let's see. Things admitted, he said: that the home may be had for Memphis, and that the home may be supported by the church, and that an organization is necessary, and whatever organization is necessary other than the church, Porter endorses. Then, he went on in connection with that with the Tipton Home. He said Tipton Home is an organization *other than the church.* Is it, Brother Woods? The Tipton Home is an organization *other than the church,* and yet you have been telling us that it is *merely the church functioning* through its members, that it is *not* an organization *other than the church.* But here you come and say that the Tipton Home is an organization other than the church. And he said such an organization is *essential.* Essential to what, Brother Woods? To salvation? To eternal happiness in heaven? *Essential to what?* You say that that kind of organization is *essential.* Essential to what? Does he mean it is essential in practicing pure and undefiled religion? Essential in meeting the requirements of God and getting to heaven after while? What's it essential to? Such as the Tipton Orphan Home. We must have an organization like that; it is essential. If it is, Brother Woods, then orphans cannot be cared for by *any other method* than that. Are you going to say they cannot. You said that organization is essential. Either one like that, or one very similar to it, is essential. And if it is, then orphans cannot be cared for under any other conditions. I want you to tell me: Can they be cared for under any other conditions? Suppose some Christian family would decide to take them into their own home and care for them. Could they do it? Not according to what Brother Woods has said, for Brother Woods said an organization like Tipton Home is essential in the caring of orphans. Well, we would like to see him get out of some of those predicaments.

Chart number fifteen, please. We will take a look at this one again. Brother Woods called it to our attention a while ago. And here we have chart number fifteen.

Porter says *this* is the same as *this* (pointing to chart). So he has one, two, three, four preachers' homes, totaling about *twenty-eight preachers' homes;* and one, two, three, up to the total of twenty-eight Memphis churches caring for *one home for the aged.* Therefore, this is the same as this. A, B, C, and D, over to Z, preachers' homes throughout the world. And over here, A, B, C, all churches sustaining one home for orphans throughout the whole world. Now that was his idea. Well, suppose we put Brother Woods' position up there. Brother Woods has a human organization set up over here, chartered under the laws of the state, and says it is essential to care for them. You can't do it any other way. Well, in this we don't have any human organizations. These are the preachers' homes, or the homes for the aged, and homes for the orphans, which I endorsed. I said not *one word* about *any such organization,* Brother Woods, and I challenge you, every inch of you, from the top of your head to the sole of your feet, to read in that letter where I said one word about endorsing an organization. I challenge you

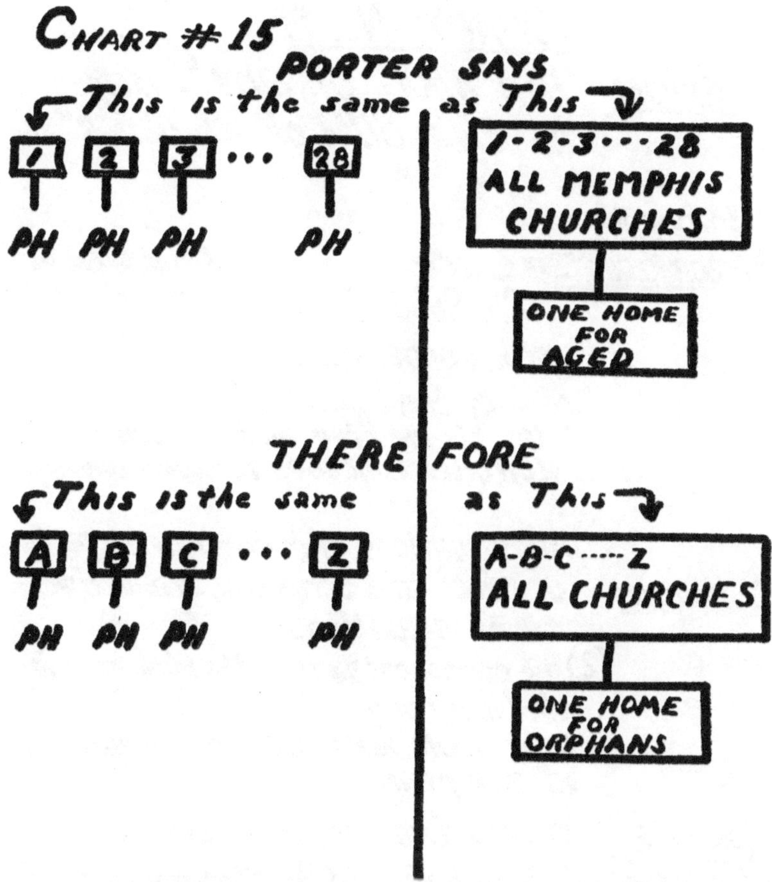

to do it. Get up here and make a play before this audience and make them think I have endorsed what you are saying; and that I have been inconsistent, and so on. *It is not there.* Nobody knows it better *than Guy Woods knows it.* Get up and tell us, Guy. Read us from that letter a statement that says so. And then, on that particular point, what homes do we have that you are defending in existence today to which all churches bear the same relation? If you don't have any, then that doesn't help your case the least bit in the world.

Chart number eleven. Here we come to Brother War-

CHART NO. 11

AXIOM: "The WHOLE of anything is the SUM of its parts"

•

PROOF MY PROP. REQUIRES: • Care Of Orph. & Aged
•Ch. Support " " " "
•Ch. Cooperation in the Support of " " "
(a) This we have already done.
(b) Porter concedes foregoing anyway.

•

Syllogism: (1.) All situations, the component parts of which are scriptural, are scriptural situations.
(2.) The component parts of the whole work involved in my prop. are scriptural.
(3.) ∴ the whole work involved in prop. is scriptural.

•

PORTER'S ALTERNATIVE: (a) Deny the major premise.
(b) Repudiate Public Statements.

ren's argument. I hope I have time. How much time do I have?

BROTHER DOUTHITT: "A little over a minute."

A little over a minute. I may not have time to get to all of this, but if I don't, I will get to it later. We will get to as much of it as we can.

Brother Warren's argument, in which "the whole of anything is the sum of its parts." The proof of his proposition requires: "first, the care of the orphan; second, church support of the orphan and aged; and third, church cooperation." And then from that he went on to prove that "all situations, the component parts of which are scriptural, are scriptural situations. Second, the component parts of the whole work involved in my proposition are scriptural." And "the whole work involved in my proposition is scriptural" is the conclusion. No man can touch either top, side, bottom, or edge of it. So declared Brother Woods. Well, let's see if we don't find a little edge sticking out somewhere that may be touched. Now, then, let us see what the issue is. What does his proposition say? Does his proposition say that the churches can support the aged, and they can cooperate in such support? And that the aged and the orphans need such support? Is that what the proposition says? No. There is a fourth point that he left out—that in that care of the orphans, and in that cooperation, and in that support of them, they have *a right to build and maintain human organizations to do it.* And that is the point that he left out, and that wrecks the whole system, or the argument, from top to bottom, edgeways and sideways, and every other way, Guy. (Time called)

Thank you.

Woods' Fifth Affirmative

Brethren Moderators, Brother Porter, Ladies and Gentlemen:

I have engaged in a good many debates; and I have seen men in difficult situations; and I say, without any effort whatever to reflect upon Brother Porter, because I regard him highly, consider him a fine Christian gentleman, and certainly one of the ablest debaters among us, that I have never heard a more feeble effort than that which has characterized him tonight. I say this without any effort whatsoever to be boastful, because if God knows my heart, I have no desire whatsoever to exhibit such an attitude; but I tell you, friends, I could sit down right now and give Brother Porter my time and my position stands unassailed. And, I think there is not a person in this audience tonight that knows it better than W. Curtis Porter!

Now, I am going to take up his speech, item by item, and statement by statement, and prove what I am saying to you right now. He said this debate would be unnecessary if there were no orphan home. I am aware of that fact.

His debate with Brother Waters would have been unnecessary if he had given up the classes and the cups. Debates with the Baptists would be unnecessary if we admitted that baptism is because of remission of sins. And, let me tell you this, friends, until 1947 there wasn't a southern preacher to my knowledge who took the position that Brother W. Curtis Porter takes here tonight. Not one of them. Last night I said to Brother Carl Ketcherside, who was in this audience, after the debate, "Well, what do you think about this fellow stealing your thunder?" And he smiled and said, "A few years ago in a debate with Brother Rue Porter, at which Brother Curtis Porter was present, I made the same arguments that Brother Porter made tonight with you in this debate." Now, of course, if we had given up our opposition to the located preacher, we would have no debates with Brother Ketcherside and Brother Garrett. And if Brother Porter would come back to the position that he held up until two or three years ago, I wouldn't be debating with him here.

He says that it will be all right for sixteen brethren to serve the Lord's supper, but asked, "Now, where is the authority for forming a corporation for such administration?" Now, friends, when a fellow has to resort to such quibbling as that, it indicates that his going is hard. In the first place, there would be no good purpose served. Such a question is moot in its nature because there would be no purpose accomplished in it. Why didn't he ask me about forming a corporation for preaching the gospel? I could tell him one about that, because it happens that I have in my possession a certified copy of the articles of corporation of the *Gospel Guardian* of which Brother W. Curtis Porter is one of the associate editors. It is organized as a corporation under the laws of the state for the purpose of propagating Christianity. Now, is that the church? We have learned a lot tonight about organizations, doing the work of the church, that are wrong. What about the organization he belongs to? Brother Porter, get busy. (Laughter.)

He said the same arguments made by me were made by the digressives. That is exactly what Ervin Waters said to him in the debate on the cups question. Exactly that. Waters charged him repeatedly with using arguments made by the digressives in defending the cups, individual cups. Now that's a mighty weak argument, Brother Porter. Mighty weak.

He said that I pleaded for a discussion of scriptural matters and turned right around and dealt with Brother Porter's letter. Well, Brother Porter, on last night I said, "Let's have a scriptural discussion"; and if you had stayed with the scriptures, I never would have introduced Brother Bill Rogers' letter. Never would. I answered with this only after you brought up matters that I made in a speech nearly twenty years ago. And I decided that what is sauce for the goose is sauce for the gander; so you got the letter. (Laughter.) And you will have it, too, from here on. I begged for a scriptural discussion. You know why we can't have it? Because these fellows can't stay with the scriptures. They've got to use the word "organization" five hundred times in every speech!

Porter's Projector
Chart No. 3

THE "HOW" VERSUS "ORGANIZATION"

MAT. 28:19 - TEACH - HOW - ORGANIZATION { CHURCH / MISSIONARY SOCIETY

1 TIM. 5:16 - RELIEVE - HOW - ORGANIZATION { CHURCH / BENEVOLENT ORGANIZATION

Now then, to the chart here. In Matt. 28: 19 our Lord said, "Teach." The *how* is not indicated. But he says we have an organization by which, through which, it is to be done, and that is the church. That doesn't answer the question. You still must have the *how.* How is the church to do it? Here is the fallacy of his reasoning. He is confusing a method with a machine. Now, the reason why it is wrong to have the Missionary Society, and why the Missionary Society doesn't inhere in the *how,* is that the *how* involves methods, and the Missionary Society is a machine. When we come to the question of benevolence we still have the same organization, the church. Just as you must have *means* with reference to teaching, you have also got to have *means* with reference to benevolence. Well, I am calling for it. Where are the *means* set out in the Bible? And when he tells us what those means are, he will describe what I am defending here tonight.

Now to his questions. But before I read them, again I say I like to be just as good to him as he is to me; so I give him some.

1. Is the work that the orphan home does wrong?

2. Is it wrong because the orphan home is an organization?

3. Is it wrong because the orphan home has a superintendent, secretary, president of the board, and other officials?

4. Is it wrong because you believe it to be an organization apart from the church?

5. Is it wrong because it is supported by cooperative efforts?

6. Would you endorse the Missionary Society if it were to become an individual enterprise, accepting contributions from individuals only?

7. What determines whether an enterprise constitutes institutionalism?

Will you give these to him, please? Thank you so much. Now then, to his questions, hurriedly. "Since you stated last night that I could not tell how the church could care for the needy without describing our benevolent organizations, did you mean to say that the only proper way to care for the needy is through such organizations?" Of course not. I said it was merely a means, by which I mean it is simply an expedient method by which to accomplish it.

"If you did not mean this, what are some of the other ways that you consider to be scriptural?" Well, now, friends, I believe it would be right and scriptural for people to take children into their own homes; but I am arguing that the Bible doesn't specify the means; therefore, it does not designate any exclusive method. That's my point exactly. Now, Brother Porter, I told you two different ways that I think is right; and you haven't told me *one* yet. Now, he said he is going to. *When* will he accomplish it?

"If our benevolent organizations, while retaining their present organizational setup, without any other change whatsoever, should decide to discontinue their work of benevolence and engage in the work of evangelism, would you endorse it as a scriptural arrangement?" You have an exact picture of that in California, and some other states, where you have to organize and have a board of directors and a president in order to exist. You have exactly that.

"If the Society for The Propagation of The Faith, a Catholic foreign Missionary Society, is not a rival to the church, would we be justified in organizing a similar society for churches of Chrst?" Well, I did not introduce that to show that everything the Catholic Church does is right. I introduced it for one purpose only, and that was to show that an organization that is different in its structural make-up that grows out of the Catholic Church is not a rival to the Catholic Church. That is the only reason I introduced it. We will have some more about that in a moment.

"As the Federal Government has a legislative branch that can pass laws to authorize a Post Office Department through which to work and the State Government has a legislative branch that can pass laws to authorize a Highway Department through which to operate, what group do we have in the church comparable to such that can pass laws to authorize benevolent organizations through which the church may function?"

Flash us the number one chart, please, and we will have that right here. Brother Porter missed the point completely on that argument last night, friends. He did not touch it at all.

Here was the argument: The Federal Government has a function to perform that involves the Post Office Department, but it is not in conflict with it. The Highway Department grows out of the State Government, but it is not in conflict with it, nor a rival of it. The homes for the aged of the Masonic Lodge do not rival the Masonic Lodge. They are merely means through which the Masonic Lodge operates. The Catholic Church operates orphanages, and they are not in conflict with the Church, nor do they rob the Church of its glory. And the church of Christ operates orphanages and homes for the aged; therefore, they are not in conflict. That was my sole point, and he did not touch

Chart No. 1
Organizations in Different Categories

Fed. Gov't. ----Post Office Dept.
State Gov't.---Highway Dept.
Masonic Lodge---Homes for Aged.
Catholic Church---Orphanages.
Church of Christ---Orphanages & Homes for Aged

Rival These? Do These

that part of it. He said, "Well, the Federal Government has the authority to legislate with reference to the Post Office Department, the State Government, and so on, also the Masonic Lodge, the Catholic Church." Now then, he wants to know the comparable authority in the church of Christ. Here it is. It is in the authority that is inherent in the Holy Spirit's teaching. You and I will both concede that it is the obligation of the church to care for the needy. In the command or example that we have to do that is the inherent authority for it. There is the authority for it, Brother Porter. A command to do a thing necessitates the means to carry that out. But you did not touch that argument at all last night. (To Brother Osborne) That is all right.

"Since you oppose church support of Christian schools, how can you endorse church support of benevolent organizations that build and maintain their own Christian schools?" I support the Christian schools in the orphan homes on the same basis that I support the idea of the church contributing to a poor family that uses some of the money to send their children to school. That's the basis on which I do it. In fact, friends, get it: (writing on the board) Let this represent the church and this the home. Let it represent the private home. Let this represent the orphan home. Now then, it is the right of an individual to have his own home. But suppose a child loses its home. Then, the church supplies that which the child no longer has. All right, it supplies that home, the orphan home. Now, in this home it had here, it had the right to an education; therefore, it is the duty of the church to supply that child with an education. There is the authority for it.

"Would you endorse a Sunday school corporation, chartered under the laws of the state, with the same organizational setup that characterizes our benevolent organizations for church edification?" No, because it is not needed. But then, when something is needed, as is characteristic of the needy, then that is a different thing. And, let me tell you this, friends, you can't operate any kind of a home without having state supervision. Brother Porter has a great deal to say about it being organized under the laws of the state. You can't operate without such. You have to have some sort of state supervision, just like you've got to have trustees for church property. All right, now. That covers it.

He says—and he got this from Leroy Garrett, because that is the only place from which it could possibly come; and I heard it a dozen times, more or less, out in California in a debate I had with him—that in the churches of California they don't have two bodies because it is still the church when organized. Now, listen. They have another organization besides that of the church. It is true that in the over-all picture there is but one organic affair, but there are two different setups organizationally speaking. There is the eldership, and then to comply with the laws of the land there is a board of directors, with a president; and you couldn't have a church of Christ in California without that. Do you endorse that, Brother Porter?

He wants to know if they could organize a Missionary Society. Brother Porter takes the position that they could, provided that they would support it privately, because he says that the orphan homes are parallel to the Missionary Society; but, he says that the orphan homes can be supported by individual contributions. If we would eliminate the church support and send the money individually, we could have the orphan homes; if the homes would just quit taking contributions from the churches, and accept private contributions, that would be scriptural. But since they are parallel to the Missionary Society, according to Brother Porter, you could support a Missionary Society by private contributions. Now, you see he is either going to do one of two things. He is ging to admit that, or he is going to back up on the idea that the parallel is there. Let him decide which he will do.

He says the orphan home is an additional body. It is. That is exactly right. But now, again, friends, it is that old fallacy of using a word in two senses. When we speak of the church as a body, we mean that it is a body in one sense. When we speak of the body that constitutes a group of people assembled for a special purpose, that is another body. But just as I showed on the chart number one, it is not in conflict with it. Let us substitute the word "organization" for "body." You have the idea exactly. "The orphan home is wrong because it is another body." Now, watch Brother Porter's predicament, ladies and gentlemen. The orphan home is wrong because it is not the church. It is another body. The private home is not the church. *It is another body!* Is it wrong, Brother Porter? It is doing a work that you say is right. Now, what about taking this child and putting him in a private home? That is another body. That's another body, Brother Porter. That is two bodies. The church is one body and the private home another body.

Is that wrong? Brother Porter, there are two bodies doing the work which you say that the church should do. He said I said the orphan home would be wrong if it were the church. Well, certainly, because we have the organic setup of the church with the elders and deacons. It is not the function of the elders to go out and sweep floors, and make beds, and cook meals for orphan children. That is not a part of their duties.

This business of universal, or at least a brotherhood-wide home would be unscriptural. He said he doubted the wisdom of it because he believes it would be wrong. Now then, Brother Porter said he *doubted* the wisdom of it. Is that as strong as he is against it? When you *doubt* something you entertain uncertainty. That is all. Brother Porter, I don't doubt that I am against things that are wrong. I don't doubt that at all. I am *certain* of this. Do you just doubt a thing that you say is unscriptural? Now, Brother Porter, you were just plain quibbling when you were on that. That is the only reason you said that; because you didn't mean that it was unscriptural *then.* You just *doubted* the wisdom of it.

He says I have taken the position that we can't care for orphans in our own homes. Let us have chart number six, please. Now, Brother Porter, I don't see how on earth you can draw such a conclusion as that. He said that I have taken the position that the organization that is characteristic of the Tipton Home is the only type of organization. Now, he misunderstood me—I am going to be charitable. I said *some such* organization. Don't you remember that? I said some such organization.

In respect to this, he said, "Yes, you can care for the needy; churches may do it; churches may cooperate in it; and churches may establish a home for such care." But he says it can't be an organization. He said I have taken the position that the only kind of organization is that which Tipton has. I took no such position. I said this; and here is the argument I made: Brother Porter admits that the Memphis churches can have a home. Now, there is going to have to be some kind of organization in a home that has twenty-eight churches pooling their resources and taking all the

CHART NO. 6—"A DEADLY PARALLEL"

Anti-Class Groups	Garrett, Ketcherside, et al	W. Curtis Porter
1. May Divide Assembly.	1. Preacher May Locate.	1. Care for the Needy.
2. Teach Classes.	2. Receive Support	2. Churches may care for the needy.
3. Use Women Teachers	3. Work with Elders.	3. Churches may cooperate in such care.
	4. Stay "50 years"	4. Churches may establish a home for such care.
"Modern Sunday School"	"The Pastor System"	"INSTITUTIONALISM"

old folks out of Memphis. You are going to have some kind of organization. I don't care what you call it. You may not call it an organization; but whatever it is, it is something. Now, that, friends, is necessary. Whatever it is that it takes to carry out the work, that is the thing that is necessary. That is what my statement was. I said some such organization. It might not have to be—I said it might not have to be exactly like this one. Now, that is what I said. Brother Porter, be a little more careful in picking up those statements.

BROTHER WATSON: "Three and a half minutes."

All right, that's sufficient. Now, he asked where he endorsed any organization in Memphis? Where did Brother Porter say he endorsed any organization? He doesn't endorse any organization for the care of the old folks in Memphis. *Not any.* But he believes the twenty-eight churches can take money from their treasuries and put it together and establish a home for destitute old people who have nobody else to care for them and take care of those old people. Well, you can do that without any kind of organization, so says Brother W. Curtis Porter. Now, I tell you friends, a fellow is certainly scared of the word "organization" to run that hard from it, isn't he? I tell you he is!

Again let us have chart number fifteen. He says I have no argument here because what he is opposing is an organization there. The Memphis churches can do that, yes; but I can't read where he said anything about an organization. No, he did not mention the word "organization." But, friends, if Brother Porter said, "I traveled from Monette, Arkansas, to Indianapolis, Indiana, a few days ago," he wouldn't have to say that he came by some means of transportation, would he? I think I would have enough reasoning ability to draw the conclusion that Brother Porter traveled in some fashion. I might not know what fashion he followed, or what kind of travel characterized it, but I would know there was some traveling involved when he made that trip. All right, he says that the Memphis churches can combine in one home. I tell you you are going to have some kind of a home down there. He said it was a *home.*

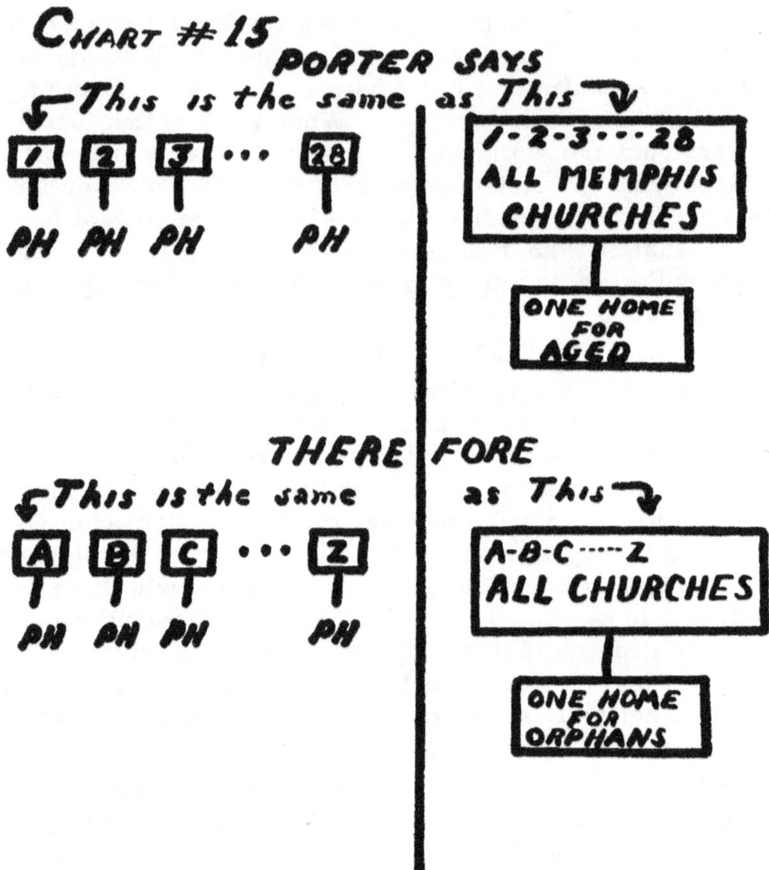

Is a home an organization or is it disorganized? Now, Brother Porter, you are in the worst situation I ever saw an able man tonight. I never saw a fellow in my life in a worse shape than Brother W. Curtis Porter is here tonight on this question, friends; and the reason is, he hasn't got the truth! If he will get back to where he was before he *backed into the Sommerite camp,* why, then he will again be a strong debater. That's his trouble. He is running away from what he thinks is institutionalism, and he has backed right into the Sommerite camp! And these brethren tonight, Brother Ketcherside and Brother Sommer, and others here know that is the truth; they know that is the thing about it. Brother Ketcherside said to me last night that Brother

Porter is making the same arguments that Daniel Sommer made years and years ago; and Brother Allen Sommer said today that these matters were first presented in 1876 or 1877. And there is the situation, and that is the reason I am against it. I have had twenty debates with the anti-Sunday school people. I am not about to accept the anti position here on this question or any other. That is sufficient now.

Now, friends, there is the issue. I maintain that Brother Porter hasn't met the argument. In fact, he hasn't taken up a single argument. All he has done is to shout, "Organization!" I am not contending for an organization that is a machine that dominates the churches. I am using the word "organization" in the sense of *means of procedure* by which benevolence is carried out. I say that orphan homes constitute a *how*. Not *the how;* but *a how.* (Time called.)

Thank you.

Porter's Fifth Negative

Brethren Moderators, Brother Woods, Ladies and Gentlemen:

I am glad to be before you again for further consideration of the question under discussion at this time, as to whether churches have a scriptural right to build and maintain benevolent organizations for the care of the needy. We are not discussing the question of whether it is scriptural for churches to care for the needy. That is entirely beside the point. We are discussing whether or not churches have the right to build and maintain benevolent organizations through which to render that care and that relief.

And I want to take up point by point the things Brother Woods has just said, and I am not greatly disturbed by his method of procedure in the beginning of his speech. He said he had a hundred or so debates, but he had never heard a more feeble effort than that which Brother Porter made tonight; that he could stop right now and give me the rest of his time, and that his position would stand unassailed. Well, that is fine for Brother Woods to tell you that. You may never have found it out if he hadn't let it be known that way. So it is very nice of him to tell you about how easily he has won the victory and how feeble Porter has been in all of his efforts; that he hasn't even taken up one single argument, he said a while ago—that Porter hasn't taken up one single argument. I wonder if he thinks that this audience is that blind. I just wonder if he does. Well, if he does, he has your intelligence far below the rank that I give it. And so I am not disturbed about that because I understand that it is *characteristic* of Brother Woods to declare the last man that he is meeting is making the feeblest effort that he has ever met. He has done that on other occasions; and whoever may be his opponent, he will tell the audience how *feeble* the man is in his efforts that is opposing him: that it is the weakest thing he ever saw. That is *characteristic* of Brother Woods. So don't be greatly disturbed if he follows that course this time. But you listen and you make your own decisions about it. I am willing for you to judge. Brother Woods doesn't have to tell you about it.

Then he said until 1947 there was not a preacher in the South who took the position that Brother Porter takes. My position, brethren and friends, tonight is that the church has no right to build and maintain organizations, a humanly organized setup, through which to render relief to those who are in need. There wasn't a preacher in the South prior to 1947 that ever took that position, Brother Woods avers. Brother Woods, did you ever see this? (Holding up a book.) You are the author of it, aren't you? *Annual Lesson Commentary* for 1946. That is back of 1947, isn't it? Now, here is a statement made by Brother Woods back in 1946. That was before 1947, and Brother Woods says on page 338 of this book: "The self-sufficiency of the church in organization, work, worship, and every function required of it by the Lord should be emphasized. This lesson is much needed today. Religious secular organizations are always trying to encroach on the function of the New Testament church, interfere with its obligations, and attempt to discharge some of its functions. The church is the *only* organization"—(And he has the word "only" emphasized in italic letters). "The church is the *only* organization authorized to discharge the responsibilities of the Lord's people. When brethren form organizations independently of the church to do the work of the church, however worthy their aims and right their designs, they are engaged in that which is sinful." That was Guy N. Woods in 1946; and yet he said that back of 1947 there was not a preacher in the South who took such a position. That is only a mite of what I have of what Brother Woods has said, even back of that date, if he wants it.

Now, he said, regarding some other matters, he talked to Brother Carl Ketcherside last night, and Brother Ketcherside told him that I did not hold these positions—or he implied that—back sometime ago; that when Brother Ketcherside met Brother Rue Porter at Ozark, Missouri, a good many years ago, Brother Curtis Porter was present at that debate and evidently endorsed Brother Rue Porter in the discussion held. It just happens, Brother Woods, that Curtis Porter didn't hear a *single word of that debate.* Curtis Porter *was not there.* I never heard a single word of that debate between Carl Ketcherside and Rue Porter. And while it was published in book form; that is, a report of it—I think it was not an exact reproduction of it—I have never even seen a copy of the book, Brother Woods. Well, what is the purpose of all that? It is simply *prejudicial.* Brother Woods seems to realize that he is up a tree or something, and he wants to create prejudice against the position I am occupying tonight by calling me a man who "has lately backed into the camp of the Sommerites." It is done for *no other reason* but for *prejudicial reasons:* to prejudice the minds of the people against the position that is being advocated. Why don't you stay with the scripture? What difference does it make whether Carl Ketcherside endorses my position or yours or whose? We will have more on that, too, because he got back to it just before he sat down. And let me look at that a moment. Yes, he said I "backed into the Sommerite camp"; and he said the arguments that Porter is making are the same arguments that Sommer made back years and years ago. Yes, Brother Woods, maybe so, in some respects; and the arguments which you make against the Missionary Societies are the same arguments that Daniel Sommer made years ago. Or were they? Did you have something in common with Brother Daniel Sommer, I wonder? I wonder if he had something in common with Brother Daniel Sommer. The same arguments he makes against Missionary Societies were also made against them. How are we to tell whether a thing is true or not? Whether it is endorsed by Leroy Garrett, Carl Ketcherside, or whether it is according to the scriptures? Just what is our plan in determining that? What is our rule, anyway, Brother Woods? Folks would seem to get the idea from what you are saying about it that if Carl Ketcherside and Leroy Garrett hold to a thing, it is wrong. But they believe that the church was established on Pentecost, and you do too. And they believe the church should have elders, and you do too. They believe that baptism is for the remission of sins, and so does Guy Woods. They believe that there is only one divinely organized church, and so does Brother Woods. They believe that singing is the only kind of music that is to be used in the church, and so does Brother Woods. They believe the church should have elders and deacons, and so does Brother Woods. And I might go on and enumerate numbers and numbers of things which they endorse that Brother Woods also endorses. So we can't determine whether a thing is right by just seeing who believes it. That has nothing to do with it.

And he said he would *never* have introduced that letter that had been written to Brother Bill Rogers if I had not *left the scriptures* and brought up some of his statements. He would never have introduced it. Then, why did you introduce the *Porter-Waters Debate* in your first speech? I hadn't said a word when you brought that up. You went back and quoted from the Porter-Waters Debate in the *very first speech* of this debate. And Porter hadn't *even said one word.* What drove you to that? Was it something Porter had done? Something that Porter had said in this debate that caused you to do that?

"Sixteen men for the Lord's supper." He said, "Now, he just resorted to quibbling." Of course, when his argument blows up, it is just a quibble. Well, we will let you decide whether it is a quibble or not. He said certainly they are not to be incorporated, chartered, and so on. He said there was no purpose accomplished. Well, they could accomplish the same purpose: they would do what the Lord said do—they would *administer the Lord's supper.* And that is what is being accomplished, you say, through the human organizations that you are contending for—the *care of the needy.* That is the purpose to be accomplished. So the same purpose would exist. I mean a *similar* purpose.

Then, he said the *Gospel Guardian* is a chartered organization, and so on and so forth. And so are the Bible schools, the Christian colleges, Brother Woods; and you endorse support for them, don't you? Not church support, but you would endorse an individual's supporting them, wouldn't you? And they are organizations.

He said that if Porter had stayed with the scriptures, he wouldn't have brought up the letter. But I have introduced that already.

Porter's Projector
Chart No. 3

THE "HOW" VERSUS "ORGANIZATION"

MAT. 28:19 - TEACH - HOW - ORGANIZATION {CHURCH / MISSIONARY SOCIETY}

1 TIM. 5:16 - RELIEVE - HOW - ORGANIZATION {CHURCH / BENEVOLENT ORGANIZATION}

Now, to the blackboard. In Matt. 28: 19 we have the commandment, "Go ye therefore and teach all nations." There is the reference, and here is the command, and the *how* is not detailed; the specifications are not given. The digressive Christian Church preacher has said that, since the *how* is not given, then we can *form organizations beside the church, in* the church or *out* of the church. I don't care where you put it. They form organizations beside the church to do that work; and so they have formed the Missionary Society. We contended the church was sufficient to do the work without those human organizations. And he said the *how* still existed. All right. Then *the organizations* and *the how* are two different things, aren't they? The *organizations* and the *how* are not the same thing, are they? No, he said we are to teach, and here is *the how,* and *the how* is not detailed. And they have the Missionary organizations in the church. But he said, "Brother Porter, after they got these organizations, they still had *the how.*" All right, then, *the how* and *the organizations* were *not the same.* Down goes everything that Brother Woods has made along this line, because he has been arguing all the time that *the organization is the how.* That is what he has been contending. Since the scripture doesn't detail *the how,* then that *includes the organizations,* and we can set them up. So *the how is the organization* here (pointing to chart), but *the how* and *the organization* up here are entirely distinct things. I wonder if he thinks that is a quibble too. (Laughter.)

Now, then, to his questions and to his answers to mine.

First. "Is the work which the orphan home does wrong?" No. The work of teaching the truth, that may be done through a Missionary Society, is not wrong either. All right.

Second. "It it wrong because the orphan home is an organization?" Not merely because the organization exists, but you are demanding and contending for a church supported human organization. That is the thing that I am opposing, just the same as I would the Missionary Society.

Third. "Is it wrong because the orphan home has a superintendent, secretary, president of a board, and other officials?" Well, that is part of it; and you are looking for the church support of it in that connection. And I want to give you another statement here regarding the matter of organization along that line. I think I will have it here in a minute. If I don't, I will get to it later. Yes, in the *Gospel Advocate* of December 21, 1944, page 830, Brother Woods said, "We deny that the mode of procedure characteristic of the average Bible school maintained by churches of Christ is the same as that followed in such denominational schools. Sectarian Sunday schools have their *boards.*" You were opposing boards then, weren't you? "Sectarian Sunday schools have their boards, conventions, rules of government, superintendents, treasurers, etc., etc., concomitants conspicuous by their absence in the Bible schools among us. If isolated instances can be produced where brethren have adopted some of these sectarian tendencies, we will offer *no defense. Apostasies* have *always occurred* in every good work." And another one is under progress. That last sentence is mine. All right. Brother Woods, back here in 1944, was *opposing boards* and treasuries and superintendents and so forth and so forth and so on, things that were "conspicuously absent from our Bible class work." And *upon that basis* he was opposing the sectarian Sunday school organizations. Yet he is endorsing the same thing today for the benevolent organizations to care for the needy. Well, let us see.

"Is it wrong because you believe it to be an organization apart from the church?" Well, I am like you were in your debate with Leroy Garrett. You said you were opposed to a Missionary Society whether it was under the elders or not. And I would be opposed to that for the church to build and maintain.

And fifth. "Is it wrong because it is supported by cooperative effort?" No, I am not opposing cooperation.

Sixth. "Would you endorse the Missionary Society if it were to become an individual, private, enterprise accepting contributions from individuals only?" I would, just to the same extent that you would, Brother Woods, when we compare your position on the Bible schools with the Missionary Societies. In the statement that you made in the *Firm Foundation* back in 1942, you reviewed Brother G. C. Brewer's book, *Contending for The Faith,* in which he advocated the idea of church supported Bible schools. Regarding those things you said, "In our view brethren surrender their contention against the Missionary Society when they espouse such a view of the colleges." All right. Can you support individually the colleges? Brother Woods would say, Yes. Or if you parallel it with the Missionary Society, then will you support the Missionary Society individually? So we are both in the same hole. We will just play around together. (Laughter.)

Number seven. "What determines whether an enterprise constitutes institutionalism?" Well, there are two kinds of institutions, Brother Woods, human and divine. I am not against institutionalism in the generic sense of the term. I believe in institutionalism, some kinds of institutions, because the church is an institution that the Lord started. I believe in that. But a human organization set up by human wisdom and human judgment and human authority, that God never authorized, is the kind of institution that I oppose. The same kind that you have opposed in days gone by. And you said *it was our stand against human institutions that brought us to our proud position today.* And that is where I stand also.

Now, then, let me see his answers to my questions if I have time to get to them. I have it here in this one. Here they are.

First. "Since you stated last night that I could not tell how the church could care for the needy without describing our benevolent organizations, did you mean to say that the only possible way to care for the needy is through such organizations?"

And then number two followed: "If you did not mean this, what are some of the other ways that you consider to be scriptural?" He said, "Well, I think it would be scriptural to take them into the home, into the Christian home, the private home, and take care of them." Well, we agree on *that how;* so you have one of them, don't you? He said, "I have given you *two hows* now." All right. I have accepted one of them; and so you have *one how* to start with at least. So we have made some progress on *the how.* Brother Woods and I have agreed on a *how* for part of it, to say the least of it. So far, so good.

Number three. "If our benevolent corporations, while retaining their present organizational setup without any other change whatsoever, should decide to discontinue their work of benevolence and engage in the work of evangelism, would you endorse it as a scriptural arrangement?" He said, "You have the exact picture of the California situation." Did you mean to say that you endorsed it, Brother Woods? Brother Woods, did you mean to say you endorsed it? Do you endorse the setup in the California law regarding churches? Do you? Do you, Brother Woods? I would like to know. You will tell me in your next speech, won't you? Please, Brother Woods. (Laughter.) Will you tell me in your next speech? Do you endorse the exact picture that you have in California regarding the incorporation of churches? Do you endorse that? If so, and you say *this is the exact picture* of it, then *you endorse this*. And, therefore, if Brother Woods endorses the California law regarding the incorporation of churches, then *he endorses this* and says, "If our benevolent corporations, while retaining their present organizational setup without any other change whatsoever, should decide to discontinue their work of benevolence and engage in the work of evangelism," he would endorse that as a scriptural arrangement. And he would have a Missionary Society that he could endorse. Would you, Brother Woods? I just can't believe that you would endorse that. Would you? You won't forget to tell us, will you? Well, if you do, I will not let you forget about it. I will keep reminding you of it.

Fourth. "If 'The Society for the Propagation of the Faith'—we want to get that chart—chart number 1, please. If 'The Society for the Propagation of the Faith' (a Catholic Foreign Missionary Society) is not a rival to the Catholic Church, would we be justified in organizing a similar society for churches of Christ?"

He said, "Well, he missed the point completely. He did not even get to my argument; that I showed that these were not rivals; that the Federal Government has a Post Office that is not a rival; that the State Government has a Highway Department that is not a rival; the Masonic Lodge has homes for the aged that are not rivals to the Masonic Lodge; and so the Catholic Church has orphanages that are not rivals. And the church of Christ may have some also; and they are not rivals." And his conclusion was that we can have any kind of organization that *doesn't rival the church.*

I showed why these do not rival, and he said that I didn't even touch it. I showed why the Post Office Department is not a rival of the Federal Government, because it has a legislative branch that can authorize it. And I showed that the Highway Department does not rival the State Government because the State Government has a legislative department that can authorize it. And then if he has the same parallel here, who in the church of Christ has the authority to legislate an organization, a benevolent organization, to care for

Chart No. 1

Organizations in Different Categories

Fed. Gov't. ----Post Office Dept.
State Gov't.--- Highway Dept.
Masonic Lodge---Homes for Aged.
Catholic Church--- Orphanages.
Church of Christ---Orphanages & Homes for Aged

Rival These?
Do These

the church? Or to care for the needy of the church? And he said I did not even touch it.

He admits the homes are additional bodies. He said, "Yes, they are additional bodies." "The home is wrong because it is not the church" (according to Porter). And he said, "The private home is also not the church, and it is wrong." (Time Called.)

Well, I thank you very kindly.

Woods' Sixth Affirmative

Brethren Moderators, Brother Porter, Ladies and Gentlemen:

If I were D. N. Jackson, a Baptist preacher whom both Brother Porter and I have met in debate numerous times, I would say that I haven't had so much fun since Christmas. (Laughter.) It is indeed a pleasure to participate in this debate, and I am glad to see Brother Porter making the effort that he is. We have advanced now to this point that he has admitted that *the home* is a method of taking care of the needy. That is the *how*. That is not answering my question, because he said that the church could take care of the needy. Now then, he has said that the private home can do it. He means that the church can do it by the home doing it, in which case what the home is doing, *the church is doing!* But he believes that the home can contribute to a Christian college; therefore, if his argument has any merit at all, if the church does it when the home is doing it, in the matter of benevolence, supporting the orphans, then the church is doing it when the home supports the Christian college! Brother Porter, you will tell us about that when you come back up here, won't you? (Laughter.) Brother Porter, you won't forget that, will you? (Laughter.) Brother Porter, I am not going to let you forget that! (Great laughter.) You remember that. Now, friends, that takes it away from him, world without end. He said, "Yes, I believe that the *how* is in the home doing it." But he said the church could do it. Now, he was either telling us how the church could do it, or he wasn't. If he wasn't, then he hasn't told us the *how* yet. But if he was telling us, then the church does it when the home does it; therefore, what the home does, the church does. But he believes the home can support the Christian college; therefore, the church can support the college, can't it, Brother Porter? Brother Porter, look up here. (Laughter.) You want to take it back? I will let you take it back right now if you want to and won't refer to it again if you want to. You want to take it back? Now, you are in a bad way on that, Brother Porter. (Laughter.) You surely are.

He said it is characteristic of me to tell that I win the victory in debates. Well, I wasn't telling you because I didn't think you knew it. (Laughter.) I was sure that you did know it, because I certainly wouldn't tell you something I didn't think was so. Certainly I wouldn't have said it. He said that seems to be characteristic of me. Well, it just so happens that I think I am always on the right side of every question, and I never saw a fellow in my life who could defend false doctrine. He always gets a whipping. I don't mean to be boastful when I say that. If Brother Porter were on the right side of this, there isn't a man on the top side of God's earth that is a stronger debater than W. Curtis Porter. Talk about telling the audience things. I have sat in the audience and I have listened to debates that Brother Porter participated in when he toyed with his opponent just like a cat toying with a mouse. I have seen him do it time and again, and there are a lot of preachers here tonight who have seen it happen. It depends, Brother Porter, on which side of the fence you are on with reference to these matters.

Friends, it is a strange thing that a man will not represent you correctly. Some of these brethren have published statements from me—have taken them out of their context—and used them in a sense I never had any idea of on this question. Right here is a good example of this. Here is what I said: "The self-sufficiency of the church in organization, work, worship, and every function required by the Lord should be emphasized. The lesson is much needed today. Religious secular organizations are always trying to encroach on the function of the New Testament church, interfering with its obligations in an attempt to discharge some of its functions. The church is the only organization authorized to discharge the responsibilites of the Lord's people. When brethren form organzations independently of the church to do the work of the church, however worthy their aims and right their designs, they are engaged in that which is sinful." I said that then (in 1946), and I say it now. I don't know of a brother associated with me in this debate, or who believes what I believe tonight, who wouldn't say *amen* to that statement. Again there I used the word "organization" in the sense of something apart from and independent of the church and as a rival to the church. But Brother Porter quit reading right there. It is significant that he stopped right there. Listen to the rest of it: "All ecclesiasticism is wrong." He didn't want to read, because by the wildest stretch of imagination he couldn't say that what I am defending is ecclesiasticism; so he stopped before he got there. He didn't read the next sentence. "Any move meant to force churches of Christ to bow to the behests of any paper, clique, or group in the church is ecclesiasticism." Look at the next one. "There is a very definite trend in this direction in the brotherhood today." And I could say the trend has grown in some circles since then. "In some of the larger cities groups of preachers meet and formulate an attitude and then demand that the churches support them in such an attitude; and if they will not, the churches are stigmatized and accused of holding to false doctrine. Preachers have no right to exercise any such powers over the free churches of Christ. Only the church itself, through its divinely authorized elders, has the right to formulate its policies, and in so doing is answerable only to the Lord. The teacher should impress these principles on their classes as strongly as possible." (Annual Lesson Commentary, 1946, p. 338.) And here is what I had in mind when I wrote that. I was thinking of the situation that then existed in Houston, Texas, when the Norhill congregation, of which Roy Cogdill was then the preacher, organized a situation down there and attempted to force the Central congregation into a cooperative effort in the Music Hall meeting, in which all the congregations cooperating turned their money over to Norhill, who then conducted the meeting. And because Burton Coffman and the Central church wouldn't go into it, they stigmatized them all over the country. *And it turns out that Burton Coffman was he only scriptural preacher in Houston during the whole deal!* Now, that is exactly the situation I was describing in that paragraph; and I remember very definitely when I wrote it.

He said with reference to the Porter-Ketcherside debate that he wasn't there. Well, I wasn't there and don't know whether he was there or not; and it is entirely possible that I may have misapprehended what Brother Ketcherside said. I, of course, withdraw that statement, because it is entirely possible that I misunderstood him. But I do know this: I have a letter in my possession from Rue Porter in which he was telling me about that debate, and he said that during that debate he threatened Carl Ketcherside with Brother

W. Curtis Porter, and Brother Porter intimated to him that he was willing to meet Ketcherside. Brother Porter, would you be willing to meet Brother Ketcherside on the orphan home question tonight? You would then, but wouldn't do it tonight. I know that to be true. I have the letter.

He said my reference to the Sommer question is prejudicial. It is not prejudicial. At least, that was not my purpose in introducing it. It was merely to identify the movement. He said that I said there wasn't a preacher in the South until 1947 who held to the view that he holds. Now, I didn't say that. I said there wasn't a preacher known to me. There may have been some, but I didn't know any then who held Brother Porter's position as it is tonight. It is a *new* position. It is true that there were differences of opinion among brethren with reference to how the homes should be organized; but, so far as I know, there wasn't a preacher who opposed the organization of the Tipton Orphan Home in 1947 within the realm of my acquaintance who was truly a southern preacher. There were two or three, perhaps, who had been transplanted down there who got some of their ideas up here and took them down there.

He says that I believe some things that Brother Sommer believed. Certainly, I do. But when we talk about Sommerism, we mean that which is peculiar to Daniel Sommer. It is true that Daniel Sommer believed in the deity of Jesus, but a lot of other people believe in the deity of Jesus. Daniel Sommer is the originator, and so his son said today, of this position in the churches of Christ; and he said that it occurred about seventy-five years ago, or somewhere around 1876 or '77. Seems to me he said somewhere about that time. That is what his son said about it right here in this pulpit today.

He says that he admits you may take orphans into a private home. That is a *how*. He believes that's right. But that is not *how* the church does it, and that still doesn't answer our question. Now, friends, Brother Porter has allowed almost two sessions to pass; and, up to now, *he has not told us how the church is to do that which he says it must do!* Do you think, if he were debating with a man who was trying to defend sprinkling and pouring, that he would spend all of his time just saying, "Sprinkling is not right; pouring is not right; that's not the way to do it; that is the wrong way to do it; you are not doing it scripturally"? Do you think he would stop with that? Do you think the Methodist preacher would have to stand up and plead with him, "Brother Porter, you are telling us how not to do it; please tell us how"? Brother Porter, I would like to know how the church is to do it. It can't do it with an organization. You said that it can do it; now then, tell us.

"Do you endorse the incorporation of the churches in California?" Well, certainly I believe that it is right for the church out there, in order to function, to conform to the laws of the state. Now, my point there was that whatever is essential to carrying on the work is scriptural; that is an expedient; and an expedient in that sense is scriptural; therefore, it is right for the church to do that. Now, even in this state, or any other state, you must have trustees to hold church property. You cannot convey property to a church, as such. You must convey it to individuals to hold in trust for the church. Well, that constitutes a different organization; and yet we all believe that is right.

Now, let us have chart number one. Again, friends, I want you to see that Brother Porter is deliberately refusing to meet the issue here. The issue is not: Is there authority in the Federal Government for the Post Office Department? There is. That was my very point. He thinks that by saying that these on this side (pointing to the chart) have the authority to formulate that it in some way militates against my position. I don't think Brother Porter has ever apprehended the argument yet. His position is that the orphanages and homes for the aged are wrong because they are organizations apart from the church, in competition with the church; and therefore, doing the work of the church, when the church itself ought to be doing it. Now, my point is that the Post Office Department, though another organization, is not in conflict with the Federal Government. The Highway Department is not in conflict with the State Government. The homes for the aged in the Masonic Lodge do not rival the Masonic Lodge. The orphan homes for the Catholic Church

Chart No. 1
Organizations in Different Categories

Fed. Gov't. ----Post Office Dept.
State Gov't.---Highway Dept.
Masonic Lodge---Homes for Aged.
Catholic Church---Orphanages.
Church of Christ---Orphanages & Homes for Aged

Rival These?
Do These

are not in competition. They are means by which these work. *Now, let him tell us how the Federal Government could operate a Post Office Department without a Post Office Department!* That is the position that he has actually taken here tonight on this; that the church of Christ can care for orphans without having some kind of an orphanage in which to care for them. He may not like the word "orphanage." That is what I am trying to get him to do; to tell us what it is. Now, he comes back and says, "Well, the authority is inherent here (Federal Government); therefore, that (church of Christ). The authority of the Federal Government is not inherent in the Federal Government; it is in the people that are back of the Federal Government. There is the source of authority. The authority is not in the Federal Government. The authority is in the people back of it. That is the source of authority. The authority of a Masonic Lodge is not in the members that make up the Masonic Lodge. It is in the bylaws that constitute the Lodge, the constitution back of it. And, in like fashion, the authority for the operation of orphanages and homes for the aged is not in the members of the church of Christ, but is in the Holy Spirit who authorized the care of the needy.

Brother Porter says he believes in the care of the needy, *but he hasn't told us how the church is to do it!* And this debate will close and he won't tell us, because he is simply on the negative side on this question. Well, all right, now, that is sufficient.

Let us take up his answers to my questions. Is the work which the orphan home does wrong? "No." Well, then, why do you oppose it? He said, "Well, because of the organization of it. That was the next question. Is it wrong because the orphan home is an organization? He said, "Well, no, not just because it is an organization, but because it is a church supported organization." Well, therefore, it is not wrong because of the organization it possesses. It is just wrong because the church supported that organization. Yet, he has been telling us for two nights that it is the organization that makes it wrong. Now he is in conflict with himself. He said all the time up until this very question here, "Yes, I am against it because it is an organization unknown to the New Testament." What is wrong with the orphan home? It is an organization unauthorized. "Brother Porter," I asked him, "is it wrong because the orphan home is an organization?" "No," he said. Well, what is wrong with it? Because it is a church-supported organization. Now he is arguing on both sides of the fence, and there isn't an intelligent person in this audience who can't see that. Nobody knows it better than Brother Porter. Brother Porter, up to now, it was the organization, wasn't it? That was what was wrong with it. Now then, it is not the organization; it is because the church supports it. Well, what is it we are talking about? Orphan homes. What is it parallel with? Missionary Society. What is wrong with it? Because it is an organization? No. What is wrong with the Missionary Society? The organization? No. What is wrong with it? Because the church supports it. *Therefore, individuals can support the Missionary Society!* Now, one of two things is true, friends. These brethren are going to have to give up the idea of private support of the orphan home or else they are going to have to admit support of the Missionary Society on the same basis. One or the other. Many of them have already given up the idea. There are preachers in the audience tonight who believe that it is wrong to support an orphan home by the church, privately, or any other way; and I can produce documentary evidence of that fact. As a matter of fact, about all they agree on along this line is that they are just against it. Brother Porter, please clarify this question for us. You have taken the position up to now that it was the organization you oppose. Now then, you answer, "No, it is not because it is an organization; it is because the church supports it." Now, will you please tell us this: Are you opposed to it simply because the church supports it, or because it is an organization? You have taken both sides. Which one are you going to settle on?

You said I was in the same hole with you. You are mistaken about the hole you are in. Not with me.

Number three: Is it wrong because the orphan home has a superintendent, secretary, president of a board, and other officials? He said I oppose the Missionary Society. I don't oppose it just because there is a superintendent, secretary, president of the board, and other officials. The light company has a president of the board and so on, and I don't oppose that because they have a president, a secretary, and so on. That is not ground for opposing it.

Is it wrong because you believe it to be an organization apart from the church? He said, "I believe it on the same basis you do the Missionary Society." That is not answering the question.

Is it wrong because it is supported by cooperative effort? "No." Now, the orphan home is not wrong because churches combine their resources and support it. Well, then, down goes another citadel that has been characteristic of these brethren. They have taken the position that it is all right for one congregation maybe to take care of its orphans, but they couldn't cooperate, churches couldn't cooperate in such support. Well, down goes that contention. Thank you. This man is step by step, and item by item, surrendering every contention which they have made.

Would you endorse the Missionary Society if it were to become a private enterprise, accepting contributions from individuals only? Well, he said, "Just like you do," because he said, "the Missionary Society and the college are parallel." And he alleges that I say that the colleges cannot be thus supported; and, therefore, since they are parallel, then the Missionary Society could not be. I did not take the position that the college and Missionary Society are parallel. I don't take that position. I don't believe they are parallel. If I believed they were parallel, I wouldn't believe in the support of a Christian college any way, because I don't believe it is right to support a Missionary Society privately.

What determines whether an enterprise constitutes institutionalism? I don't know exactly what he said about it. He wasn't very clear on that.

Now let us see, friends, what we have arrived at here. Let us see what has been admitted here tonight. Brother Porter has taken the position, item number one, that it is right to care for the needy. Secondly, that it is right for churches to care for the needy. Thirdly, that it is right for churches to cooperate in the care of the needy. Fourthly, that it is right to have an organization for the care of the needy, only that organization must not be supported by the church. Next, it is right for the private home to take care of the needy. *Now then, I ask him the question: How is the church to discharge that care?* I emphasize, ladies and gentlemen, this point. Brother Porter admits that it is right to take a child into the private home. Now, that is either the church doing it, or it is not. You remember that. If it is the church doing it, then when the individual performs an act, it is the church doing it. But he believes an individual can support the Christian college; therefore, the church could then support the Christian college through the individual. But if he says, "No, the church doesn't do it through the private home," then he hasn't told us *how the church does it,* has he?

Friends, I have introduced argument after argument that Brother Porter has not answered; first of all, a leading argument, one that I think is absolutely irresistible, the one on the axiom that the whole of a thing is the sum of its parts. He said, "I have only a minute." Then he ran over here and said two or three things about it and passed it and said no more. I wonder if you think that is actually meeting the issue. I tell you, Brother Porter, all of us were expecting more of you than that. We thought you would be able to take the things up and answer them. (Time called.)

Porter's Sixth Negative

Brethren Moderators, Brother Woods, Ladies and Gentlemen:

If Brother Woods were allowed to render the verdict for this audience, of course, the debate is over. But I am certain of the fact that he is not the jury in this case, and we will let you make your own decision about whether or not Brother Porter has made any effort to answer his arguments, and touched top, edge, side, or bottom of them, or whether he has just quibbled all the way through. That is not Brother Woods' business to make that decision for you. You make your decision for yourselves.

Then regarding the matter of the college, and I want to get to that just now at the beginning. He had not made the Christian college parallel with the Missionary Society; therefore, he was not in the hole that I was in. Well, we are going to read. I am going to read more of the statement. I read a portion of it a while ago. I am going to read the entire statement to you and let you draw your own conclusions. He was reviewing Brother Brewer's book, *Contending for The Faith;* and this review was published in the *Firm Foundation* of February 3, 1942. And here is the quotation from Brother Woods' article:

"The section on colleges and Missionary Societies in which the author attempts to prove that it is scriptural for the churches, as such, to contribute from their treasuries funds for the support of Christian colleges, falls, in this writer's opinion, far short of the mark. Brother Brewer insists that there is a difference in sending funds to a Christian college, a human institution, and in doing the same with reference to a Missionary Society. Through long dreary pages this is argued at length, all of which, to this writer, is a sea of mud! Perhaps it is our own denseness; and if Brother Brewer and those who profess to see such a difference wish to consider our inability so to do a manifest mark of immaturity, they are at liberty to do so. We can write only as the matter appears to us at present. We are frank to confess that we lack the inner wisdom, or whatever it is, that enables one to accept without question the theory that it violates no principle of reason or revelation to support a human institution designed to educate young men for the ministry, and yet insist that it is subversive of both reason and revelation to support an institution similarly organized to keep these young men in foreign fields preaching the gospel they learned in the college. In our view, brethren surrender their contention against the Missionary Society when they espouse such a view of the colleges."

Brother Woods, if you were not paralleling the Missionary Society and the Christian colleges in that, why was it your view that brethren were *surrendering their contention against the Missionary Society?* Will you tell us? Why were they surrendering their position against the Missionary Society if you were not paralleling them? To contribute to the colleges out of the church and also to the Missionary Society out of the church? Now, if anybody can read that and decide that Brother Woods was not making a parallel between the Missionary Society and the Christian colleges, you can excuse me because of my "manifest mark of immaturity," not being able to see that thing which is "a sea of mud" to me.

Brother Woods began by saying, "If I were D. N. Jackson, whom Brother Porter and Brother Woods both have met a number of times, I would say that I never had so much fun in my life." Yes, but you weren't D. N. Jackson; and you didn't have the fun, Brother Woods. You have indicated that Jackson was having some fun. Maybe he thought he was, and maybe he thought he wasn't. Maybe he was putting up a front like some other preachers I have known to do sometimes. Maybe that was it. But I am certain of the fact that there was not as much fun in it as you intended to indicate.

Now, then, regarding the matter of the contributions from the church and how it is to be done, he said, "Well, if the individual takes them into his own home, that's not the church, unless the church does it when the home does it; and if the church does it when the home does it, then whatever the home does the church does; and since the home can support the college, then the church can support the college; and, therefore, Porter has endorsed church support of colleges." Well, I took *what you said.* That was your statement, Brother Woods. That was the answer *you gave.* You said the home does it. In answer to the question about *the how,* you said the home could do it; that it could be done in the private home. Did you parallel the home with the church and make whatever the home does the church does? If so, then you are in that hole yourself, whether you see the hole or not. The audience, I think, may be able to see it.

He said, "I did not tell you that I am winning a victory just because I thought you didn't know it." I wonder why he was telling you then. I suppose he thought if he would tell it often enough he might convince himself that he was doing it; if he would just repeat it over and over, he might make himself believe that he was. Maybe that was the reason for it. Well, anyway, we will let you decide how the victory has been won.

And he said he had seen Brother Porter "toy with denominational preachers as a cat would with a mouse, but he is on the wrong side of this thing." Just as Brother Woods and others are on the wrong side when they oppose the Missionary Society. I am on the same side of this thing that he is with respect to the Missionary Society. And if the position I occupy is wrong tonight respecting this, then his position with respect to the Missionary Society is wrong. So we will both be on wrong sides, according to that.

And, of course, he has been woefully misrepresented,

and he did not say there was no preacher prior to 1947 that took my position—no preacher in the South—but "no preacher known to him." Of course, I read to you a statement from a man by the name of Guy N. Woods, but my opponent didn't know him. My opponent didn't know him. All right. Now, he said where the misrepresentation was in this that I read a while ago, from the *Annual Lesson Commentary,* was that he said institutions or organizations that were "formed independently of the church"; that that was the kind of organizations he opposed. Well, that is one kind. I oppose that kind too. But that isn't all that Brother Woods opposed. That isn't the only statement he made about the matter, and we are going to see if that is true or not. In this Abilene Christian College lecture, in 1939, on page 53, Brother Woods said, "The tendency toward institutionalism. The ship of Zion has floundered more than once on the sandbar of institutionalism. The tendency to organize is a characteristic of the age. On the theory that the end justifies the means, brethren have not scrupled to form organizations (i-n) in (t-h-e) the (c-h-u-r-c-h) church." "Organizations *in the church.*" Not only did he oppose organizations formed "independently of the church," but he opposed organizations "in the church." All right. They "have not scrupled to form organizations *in the church* to do the work the church itself was designed to do. *All such organizations*"—What kind? "In the church," Brother Woods. That is what you said here. "In the church." Not only those "independent of the church," but those "in the church." All right. "All such organizations usurp the work of the church and are unnecessary and sinful." Who was that? A man by the name of Guy N. Woods, back in 1946. My opponent never heard of him. No preacher known to him ever took a position like that.

Then he came up with the Music Hall meeting and said the opposition against Burton Coffman and the church he was with over there, because they wouldn't come in and cooperate with the other churches and have a meeting, and so on, and so on, was what he had in mind when he wrote some of these statements. Well, the charge that Burton Coffman was opposed because they wouldn't cooperate in the meeting just isn't true. But it was the attitude that they took concerning the preacher who was going to conduct the meeting. All right.

Then he said, regarding the Rue Porter-Ketcherside debate, that I had said I wasn't there. But he said, "I do know that Rue Porter told me that he threatened Ketcherside with Curtis Porter." Well, I don't know what Rue threatened Brother Ketcherside with. I wasn't there. I gave him no authority to make any threat. I don't know anything about that, and I am entirely unresponsible for anything Brother Rue may have said along that line. He was speaking on his own; and whether he threatened him with me, I don't know. That is entirely beside the point.

Then this preacher in the South. He said, "There was no preacher known to me at that time that would oppose the *Tipton Orphan Home.*" Well, he mentioned that in this book here, that ACC Lecture in 1939. He endorsed the Tipton Orphan Home, but Brother Woods did not regard the Tipton Orphan Home as an organization. He took it out of the realm or the class of organizations at that time and said it wasn't. It was merely the elders working. "It wasn't an organization at all in the church as these others were." Now, I asked you last night, Brother Woods, and you didn't answer me. I wonder if you forgot it. Did you in 1939 endorse the Boles Orphan Home? What did you tell me about that? You said they did not oppose the Tipton Orphan Home, and you said in 1939 that that was the one that you endorsed. Now I want to know: Did you endorse the Boles Orphan Home in 1939?

And "Brother Daniel Sommer's son said today that his father was the one who originated the position that Porter occupies"; that is, the position that the church is an all-sufficient institution to do the work that God designed the church to do, originated with Daniel Sommer. Do you believe that? Do you believe that, Brother Woods? That the position that the all-sufficiency of the church to do the work that God assigned the church to do originated with Daniel Sommer? I am afraid you may have *misapprehended* what Brother Sommer's son said about it. I did not hear that statement.

He comes back, then, to the matter of *how.* He says, "He has not told us how." Well, I showed on this blackboard over here a while ago that he had said that *the organization* and *the how* are *two different things.*

Porter's Projector
Chart No. 3

THE "HOW" VERSUS "ORGANIZATION"

MAT. 28:19 - TEACH - HOW - ORGANIZATION { CHURCH / MISSIONARY SOCIETY

1 TIM. 5:16 - RELIEVE - HOW - ORGANIZATION { CHURCH / BENEVOLENT ORGANIZATION

Why didn't you notice that, Guy? You have been arguing all the time that since the Book doesn't tell *how* to care for the needy, then the church has the right to *form a human organization* to do it, and that *the organization comes within the how.* Then you turn around and say *the how is one thing* and *the organization is something else.* That is what Porter has been contending for. You don't know which side you are on, do you? Which side of this are you debating, anyway, Brother Woods? You came back and you said that the how and the organization are not the same thing, but that is the basis of your argument all along—that if *the how* is not detailed, you can make the organization to suit your own conveniences and your own judgment and your own discretion. Well, that is the same basis upon which the Christian Church preachers operated a hundred years ago when they developed the Missionary Society that led into the Christian Church. They worked upon the matter of *how. How* are you going to preach? The Bible said teach; it didn't tell *how. How* are you going to do it? Could you tell them, Brother Woods? Now, if some fellow would come up to you and say, "I believe sprinkling is baptism," you would say, "No, it isn't." He said, "I would tell him what it was then." You would tell him, would you? All right. When the Christian Church preacher comes along and says, "Here is the command to teach, and it doesn't tell *how*—doesn't tell *how,*" then would you tell him *how* to do it? How would you tell him? How would you tell him?

Would you tell him that it must be done by the church operating in its local capacity without the use of human organizations through which to operate, and which are to be built and maintained by the church? If you make the *how* mean that, *then that is the how.* The church can care for its orphans without setting up a chartered organization, a human organization, with any kind of board. The church itself can care for its orphans just like it cares for a preacher, or anybody else that may be in need, operating in its local capacity as a congregation. It can certainly do it. That gets to his "how" matter.

He endorses the California laws, he said. Well, then, you endorse the setup that I mentioned a while ago, because you said one is the exact picture of the other. So you endorse the idea that if our benevolent organizations today would change their purpose of work from benevolence to evangelism, retaining their present setup of organization, making no change whatsoever, that you would accept that as a Missionary Society to do evangelism. That is what you have done, because you say they are exact pictures, and you have endorsed one; therefore, you endorse the other. Thank you, Brother Woods.

Chart number one, let us have that. We want to take another look at chart number one just here.

And he says it hasn't been touched; that I have missed the point in the whole thing. He says the issue involved here—Porter has refused to meet the issue—and the issue involved is *not the authority.* Well, the issue involved, he says, is whether this over here (pointing to chart) rivals this over here. And that is the very thing that I have been dealing with. I showed *why*—why the Post Office Department did not rival the Federal Government; and the reason it did not is because the Federal Government had the legislative branch that could make the law to authorize it. Therefore, it wouldn't rival it. And the same thing is true of the State Government and the Highway Department. The Masonic Lodge that makes its own rules and regulations can authorize the institutions which they have. And the Catholic Church, with the pope as its head, can make its laws to govern, to authorize, the institutions it has; and,

Chart No. 1

Organizations in Different Categories

Fed. Gov't. ----Post Office Dept.
State Gov't.---Highway Dept.
Masonic Lodge---Homes for Aged.
Catholic Church---Orphanages.
Church of Christ---Orphanages & Homes for Aged

Rival These? Do These

therefore, they don't rival. And upon the same basis he says these don't rival the church. Then, in that case, somebody in the church must have the right and the authority to legislate, to give a law somewhere, or rule, to operate or organize and build and maintain human organizations in order that they may not *rival the church.* Now, then, I called attention to this last night. Brother Woods did not say a thing about it. Not only does the Catholic Church have orphanages, but it also has Missionary Societies. And I gave you the name of one of them a while ago, the Society for The Propagation of The Faith. That is a Foreign Catholic Missionary Society. I want to know, Brother Woods: Is that a rival of the Catholic Church? Is it? Does that Missionary Society of the Catholic Church, as an organization, rival the Catholic Church? And if it doesn't, could we have a Missionary Society that wouldn't rival the church of Christ? Could we? If we can, why, give us its constituent parts. Tell us how to organize it. So that's the very point.

Now, he said, of course, back up here, with the Post Office Department, the authority is not in the government, but in the people back of it. And in the State Government, it is the people back of it. And, of course, on the same basis of his argument, why, you have to get down here (pointing to "church of Christ") and say the authority for this is not in the church, but it is in the people back of it. And I suppose that is it. So it is the people back of it, and not the church at all that he gets his authority from in order to set it up. And there is his parallel with his argument on the very chart that he has made. Thank you, Brother Woods, for the chart. All right. How much time do I have now?

BROTHER DOUTHITT: "About four minutes."

Four minutes. Thank you.

About these questions I answered. What is wrong with the Bible College? What is wrong with these things? Organization? He said, "Well, Brother Porter said that it is wrong because it is a church supported organization." He said, "All the time he has been claiming the *organization itself* is wrong." Why, the church support of it is the thing that has been involved all the way through, Brother Woods. Your very proposition says that—that "churches" may scripturally "build and maintain benevolent organizations." The very thing involved in the proposition is organizations built and maintained by churches. Did you know what you are affirming? Why, that is where the fight has been from the very beginning of this discussion. *Organizations built and maintained by churches.* That is what your proposition says. That is what we are debating. So I haven't sidestepped at all, and I am not on two sides of the question at all for the simple fact there are many organizations that might exist that would not be sinful within themselves. Do you believe in endorsing every organization that is not sinful within itself? Even if they have boards? Why, he said, "You take the light company." He said, "I don't oppose the light company." No, I don't either, Brother Woods. It is an organization. Neither of us opposes it. But, Brother Woods, I would oppose turning the church's money over to the light company and telling it to go ahead and use it like they want to. Wouldn't you? Or would you? Would you, Brother Woods? Would you oppose the church's turning its money over to the light company and telling them to go ahead and furnish lights for the people wherever they see it is needed? Just let them take charge of it and furnish the people that need lights with lights? We will just turn our contributions to you. What would be wrong with that, Brother Woods? Would it be the fact that it is an organization, or that it is a church supported organization?

That gets back down to the statement he made with which to begin—that he didn't believe the Missionary Societies and colleges, or schools, were parallel.

Now, just for a moment I want to get back to these questions if I have time. I asked him the question: "Since you stated last night that I could not tell how the church could care for the needy without describing our benevolent organizations, did you mean to say that the only possible way to care for the needy is through such organizations?" He said, "No; no, you can take them into your homes." And he said, "I have given *two hows.*" And then he turned around, when I had accepted one of them, and said, "That is not *a how at all.*" He had "given two," as long as nothing was said about it; but when I accepted one of them, he said, "No, that isn't a *how* any more."

Then on number four: "If the Society for The Propagation of The Faith (a Catholic Foreign Missionary Society) is not a rival to the Catholic Church, would we be justified in organizing a similar Society for churches of Christ?" He never did tell us. But he did say in his debate with Brother Garrett, "You can determine a man's sincere approach to a problem by how he answers questions." He said if he wants to come up and discuss the issue, he will not evade it; he will not dodge it; he will not do anything like that; he will just come right up and answer fully and clearly. It is the very thing that he hasn't done during this debate. I wonder why. Maybe somebody else is on the wrong side. Maybe he would do a better job if he were meeting a Baptist or a Methodist. And I am sure he would, because he would have the truth on that; but here he doesn't have the truth—he is defending something that is not authorized in all the Book of God and can no more defend it than the Christian Church preacher can defend the Missionary Society for the work of evangelism. In fact, he has already accepted it.

(Time Called.)

Thank you.

SECOND PROPOSITION

It is contrary to the Scriptures for churches to build and maintain benevolent organizations for the care of the needy, such as the Boles Home, the Tipton Home and other Orphan Homes and Homes for the Aged that are among us.

Affirmative: W. Curtis Porter

Negative: Guy N. Woods

Porter's First Affirmative

Brethren Moderators, Brother Woods, Ladies and Gentlemen:

I am grateful to God almighty for the blessings of the day that has passed and for this privilege of entering into this discussion tonight regarding the issues that are confronting us at this time.

We are upon the same subject that we have been for the past two sessions, except, of course, we have merely changed positions, and I take the affirmative tonight on the proposition that has just been read. The proposition seems clear to me and needs but little defining; but by its being "contrary to the Scriptures," we mean that it is out of harmony with them, or in conflict with them. By "the Scriptures," we mean, of course, the Word of God, the Bible, and especially the New Testament Scriptures in this discussion. By "churches," we mean the local congregations of the body of the Lord Jesus Christ, of which He is the head. "To build and maintain," that is, to set up and to support and to keep in existence or keep going. "Benevolent Organizations," that is, organizations for the work of benevolence or for the work of charity. "For the care of the needy," that is, those, of course, in need—to give them relief in their distressed condition. "Such as Boles Home, the Tipton Home, and other Orphan Homes and Homes for the Aged that are among us"—these simply give to us two of the Homes involved and other similar Homes that we have today, either for the Orphans or the Aged. "That are among us," or, that is, that are among those who make up the churches of Christ throughout the country. I think that will be sufficient by way of definition, but I do want to call to your attention some matters regarding organization in just a moment.

But I want to have this to say just here, that during the past two evenings Brother Woods has been telling you repeatedly how victorious he has been over Porter and how feeble Porter's efforts have been in all of this discussion, and things of that nature. And he came up last night with a chart and with an argument that he had obtained from Brother Warren, which Brother Thomas Warren and Roy Deaver spent about two and a half years constructing. Brother Woods said it was the finest argument he had seen in twenty-five years of debating and approximately a hundred debates, and he felt it was absolutely *unanswerable* and *irresistible.* And this argument that he thought was so unanswerable and irresistible, that was the best he had seen in twenty-five years and a hundred debates, and which had been consuming the time of two and a half years for the men who had constructed the argument, fell in less than one minute. If I were going to turn prophet tonight and make a little prediction, I would predict that Brother Woods is through with that argument, that it may not appear before us again during this discussion.

Now, I want to invite your attention to the discussion of "organization." We have mentioned in the proposition the matter of "benevolent organizations." The word "organization," I am sure, as both Brother Woods and I will agree, is used in two different senses. Sometimes it means only *a systematic arrangement,* and on other occasions, the word means more than that. It means *a body politic and corporate.* It refers to a body, another body that is set up, another organization, in that sense of the term. And I want to read to you with that in mind just here a few statements relative to the homes that are involved in this. I have lying on my desk here the copies of charters of twelve orphan homes and four of the homes for the aged that are among us today; and from these charters we get the definite statement that these homes are set up under *corporate bodies,* that they are more than just a *systematized arrangement,* or something of that nature—that they are other bodies. I want to read to you a statement or two from the charters.

First, from Boles Home, of Quinlan, Texas. It begins by saying that, "We hereby associating ourselves together for the purpose of forming a corporation under the laws of the state of Texas, do declare: The name of this corporation shall be Boles Orphan Home, Greenville, Texas." And then from the charter of the Tipton Home, of Tipton, Oklahoma, I read, "That the undersigned citizens of the state of Oklahoma, do hereby voluntarily associate ourselves together for the purpose of forming a private corporation under the laws of the state of Oklahoma." And then gleaning from these charters a number of points, we have this found and located in the charter of Boles Home. First, it was formed as a "Corporation" under the name of Boles Orphan Home on May 4, 1937. Second, it was to exist for a period of "fifty years." Third, it is operated by a Board of Directors from various localities. Fourth, the Board Members are selected in a joint meeting by the elders of the Johnson Street church in Greenville and by the elders of the church at Terrell, Texas. Fifth, to be qualified the Board Members must believe that such organizations are wrong. Sixth, the same qualification is stipulated for the Superintendent. Seventh, the failure to possess this and other qualifications mentioned will automatically terminate the service of such persons. Eighth, the *Corporation* owns property, personal and real. Ninth, the qualifications for the Board Members can never be changed. Tenth, the name of the "Corporation" is "Boles Orphan Home"—not the church of Christ. And eleventh, the Home is provided by "this corporation," and not by the church. I have other points regarding the Tipton Home that I don't have time to read just now.

But now I want to come to my projector chart number one, please, and take a look at some of this matter. In this connection I want to deal with the Memphis situation. And I might make this statement, that word has been passed around that Brother Bill Rogers resorted to some underhand trick in getting this letter written, but I feel sure that is not true with Bill. Bill and I have been the very closest of friends through the years, and at the time I wrote the letter I had no arrangement for any debate under way anywhere. And so I feel sure that that isn't so concerning Bill. And besides, there is nothing in the letter after all that gives any consolation whatsoever to the position advocated by my opponent, as will become evident as we proceed.

Now, then, we have here a chart that shows *systematic arrangement* on *one* hand and a *body politic* on the other. In this case we are going to say there are a number of churches in Memphis that are going to conduct a meeting out here in a locality where there is no church in Memphis, and these churches are going to cooperate in a systematic arrangement for that kind of meeting; and here, the church over here, (pointing to chart) furnishes a part of the support for the preacher to conduct a meeting. This church furnishes the other part of his support. Church number three furnishes the singer with his support for the meeting. Church number four furnishes the tent in which the meeting is to be conducted. And church number five furnishes the seats and utilities and things of that kind for the meeting. Each of them deals directly, and the meeting is conducted out here, and there is no need of a board to be organized under which that is to be done. Each one retains the same relationship to that without the organization of a board, though Brother Woods claimed last night that the thing that I had in mind could not be set up without the organization of a Board. Here we have a *systematic arrangement* in the conducting of a meeting. But here (pointing to other part of chart) we have the other sense of the word "organize," *a body politic.* We take those same five churches in Memphis, or any other number of churches, and down here we organize a Missionary Society, and that is *a body politic.* That's *a corporation.* That, my friends, is the thing that we are discussing along this line that is set up and chartered under the laws of the state. And these congregations send their contributions to the church here, or rather to the Missionary Society here, the *body politic;* and it takes charge of it and goes out here and conducts the meeting—hiring the preacher, hiring the singer, furnishing the tent and the seats and all the things that pertain thereto; and thus the meeting is conducted, or even a number of them, so far as that's concerned. Now, here we have *a Board;* here we have *a Missionary Society;* here we have *a body politic.* That's one

Porter's Projector
Chart No. 1.

ORGANIZATION

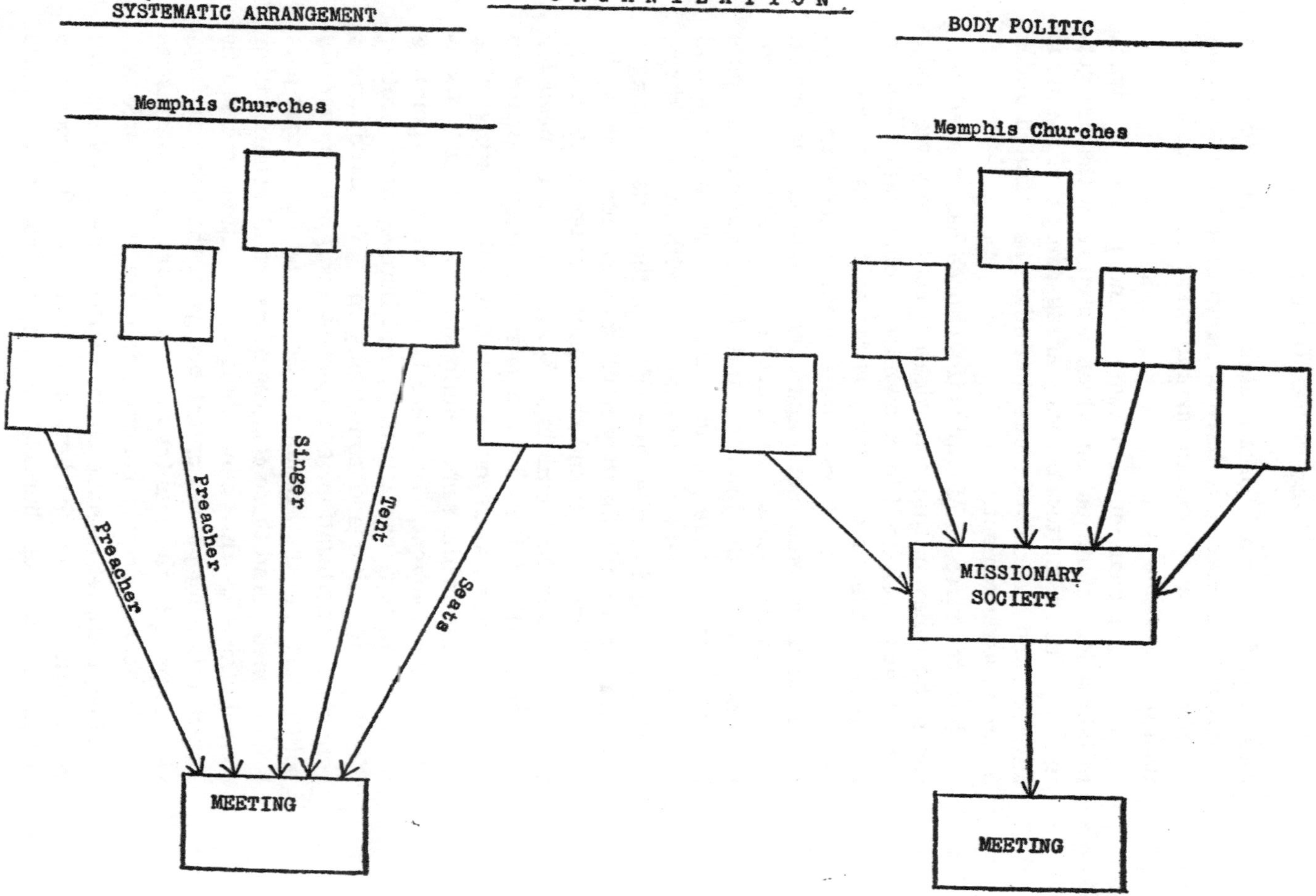

SYSTEMATIC ARRANGEMENT

Memphis Churches

Preacher

Preacher

Singer

Tent

Seats

MEETING

BODY POLITIC

Memphis Churches

MISSIONARY SOCIETY

MEETING

meaning of the word "organization." Over here (pointing to left side of chart) we have a meeting that is conducted simply under a *systematic arrangement* that *requires no such organization.*

Now, then, chart number two of mine, please. We want to take a look at it, just an advance step from that, in getting these other matters before you regarding that Memphis situation and the kind of home that might be operated under a similar arrangement.

Now, of course, in Memphis if a church has an aged person to be relieved, that congregation could very well take care of the person itself in its own local congregation, among members of the congregation, as far as that is concerned, perhaps; but if it becomes more economical for them to obtain a building somewhere, and church number one has an aged person that needs care, it may hire somebody out there to do the work in this building, and church number one puts its aged person there. Church number two has one and places the aged person there; and so with number three, number four, and number five. Each of them places an aged person in that building they have obtained and sustain the same relationship to it; and each church supports its needy that it places in that building. Now, there is no need for "an organization" there—there is no need for a Board to be set up there whatsoever. It is just like the meeting. The churches sustain the same relationship to it. That's a *systematic arrangement.* But here is what we have (pointing to "Benevolent Organizations"), and here is what Brother Woods is affirming and contending for. We have here a benevolent organization, a *corporate body* set up, a *body politic,* just like the Missionary Society so far as that part is concerned. And these congregations are all sending their contributions to this benevolent organization under this Board, this *body politic,* and it brings in the orphans from various parts of the country and takes care of them, just as the Missionary Society conducts the meeting. Thank you.

Now, then, let us have chart number three; and we will get a little more on *the how;* and then we will proceed to another matter just here. You can see from these charts

Porter's Projector
Chart No. 2.

O R G A N I Z A T I O N

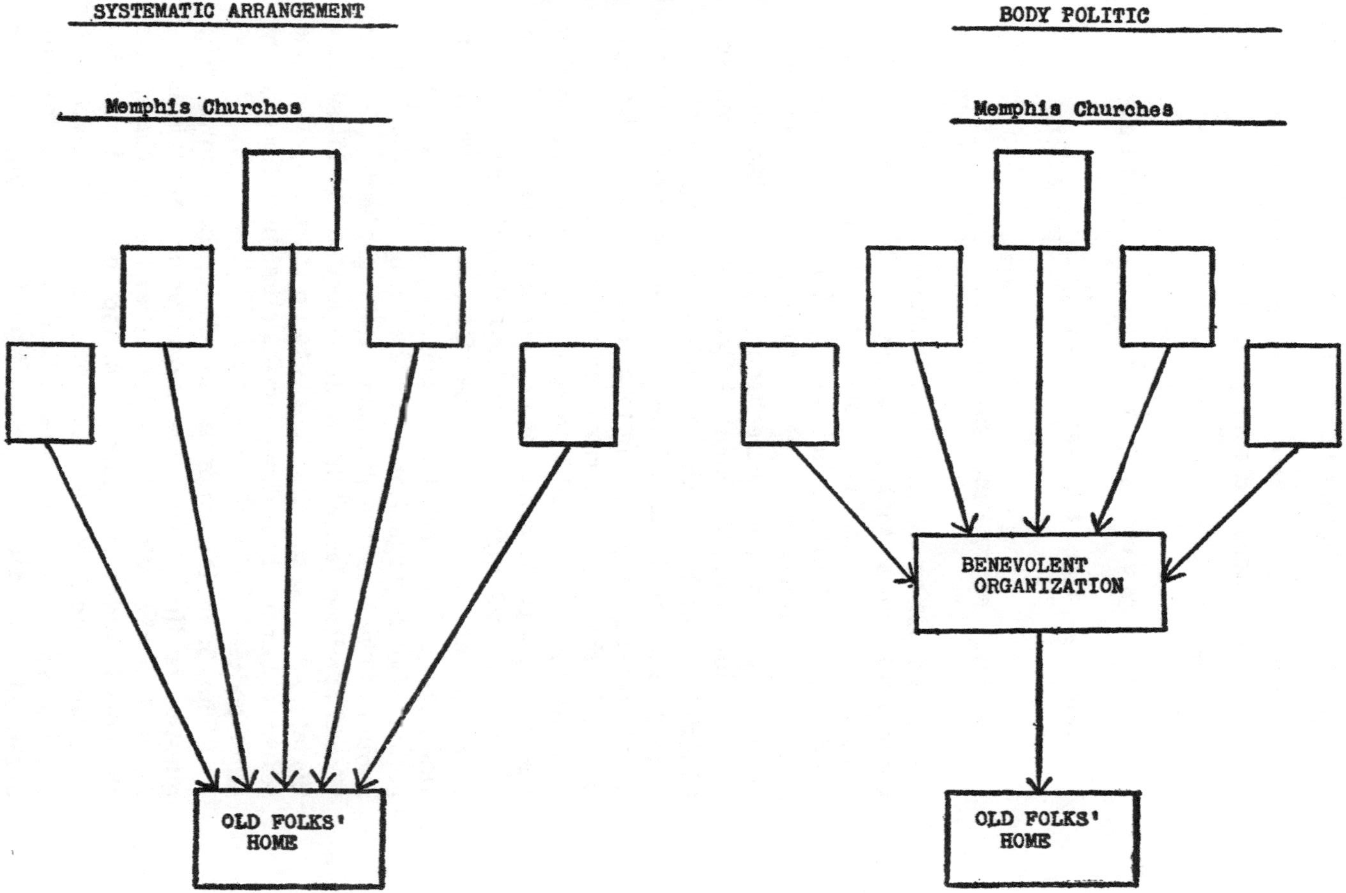

SYSTEMATIC ARRANGEMENT

Memphis Churches

OLD FOLKS' HOME

BODY POLITIC

Memphis Churches

BENEVOLENT ORGANIZATION

OLD FOLKS' HOME

already used that there is a difference between a mere *systematic arrangement* and a *body politic.*

Porter's Projector
Chart No. 3

THE "HOW" VERSUS "ORGANIZATION"

MAT. 28:19 - TEACH - HOW - ORGANIZATION { CHURCH / MISSIONARY SOCIETY

1 TIM. 5:16 - RELIEVE - HOW - ORGANIZATION { CHURCH / BENEVOLENT ORGANIZATION

We had this on the blackboard somewhat last night, but I put it up here so that others may be able to see it. We have at the top of it, "The How." I gave Matt. 28: 19; the Lord said "go therefore and teach." So we have "Teach." And the question comes: "How" to teach? Then we have "Organization" and out there "Church" and "Missionary Society." Now, then, the Book of God says "teach"; and the Christian Church preachers came along, and they said, "How? *How* to teach? Where are you going to get *the how?* Where are you going to find out *how* to do it?" So they said *the how* authorizes setting up a Missionary Society organization in order to do it. We have insisted that the church was the sufficient organization. Brother Woods came along last night and admitted that *the organization* was different from *the how;* therefore, his *how* and his organization are separated now, and they can't get back together. So the organization is one thing, and *the how* is another. *The how* doesn't include the organization, Brother Woods admitted last night, with respect to the Missionary Society. And so the church was to do the work, to do the teaching, but not turn it over to the Missionary Society, *another body.*

1 Tim. 5: 16, the command to relieve the widows. The question is: How? Well, the matter of organization comes up; and Brother Woods, like the digressive preachers, says *the how includes an organization,* another organization besides the church. We are insisting, just like we have with the digressive church preachers, that the church is the only organization needed; and we don't need to set up a benevo-

lent organization out here, *another body,* to do it. And so *the how* is that way. And *the how* can be settled by each congregation doing its own work as a congregation, without resorting to *any other body politic* or anything of that nature. All right. Thank you for that.

And I want to call your attention then to a chart I have on the roll, if I can get to it presently. I have here the chart on "Law and Expediency." Brother Woods presented something along that line last night. And he has been claiming we occupy the same position as the anti-Bible class folks. Let's take a look at it now.

"To be expedient," of course, a thing "must first be lawful." 1 Cor. 6: 12. And in this chart we have five columns: one embracing "Commands"; number two embracing "Inclusions"; number three, "Perversions"; number four, "Incidentals"; number five, "Additions." And over in Gen. 6: 14-16 God commanded Noah to build an ark. That's a commandment that God gave. But in giving that command there were certain things "included," among which was the fact it was to be built of "gopher wood." Furthermore, that it was to be "three stories" high. There are other things besides that included, but we don't have room for all of them; just that in order to get it before you. These are "inclusions" in the command. Then that command might be "perverted." If Noah, instead of using "gopher wood," had used "cottonwood" to build the ark, supposing that "cottonwood" and "gopher wood" are not the same—we don't know just what the *gopher wood* was—at any rate, if "cottonwood" is different from "gopher wood," and he had used "cottonwood," that would have been a "perversion" of the command"; therefore, a violation of it. Or if he had built the ark "ten stories" high instead of "three stories," that would also have been a "perversion," or a violation. But in that "command" there are also "incidentals," such as what "tools" may be used in getting the materials ready, what was to be the "size" of the trees from which he obtains the material to go into the ark, and what were his means of "transportation" to get them to the proper place. These are but "incidentals," belonging in the *realm of "expediency."* But suppose that Noah had decided to take the same kind of material of which he built

Porter's Roll
Chart No. 2.

LAW AND EXPEDIENCY

To Be Expedient - Must Be Lawful. 1 Cor. 6:12.

COMMANDS	INCLUSIONS	PERVERSIONS	INCIDENTALS	ADDITIONS
Build Ark Gen. 6:14-16	Gopher Wood Three Stories	Cottonwood Ten Stories	Tools - Size Transportation	Another Building
Teach Mat. 28:19	Whole Counsel Truth	Human Traditions Doctrines of Men	Blackboard - Radio Charts - Press	Christian Missionary Society
Baptize Mat. 28:19	Water - Believers Burial	Wine - Infants Sprinkling	Ocean - River Pool - Baptistry	Christian Baptizing Association
Sing Eph. 5:19	Spiritual Songs Melody in Heart	Worldly Songs Melody on Harp	Books - Tuning Fork Voice Parts - Notes	Singing Saints Society
Partake Lord's Supper 1 Cor.11;Acts 20:7.	First Day - Bread Fruit of Vine	Midweek - Beef Buttermilk	Plates - Cups Place - Hour	Christian Communion Confederation
Pray Phil. 4:6; Jas. 1: 6.	To God In Faith	To Virgin Mary In Pretense	Length of Prayer Posture	Christian Praying League
Give 1 Cor. 16:1,2; 2 Cor. 9:6, 7.	As Prospered Cheerfully	Sparingly Grudgingly	Collection Plates Envelopes	Christian Fellowship Federation
Visit Orphans Jas. 1:27.	Food - Clothes Shelter	Oppress - Vex Neglect	House - Tent City - Country	Christian Benevolent Corporation

the ark, some gopher wood, and construct "another building," and in this other building he had put some of the goats and sheep and things of that kind—goats and sheep and pigs and things of that nature, and placed them in this building here. Now, then, I am asking you: Can I put this *other building* in the *realm of incidentals?* Where does it belong? All right.

Then, in the next place, we have the "commandment" to "teach" in Matt. 28: 19. In that "command" to "teach" there is "included" that we teach the "whole counsel" of God, that we teach the "truth." Furthermore, that "command' may be "perverted" by teaching "human traditions" or the "doctrines of men" instead of teaching the "whole counsel" of God and the "truth." But in that "command" to "teach" there are certain "incidentals" involved, such as the use of the "blackboard" or the "radio," or the "chart," or the "press." These are but "incidentals" by which the teaching may be done, and belong to *the realm of expediency.* But suppose somebody decides to take some of the same material from which this divine building, the church, is constructed and build another building called the "Christian Missionary Society," and do some of the teaching through that. Can we put this over in the *realm of incidentals,* in the *realm of expediency?* That is where the Christian Church has been trying to put it for years. They say that is where it belongs. Right there is where they have put it, and we have fought them over it for a hundred years. All right, and the same thing would be true of the anti-Sunday school brethren who try to make of it an organization, a Sunday school organization (and argue that we have one), whereas we have only Bible classes without that organization, that separate body set up. But if it were a separate body, it would have to go over here just like the Christian Missionary Society.

Then we have in the same Scripture, Matt. 28: 19, the "command" to "baptize." Certain things are "included," as "water" as the element, "believers" as the subjects, a "burial" as the act. It may be "perverted" or violated by using —Did I skip one? No. Yes, by using "wine" as the element and by using "infants" as the subjects and "sprinkling" as the mode. There are certain "incidentals" involved in it, as to whether you baptize in an "ocean," a "river," a "pool," or a "baptistry." But suppose that we take some of the members and organize a "Christian Baptizing Association." When we get that organized, we notify churches throughout the area that we have organized a "Christian Baptizing Association." When you have any baptizing to do, let us know, and we will send a delegation from our Association to do it for you. Now, that, my friends, would be *another body.* And, of course, we will need some money to stay in business; so send us along the fifth Sunday contribution, please.

We have also the "command" to "sing" in Eph. 5: 19. That command "includes" "spiritual songs" and making "melody in the heart." And it may be "perverted" by singing "worldly songs" and making "melody on the harp." There are certain "incidentals" included, such as the "songbooks" and the "tuning fork" and the "voice parts" and the "notes" and so on. But suppose we organize from the members of the church what we call the "Singing Saints Society." When we get this separate body set up, we notify churches that we have the Singing Saints Society in operation; and if you have some singing to do, let us know, and we will send a delegation from our Society to do it for you. All right, does that go in the *realm of incidentals?*

Then we have also the "command" to "partake of the Lord's supper" in Matt. 26: 26-28, Acts 20: 7. It "includes" the "first day" of the week as the day, "bread" and "fruit of the vine" as the elements. It may be "perverted" by making of it a "midweek" service or using "beef" and "buttermilk" as the elements of food. There are certain "incidentals" involved in it, as the "plate" or the number of "cups" that may be used, the "hour" of the day, or the "place" where the meeting may occur. But suppose we organize a "Christian Communion Confederation." We get it set up and notify brethren that we have this Confederation set up; and if you want the Lord's supper administered, let us know, and we will send a delegation from our Confederation. Shall we put that in "incidentals"?

The same with praying. To pray "to God" and "in faith" is "included" in the "command." And praying "to the virgin

Mary" "in pretense" would be "perversions" of it. The "length of prayer" and the "posture" of body would be the "incidentals." But if we were to organize the "Christian Praying League"—set that up to do the praying for the churches—then we have something that cannot go in *the realm of incidentals.*

We have the "command" to "give," 1 Cor. 16: 1, 2, and 2 Cor. 9: 6, 7. We are to give, and that which is "included" in the command is to give "as prospered" and give "cheerfully." We might "pervert" that command by giving "sparingly" or "grudgingly." And certain "incidentals" are involved, such as the "collection plates" and the "envelopes." But suppose we put up the "Christian Fellowship Federation" as an organization to do the giving or to take charge of it; and if you have some money to give, send it to us. We will specialize on this matter; and we will take charge of it and spend the money for you. Send us a contribution for our own benefit, because we need to stay in business.

And then we take the final one, "visiting the orphans," James 1: 27, just admitting, for the sake of argument, that it is a collective duty revealed there, not a private, individual duty. There are the "inclusions," "food," and "clothes," and "shelter." There are certain "perversions" of it, such as, you may "oppress," you may "vex," or you may "neglect." There are certain "incidentals" involved in it: whether to take care of them in a "house" or in a "tent," in the "city" or in the "country." But we set up a "Christian Benevolent Corporation," and brethren say this "Christian Benevolent Corporation" goes in *the realm of incidentals.* If you put the "Christian Benevolent Corporation" in the realm of incidentals, then we can put the "other building" by Noah in the same place, and the "Christian Missionary Society" in that realm. The "Christian Baptizing Association," the "Singing Saints Society," the "Christian Communion Confederation," the "Christian Praying League," the "Christian Fellowship Federation" all go in the same lot. If you can keep *all of these* out, then upon the same basis I will keep *that one* out. And if these are wrong, if these are contrary to the scriptures, down to this point (pointing to chart), then *this one is also contrary to the scriptures* because they are parallel. (Time Called.)

And I thank you very kindly.

Woods' First Negative

Brethren Moderators, Brother Porter, Brethren and Sisters, and Friends:

I am again thankful that in the providence of God I am privileged to be before you and tonight in the negative of the proposition which Brother Porter seeks to establish. He directed attention in the outset of his speech to the fact that it is the same subject as before, and I might say that he is still approaching it in the same fashion as before. He is still in the negative. Brother Porter hasn't changed positions as they relate to this debate. All he is doing tonight is making negative speeches in the affirmative! That's all.

He said that I had "turned prophet"; and thus far my batting average is one hundred per cent. I told you in the outset of this debate that, notwithstanding the fact he had promised, inasmuch as he thought our way of doing it is wrong, to tell us the right way; but up until this very moment we don't know what the right way is, according to Brother Porter, do we? We are now in the third night of this debate, and yet he has not fulfilled his promise to tell us *how* the scriptures teach that the church is to provide for its needy. Brother Curtis Porter believes that those of us who support orphans in orphan homes and who defend the benevolent institutions are on the road to apostasy—that we are on the way to hell. And notwithstanding the fact that three nights now have been up in this debate, until this moment *he hasn't explained to us the right way to do it!* Ladies and gentlemen, some of us are going to begin to wonder *when* Brother Porter will come out with the scriptural way to do it.

He said I introduced an argument a night or two ago that I said was the best I had ever heard. Well, I think I didn't say that. I said it was one of the best. He said that Brother Thomas Warren and Roy Deavers spent two and a half years working it up. Well, up until about two months ago they were over on Brother Porter's side of this thing!

If they worked it up, they worked it up while they were on his side of it, for they just changed about two months ago. In the next place, they didn't work up this argument. I said they stated the principle, and I took it and adapted it to this position. He said that it went down in one minute and he was going to predict that we wouldn't see any more of it! Let us see chart number eleven, please.

CHART NO. 11

AXIOM: "The WHOLE of anything is the SUM of its parts"

•

PROOF MY PROP. REQUIRES:
• Care Of Orph. & Aged
• Ch. Support " " " "
• Ch. Cooperation in the Support of " " •

(a) This we have already done.
(b) Porter concedes foregoing anyway.

•

Syllogism:
(1.) All situations, the component parts of which are scriptural, are scriptural situations.
(2.) The component parts of the whole work involved in my prop. are scriptural.
(3.) ∴ the whole work involved in prop. is scriptural.

•

PORTER'S ALTERNATIVE:
(a) Deny the major premise.
(b) Repudiate Public Statements.

Chart number eleven. Brother Porter was hoping he wouldn't see any more of it. Now, you get it, friends: Here is the axiom: *The whole of anything is the sum of its parts.* There are certain fundamental principles that are obligatory upon me in sustaining my contention; *first*, that it is right to care for orphans and aged; *secondly*, that the church is obligated to such care; and *thirdly*, that churches may cooperate in such care. Now, I have already shown that; and Brother Porter conceded every one of those three points. *Every one of them*. It wasn't necessary for me to prove it because he had already admitted it. Now, get the syllogism: All situations, the component parts of which are scriptural, are scriptural situations. Brother Porter and I agree that the component parts of the whole work involved in this proposition are scriptural. Now, the irresistible conclusion is that, therefore, the whole work involved in this proposition is scriptural. Now, he can do only one of two things: Either he must deny the major premise, in which case he makes himself ridiculous; or else, he must repudiate his public statements. He came back and said there was one point missing; it ought to have in it a statement with reference to organized work. He came along tonight and defined organized work in the sense in which I intended here as *systematic procedure*. Let us just add point number four: There must be systematic procedure involved in the support. That is exactly what I said, and that is my proposition. And so down you go, Brother Porter! Ah, no, you haven't touched it. You can't do it in a hundred years. I could sit down right now and my proposition stands proved. I have never seen a more feeble effort than Brother Porter put forth in trying to reply to that. All right, now. That is sufficient.

Now, friends, I am very happy he gave us a definition of organization. He said there is one definition of the word "organization"; *systematic procedure*. That is exactly what I meant by it.

He cited us to the charters of Tipton and Boles and showed that these homes are organized, and that they are corporations; and that is exactly right. And a little more about that when we get to his charts.

And now, before I get too far into the speech, in order to give him time to look them over, I have some questions.

1. If the churches in Memphis can build an old folks home for the aged, cannot these same churches also build a

home of the same type as you endorse for old folks for homeless children?

2. In whose title should the property of such a home as you have in mind for old folks in Memphis rest? In one man, a group of men composed of all the elders of the churches in Memphis, or to all the churches equally?

3. May such a home as you endorse have a manager, a treasurer, or secretary?

4. Will the churches or the home take legal custody and guardianship of those to be provided for in this home?

5. In the case of the home for the homeless children, who will administer discipline?

6. Do you believe that a California congregation should comply with the law and incorporate in order to exist legally there?

7. Is the legal organization which results from such incorporation the same as the organization which the New Testament teaches?

8. If the incorporation of a congregation, with its president, vice-president, secretary, and essential directors does not form a new body or change its status before God, does the incorporation of a home make it a new body or change its status in God's sight?

Hand these to him, please. Thank you.

Now then, let us have chart number one of Brother Porter's. Here, friends, is the occasion for this discussion with reference to this Memphis home. In a letter dated January 27, 1955, Brother Porter said this: "Of course, Paul's instruction to Timothy regarding widows that should be taken care of by the church is pretty definite. If, however, there are enough old folks in Memphis to justify a home, old folks, I mean, who have no relatives to care for them, I suppose the Memphis churches could maintain a home for such if they sustain the same relationship to the home. But if a brotherhood project is to be set up to take care of old folks from all over the nation, I doubt the wisdom of such undertaking."

Now, here is what he admits: (1) A home may be maintained in Memphis for old folks; (2) this home may be supported by Memphis churches; (3) the home may be main-

Porter's Projector
Chart No. 1.

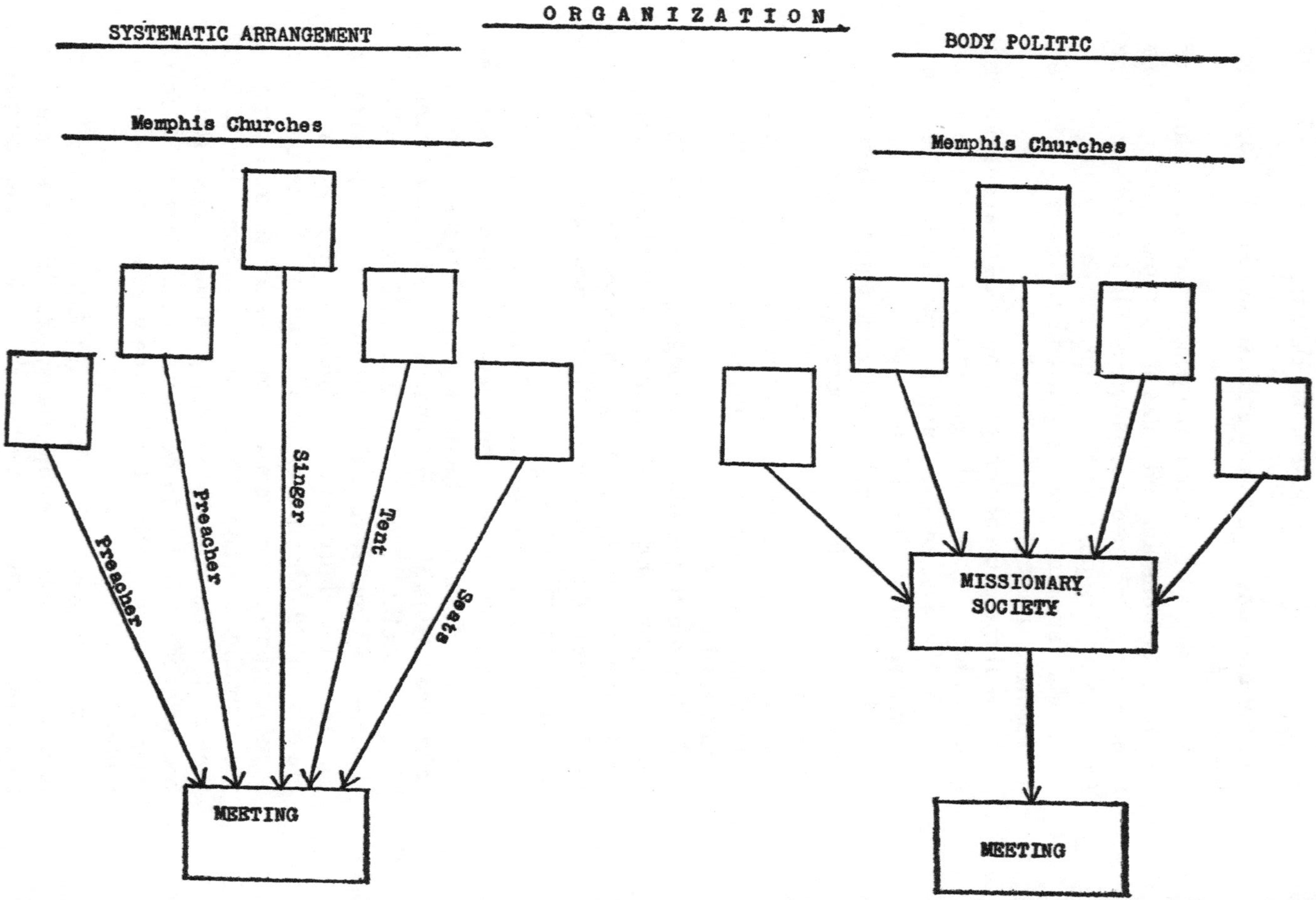

O R G A N I Z A T I O N

SYSTEMATIC ARRANGEMENT

Memphis Churches

Preacher

Preacher

Singer

Tent

Seats

MEETING

BODY POLITIC

Memphis Churches

MISSIONARY SOCIETY

MEETING

tained, though not under an eldership of some Memphis church. He comes back tonight and says, "Here is the parallel." He has changed positions on me. Let us have chart number fifteen before we consider this—my chart number fifteen. Bear in mind while we are getting that chart that this is supposed to represent a parallel here (pointing to Porter's chart); then we are going to examine it after we examine chart number fifteen. We will have it in just a moment. Here we are.

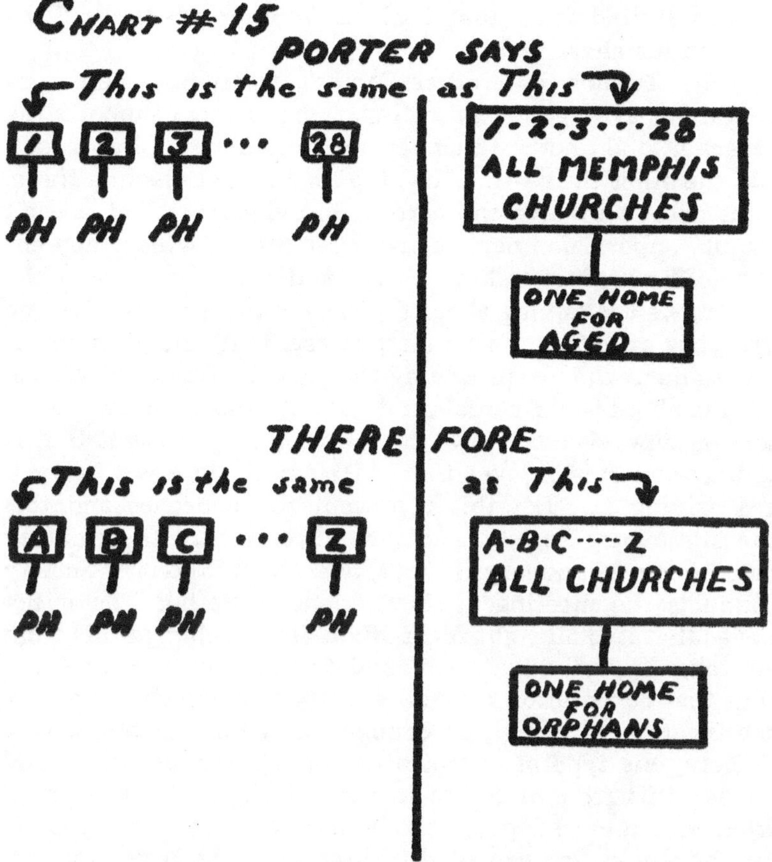

Now then, Brother Porter said that what he had in mind was this: All the Memphis churches, some twenty-eight of them, could combine their resources in the support of *one*

home for the aged. He said that is parallel now with all those twenty-eight churches owning twenty-eight preachers' homes! I said, "Brother Porter, that is pure quibbling. You know that that is not a parallel." If that were so, then let this (pointing to the chart) represent all the churches in the world and this represent all the preachers' homes in the world; therefore, that would be parallel to all the churches of Christ in the world having *one home* for orphans all over the world; and we would have what he calls the universal church activated. Now, that, friends, is his position. Now, he has shifted from that back to another position. Turn back to his chart number one.

Here, friends, is Brother Porter's position. These congregations arrange for a meeting. One of them supports the preacher, and another a singer, and another supplies a tent, and the other the seats. Now, that is a gospel meeting there. That doesn't involve the care of individuals. That doesn't require supervision particularly over that in which they engage. We are not talking here about the preaching of the gospel; we are talking about the care of individuals. Let me call your attention to this fact, please, that this meeting involves men who are preaching the gospel. But what we are talking about is individuals, individuals who must have some sort of supervision. Now, the question is: Who is it that is to take supervision over that? He says, "Here is what you are driving at. Let this represent the churches and this the Missionary Society, and the churches turn their money over to the Missionary Society, and the Missionary Society conducts the meeting." Now, friends, Brother Porter believes that it is all right for individuals—to change this from churches to individuals—to send to a corporation in order that that corporation may do exactly that which is done in the meeting. Let us just change this from the Missionary Society, one type of organization, to a religious paper, and change this from churches to individuals, and the meeting from one hundred people to a hundred thousand people; and he thinks you can send it directly to the paper for this preaching. But he says that the paper and the home are organized on the same basis. At least the *Guardian* takes that position. If that be true; if it is all right to send money

Porter's Projector
Chart No. 1.

ORGANIZATION

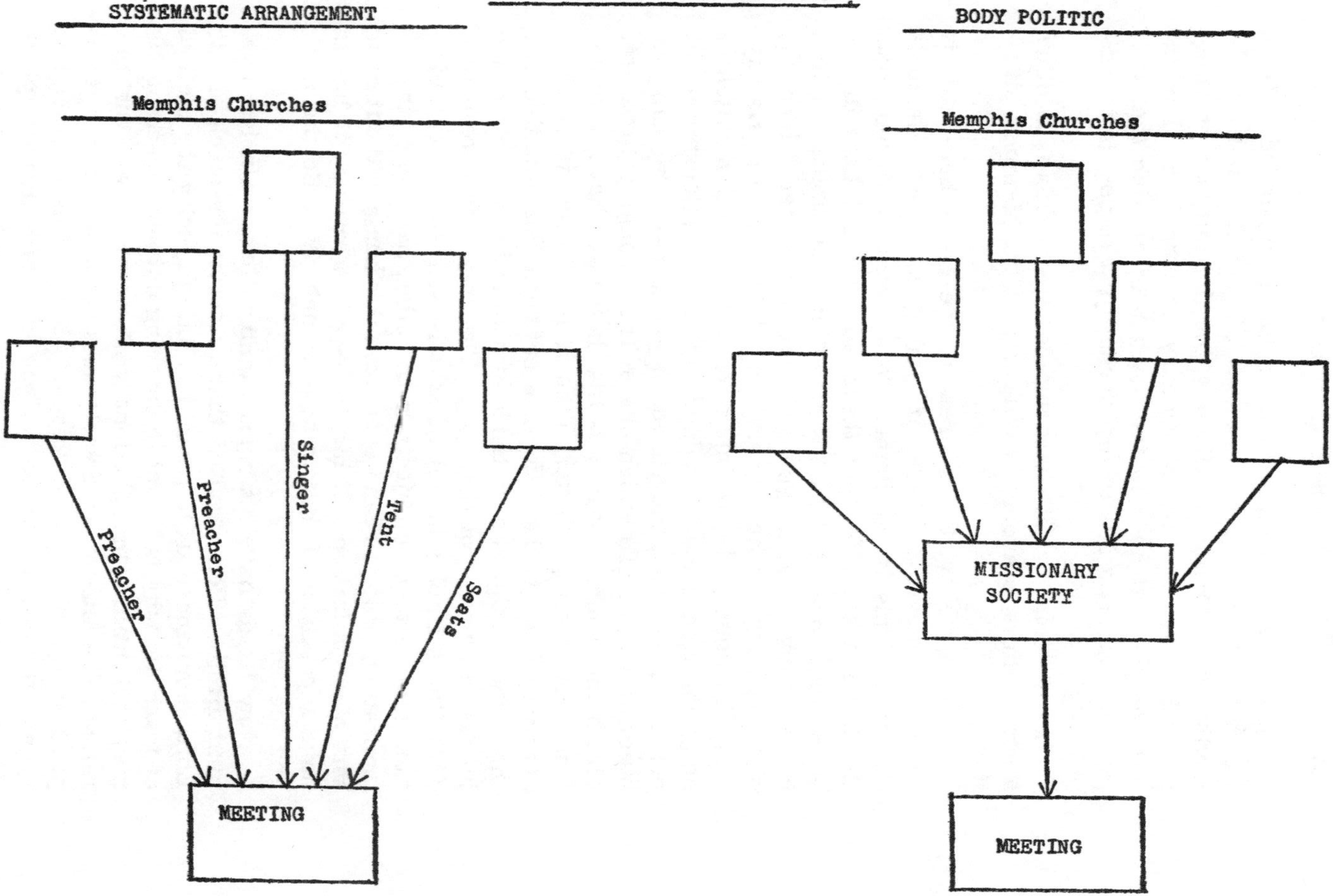

SYSTEMATIC ARRANGEMENT

Memphis Churches

Preacher
Preacher
Singer
Tent
Seats

MEETING

BODY POLITIC

Memphis Churches

MISSIONARY SOCIETY

MEETING

to a paper, or a school, or to an orphan home *as individuals,* which he concedes, then he has this parallel to individuals' sending to a Missionary Society for the purpose of doing that which he says the Missionary Society does! *I maintain tonight that he is in the position of arguing that it is right to support a Missionary Society just so you do it individually!*

Let us look now at chart number two. This is Brother Porter's effort to avoid the difficulty of the Memphis situation.

He said, "Now, this represents the home here; this is what I believe." These, if you please, are Memphis churches. This is the home. Now, what have you done, Brother Porter? You put these old folks out here in this home; each one of these congregations contributes to that home. Now, what do you do? Brother Porter, which one of those churches has supervision of that home? He says that, "I suppose the Memphis churches could maintain a home for such if they sustained the same relationship to the home." Now then, they have all got to have the same relationship to it. To which one of those congregations does that home belong? *Whose* is that home you have in mind? I ask you, Brother Porter: Who is it that has jurisdiction over it? What is the difference between this situation and that which tonight he contended for in the matter of orphan homes and homes for the aged? The only difference is this: This (the Memphis home) he says is without any organization; and he says he objects to the other because of the organization. But you can't even have this home without *some* sort of organization. It has to have a treasurer; it has to have supervision; it has to have somebody to do the work and the care.

Now let us have his chart number three. On last evening, Brother Porter raised this question: Inasmuch as the Lord commanded us to teach, but didn't specify the method of teaching, why is it that in carrying out such teaching we may not utilize the Missionary Society? Well, for this reason: The Missionary Society does not inhere, nor is it implied at all, in the word "teach." But, in the command to relieve the orphans there is *some kind* of a home implied.

Porter's Projector
Chart No. 2.

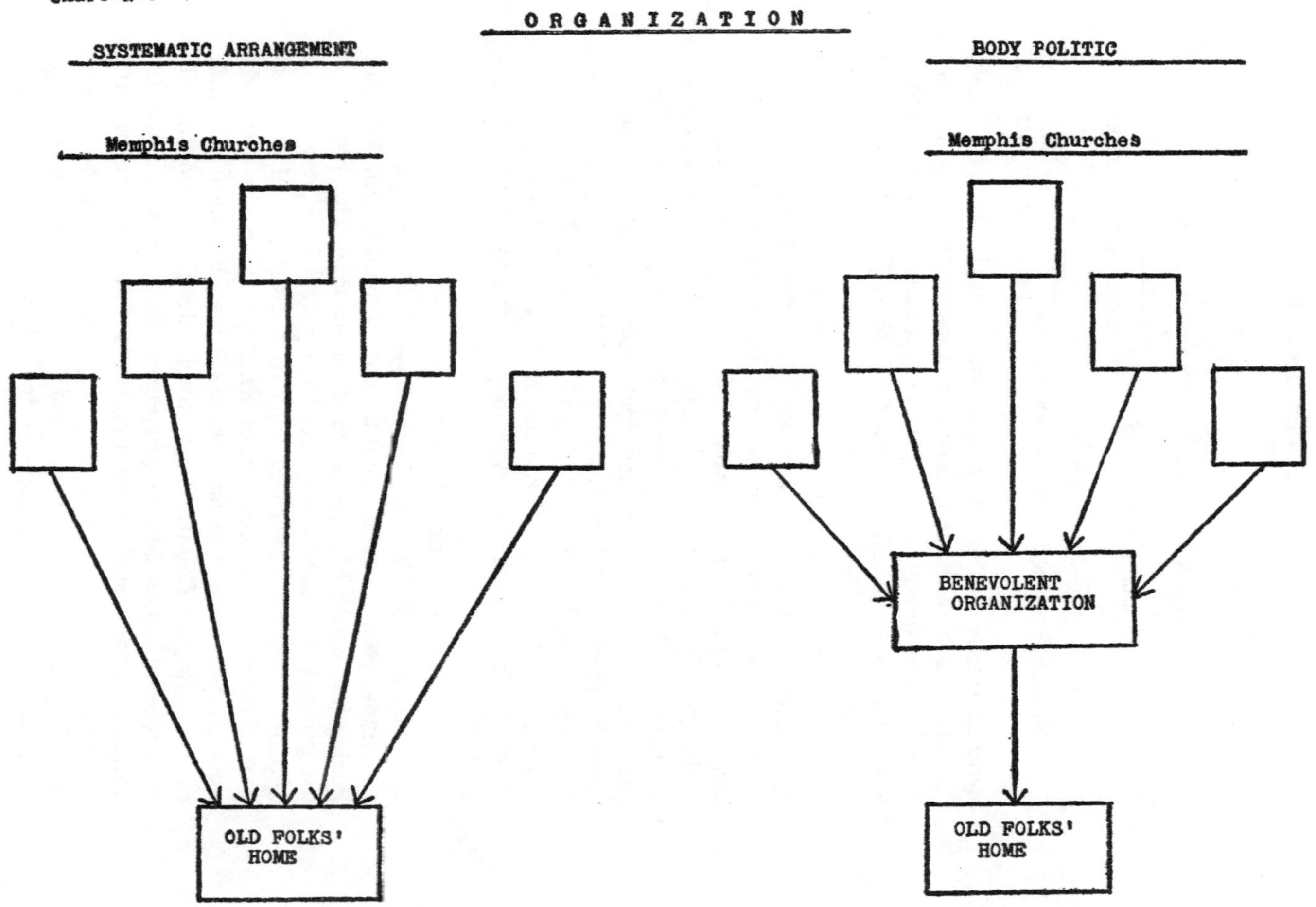

O R G A N I Z A T I O N

SYSTEMATIC ARRANGEMENT

Memphis Churches

OLD FOLKS' HOME

BODY POLITIC

Memphis Churches

BENEVOLENT ORGANIZATION

OLD FOLKS' HOME

Porter's Projector
Chart No. 3

THE "HOW" VERSUS "ORGANIZATION"

MAT. 28:19 - TEACH - HOW - ORGANIZATION { CHURCH / MISSIONARY SOCIETY }

1 TIM. 5:16 - RELIEVE - HOW - ORGANIZATION { CHURCH / BENEVOLENT ORGANIZATION }

Brother Porter admitted it and put it on the board. Now, you can teach without a Missionary Society; but you can't care for the needy without *some place* to care for them. What I am contending for tonight is this: *The place to care for them.*

Let us have the lights on just a moment. Right here is the situation: Let this represent the church and this the normal home. Now then, what is the orphan home? *It is simply an effort on the part of the church to supply that which the child lost!* Now here, friends, is the difference between the Missionary Society and the orphan home. The church is its own Missionary Society, and, therefore, doesn't need another. But the church is not its own orphan home, because the home and the church are two different things. Therefore, the church replaces that which the child lost. There is the difference. Anybody ought to be able to see that.

How much time do I have?

BROTHER WATSON: "You have four minutes."

Thank you. I want you to note friends, that Brother Porter has made his whole condemnation of the homes on the ground that they constitute incorporated bodies. I have here in my hand a certified copy of the articles of corporation of the *Gospel Guardian,* of which he is an associate editor. Here is what it says: "Know all men by these presents, that we, Roy E. Cogdill," and so on, "do hereby voluntarily associate ourselves for the purpose of forming a private corporation under such laws upon the following terms and conditions: The name of the corporation shall be Gospel Guardian Company, Incorporated." Now let us see what the purpose of it is: "The purpose for which it is formed is to

THE CHURCH and the HOME MOVE ON PARALLEL LINES

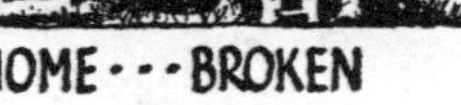

(Chart #18)

support a religious, charitable, literary, and educational undertaking." A what? "A *religious*" and even a "*charitable, literary*, and *educational* undertaking." What have we got here? A *corporation*. What is its purpose? On the masthead of the paper we have this statement, "Dedicated to the propagation and defense of New Testament Christianity." What is the function of the church? It is the pillar and ground of the truth. It has then, the same aim as the church of our Lord. But what is it? It is a corporation. It is not the church by the wildest stretch of imagination. Yet, it is an incorporated body; hence, according to Brother Porter, *another body* doing the work of the church! Now, Brother Porter, put down this question: Does the *Gospel Guardian* do a work of the church? It either does or it doesn't. We will see now whether it is organized in the interest of the church or not.

Now, Brother Porter, you talk here (pointing to the chart) about, for example, a Christian Baptizing Association. I haven't time to take all of this up. I will do it gladly in later speeches. But I direct attention here to the fact that he says we are commanded to baptize; and the inclusions: water, and so on; the perversions: wine, infants, sprinkling; and incidentals: ocean, river, pool, baptistry; over here the addition: a Christian Baptizing Association. *I don't see any place on there for Brother Porter!* Now, where is he on it? I want to know where Brother Porter is on that chart. He is on there somewhere, because he baptizes. Now, where are you, Brother Porter, on the chart? I notice down here that he talks about a Christian Benevolent Corporation. But he has told us you can put children into private homes. *I want to know where his private home is on that chart!* It is bound to be somewhere. Where is it, Brother Porter?

Now, Brother Osborne, we will have in that connection a chart that I will get to in just a moment here, a chart that will indicate to you exactly—here it is, chart number twelve. Here is the chart simplified in order that you may see exactly what his argument is.

Porter's Roll
Chart No. 2.

LAW AND EXPEDIENCY

To Be Expedient - Must Be Lawful. 1 Cor. 6:12.

COMMANDS	INCLUSIONS	PERVERSIONS	INCIDENTALS	ADDITIONS
Build Ark Gen. 6:14-16	Gopher Wood Three Stories	Cottonwood Ten Stories	Tools - Size Transportation	Another Building
Teach Mat. 28:19	Whole Counsel Truth	Human Traditions Doctrines of Men	Blackboard - Radio Charts - Press	Christian Missionary Society
Baptize Mat. 28:19	Water - Believers Burial	Wine - Infants Sprinkling	Ocean - River Pool - Baptistry	Christian Baptizing Association
Sing Eph. 5:19	Spiritual Songs Melody in Heart	Worldly Songs Melody on Harp	Books - Tuning Fork Voice Parts - Notes	Singing Saints Society
Partake Lord's Supper 1 Cor.11;Acts 20:7.	First Day - Bread Fruit of Vine	Midweek - Beef Buttermilk	Plates - Cups Place - Hour	Christian Communion Confederation
Pray Phil. 4:6; Jas. 1: 6.	To God In Faith	To Virgin Mary In Pretense	Length of Prayer Posture	Christian Praying League
Give 1 Cor. 16:1,2; 2 Cor. 9:6, 7.	As Prospered Cheerfully	Sparingly Grudgingly	Collection Plates Envelopes	Christian Fellowship Federation
Visit Orphans Jas. 1:27.	Food - Clothes Shelter	Oppress - Vex Neglect	House - Tent City - Country	Christian Benevolent Corporation

CHART NO. 12

ITEM	ESSENTIAL	INCIDENTAL	ADDITION
Ark	Gopher Wood	Tools, Size of Trees, etc.	Little Ark
Benevolence	Doing Good	Money, Food, Clothes	Orphanages, Homes for Aged
Teaching	Truth	Oral, Written Radio, Tracts	Sunday School
Preaching	Gospel	Pulpit, Radio, Bldg.	Gospel Guardian!
	(1)	(2)	(3)

Where is the Private Home?

1. ______ ?
2. ______ ?
3. ______ ?

He has the item on this side, the ark; and the gopher wood the essential; and the incidental: tools, size of trees, and so on; and addition: another building, or a little ark. Now then, his parallel of benevolence: doing good, money, food, and clothing; and his addition: orphanages, homes for the aged. Now let us try that illustration: I put here the teaching; the essential of it is the truth; the incidental of it: oral, written, radio, and tracts. Then the anti-Sunday school people say the addition is the Sunday school. I put here preach; and here the gospel; and the incidental: pulpit, radio, and building, and so on; and over on the other hand, the *Gospel Guardian!* (Time called.)

All right. Thank you.

Porter's Second Affirmative

Brethren Moderators, Brother Woods, Ladies and Gentlemen:

I appreciate the privilege of returning to the stand to continue my discussion, my part of this discussion, of this particular proposition tonight. And if I were inclined to do a little bit of boasting and crowing, as Brother Woods has been doing through the debate, I could say that is the feeblest effort I ever saw.

Now, I want to answer his questions first; and then I have some for him.

First. "If the churches in Memphis can build an old folks home for the aged, cannot these same churches also build a home of the same type that you endorse for old folks for homeless children?" Yes, of the same type.

Second. "In whose title should the property of such a home as you have in mind for old folks in Memphis rest: in one man, a group of men composed of all the elders of the churches in Memphis, or in all of the churches equally?" The matter of who owns the property is merely an incidental matter. It might not be owned by any of them, as far as that's concerned.

Third. "May such a home as you endorse have a manager, a treasurer, or a secretary?" It is already under the elders as the managers, and they have charge of the treasury of each congregation.

Fourth. "Will the churches or the home take legal custody and guardianship of those to be provided for in this home?" Each church is responsible for the one that it places in the home.

Fifth. "In the case of the home for the homeless children, who will administer discipline?" Well, we might ask the same question: Who would feed the persons in there; or who would prepare the meals? Why, certainly, they may hire somebody over there to do the work, just as they may hire a preacher, without setting up a Board or Organization of any kind.

Sixth. "Do you believe that a California congregation should comply with the law and incorporate in order to exist legally there?" Well, I deny that they have to incorporate in order to exist.

Seventh. "Is the legal organization which results from such incorporation the same as the organization which the New Testament teaches?" I have never seen a copy of the charter required by the California laws. I'd have to look it over in order to tell you anything in detail about that particular charter, or articles of incorporation.

Eighth. "If the incorporation of a congregation with its president, vice-president, secretary, and essential directors does not form a new body or change its status before God, does the incorporation of the home make it a new body or change its status in God's sight?" Whether or not that is true, Brother Woods, you have already admitted that the home *is another body.* You stated definitely last night that the home is an *additional body.* You have already gone on record as that. It is on the tapes, Brother Woods, that you said the home is an additional body; and so all of the twisting and all of the squirming that you may do in order to try to get out of it is not going to help you because it is still there.

Now, will someone hand him these questions, please?

1st. Do churches have a scriptural right to contribute funds to the needy in private homes that are denominational?

2nd. Do churches have a scriptural right to contribute funds to the Buckner Orphan Home of Dallas, Texas?

3rd. Do we need Benevolent Organizations to care for

orphans because not enough private homes are willing to take orphans into them for care?

4th. If it is impossible for the needy to be cared for except in some such organization as Tipton Home, were the churches unable to do the work of benevolence for nearly nineteen hundred years of its existence?

5th. If they were able to do such work, where is the New Testament record of any such organization?

6th. Did you endorse such organizations as Boles Home in 1939?

7th. If you did not, what New Testament teaching caused you to oppose them?

8th. If you did endorse such organizations at that time as Boles Home, then what is the name of one of the organizations which brethren formed "for the care of orphans" that you opposed?

Now, I shall get to the speech that he made and pay my respects to the things said. He said that Porter had not changed positions at all in this debate. "He is still in the negative as he has been all the way." Well, that is the way my proposition forced me to be. We couldn't get any other proposition to debate except negative propositions; and, therefore, I had to approach it from a negative point of view in order to have the debate at all. Now, then, it makes no difference about that particular thing. My proposition says it is "contrary to the scriptures"; and if I show that it is contrary to the scriptures, that is, what he is doing is *contrary to the scriptures,* after all, I would be under no obligation, so far as the proposition goes, to go anything beyond that. But I have gone beyond that, and I have showed some *hows* that he has been calling for, and there will be more of that as we go. But he said, "Porter *still hasn't told us how.*" Both of us have admitted that children can be cared for in private homes. That is *one how* by which the needy can be cared for; but since "that is individual action and not collective action on the part of the church, then we want *another how.*" And I gave you *another how* in this Memphis situation a while ago, in which churches could maintain a home, a place for a residence, where the aged might be cared for with each church sustaining the same relationship to it, with no Board whatsoever set up over it; and, therefore, that is *another how* by which it can be done. Brother Woods, would you endorse an arrangement like that? Tell me, Brother Woods, would that kind of arrangement be within scriptural principles? Would you accept that? Do you believe that method is contrary to the Bible, contrary to New Testament authority? Tell me, Brother Woods, when you come to the stand.

Then he came to Brother Warren's argument, one that he had adapted from Brother Warren. Brother Warren made it on another line, but he took it and applied it to this principle. And I want Porter's chart number four, please, in this connection. And I said if I would turn prophet a while ago, I would predict that we had seen the last of that chart; and Brother Woods said, I was "hoping I wouldn't see it." No, I was hoping that I could induce him to put it up here again. That is exactly what has happened.

Porter's Projector
Chart No. 4

WOODS SAID ABOUT CHART NO. 11:

"HERE IS ANOTHER ARGUMENT. I CONSIDER THIS, FRIENDS, ONE OF THE FINEST ARGUMENTS THAT I HAVE, IN 25 YEARS OF CONTROVERSY AND IN 100 DEBATES, APPROXIMATELY, I HAVE EVER SEEN. . . BUT I CONSIDER THIS ABSOLUTELY UNANSWERABLE AND IRRESISTIBLE."

- WOODS - From Tape.

Here is what Brother Woods said—this is taken from the tape recording: "Here is another argument. I consider this, friends, one of the finest arguments that I have, in twenty-five years of controversy and in one hundred debates approximately, ever seen. But I consider this absolutely unanswerable and irresistible." Now, that's what Brother Woods said about this argument that he adapted from Brother Warren—that it is one of the best that he had seen in twenty-five years of controversy and approximately one hundred debates. He considers it absolutely *unanswerable* and *irresistible*.

Now, I want chart number eleven of Brother Woods,' please. We want to get that chart now in this connection that he used a while ago. We will take a look at it and see how *unanswerable* and *irresistible* the thing actually is.

CHART NO. 11

AXIOM: "The WHOLE of anything is the SUM of its parts"

PROOF MY PROP. REQUIRES: • Care Of Orph. & Aged
•Ch. Support " " " "
•Ch. Cooperation in the Support of " " •
(a) This we have already done.
(b) Porter concedes foregoing anyway.

Syllogism: (1) All situations, the component parts of which are scriptural, are scriptural situations.
(2.) The component parts of the whole work involved in my prop. are scriptural.
(3) ∴ the whole work involved in prop. is scriptural.

PORTER'S ALTERNATIVE: (a) Deny the major premise.
(b) Repudiate Public Statements.

Here we have it now. "The axiom: The whole of anything is the sum of its parts. Proof of my proposition requires: Care of the orphans and the aged; church support of the orphans and aged; and church cooperation in the support of the orphans and aged. This we have already done," that is, already shown this to be true; and second, "Porter concedes the foregoing anyway." Now then "Syllogism: First, all situations, the component parts of which are scriptural, are scriptural situations. Second, the component parts of the whole work involved in my proposition are scriptural. Third, the whole work involved in the proposition is scriptural." And "Porter's alternative." First, Porter must either "deny the major premise" or he must "repudiate" the statements that he has made about it—the "public statements." Now, he said that is *unanswerable*.

Now, I want Porter's chart number five. We want to take a look at this. I am very glad, Brother Woods, that you had the disposition to bring that chart up again. I wanted to see it again, and I wanted the congregation to see it again and see just how *unanswerable* the thing actually is.

Porter's Projector
Chart No. 5.

A "DEADLY PARALLEL" TO WOODS' CHART NO. 11

AXIOM: "The WHOLE of anything is the SUM of its parts."

PROOF FOR MISSIONARY SOCIETY REQUIRES:
1. Obligation to preach the gospel.
2. Obligation of church to support preaching of gospel.
3. Church cooperation in supporting preaching of gospel.
(a) This has already been done.
(b) Woods concedes foregoing anyway.

SYLLOGISM:
(1) All situations, the component parts of which are Scriptural, are Scriptural situations.
(2) The component parts of the whole work involved in Missionary Society are Scriptural.
(3) The whole work involved in Missionary Society is Scriptural.

WOODS' ALTERNATIVES:
(1) Endorse Missionary Society.
(2) Repudiate best argument of 25 years and 100 debates.
(3) Repudiate proposition and admit defeat.

Now, then, we have A Deadly Parallel to Woods' Chart Number Eleven. "The axiom: The whole of anything is the sum of its parts." That is exactly what his chart says. All right. "Proof for a Missionary Society requires: First. Obligation to preach the gospel. Second. An obligation of the church to support the preaching of the gospel. Third. Church cooperation in the supporting of the preaching of the gospel." All right. "This has already been shown to be true"; and besides "Brother Woods concedes all those points anyway." He won't deny one of them. All three of those points he concedes to be scriptural. All right, then, the "Syllogism: All situations, the component parts of which are scriptural, are scriptural situations. Second. The component parts of the whole work involved in proof of the Missionary Society is scriptural. Third. Therefore, the whole work involved in proof for the Missionary Society is scriptural." And Woods has three "alternatives" here. "First, he must endorse the Missionary Society; or second, he must repudiate one of the best arguments of twenty-five years and a hundred debates; or third, he must repudiate his position and admit defeat—his proposition and admit defeat." Just leave it there a moment, please. Now, then, friends, there is the parallel, a *deadly parallel to his chart*. The only change made is up here in these matters of *preaching the gospel*. Where he had "care for the aged and orphans" we placed "*preaching the gospel.*" We have the very same component parts with respect to preaching of the gospel that he had on his chart respecting the care of the needy, and *every one of them is scriptural*. Will you deny, Brother Woods, that either one of those component parts is scriptural? Will you? All right, if you don't, then the *syllogism* stands, according to your argument, that "all situations, the component parts of which are scriptural, are scriptural situations." There they are. "Second, the component parts of the work involved in proof of the Missionary Society is scriptural. Third, the whole work involved in the proof of the Missionary Society is scriptural." And Brother Woods must *endorse* the Missionary Society, or he must *repudiate* one of the best arguments he has ever heard, or he must *repudiate* his proposition and admit his defeat. I *challenge* him, every inch of him, from the top of his head to the bottom of his feet, to show just *what is wrong with that chart*. Will you do it, Brother Woods? Tell me what is wrong with that chart. I *challenge* you to do it. Here is the very same line of proof, word for word, item for item, that he used in substantiation of his benevolent organization. I challenge him to show me *what is wrong* with that chart. And the very minute he does, I will find the *same defect* in his. I will guarantee that I will. The best argument Brother

Woods ever heard, one of the best he has ever heard, in twenty-five years of debating, has gone with the wind. We need some more lights up here, please.

He came to my chart number one. Let us have that again, please. My chart number one regarding the systematic arrangements. I showed there were two definitions, or two meanings, of the word "organization": that sometimes it means *a systematic arrangement,* and sometimes it means *a body politic and corporate.* Chart one, I believe is right.

Here we have "a systematic arrangement" on one side. Here is "a systematic arrangement"; over there is "a body politic." Now, these churches may conduct a meeting out here and each of them sustain the same relationship to it, each of them bear its part of the support of that meeting, without setting up any Board whatsoever. That is "a systematic arrangement." In that sense nobody ever opposes "organization." But over here we have another meaning of the word "organization"—"a body politic and corporate." The organization is a Missionary Society that becomes chartered under the laws of the state, placed under a Board, and contributions are sent to it, and *it* conducts the meeting. That is another type of "organization"; and that is the type of "organization" which we oppose. It is "a body politic and corporate." All right.

Now, then, chart number two again. We will see about the Memphis home again. Of course, he said in this case we had a gospel meeting. That was a gospel meeting we were talking about; not caring for the orphans; not caring for the needy. That's a gospel meeting. Well, can't you have *a systematic arrangement* in a gospel meeting, Brother Woods? If what you mean is just a systematic arrangement, that the benevolent organization is just a systematic arrangement, don't you believe in having a systematic arrangement for preaching the gospel? All right, if you do, and taking your meaning of systematic arrangement, then that thing we just had is what you will have to endorse.

Here is the home; and each of the churches has an aged person needing relief to be placed in that building to be cared for, all sustaining the same relationship to the home, so to speak, and each one bears its own burden, supports its

Porter's Projector
Chart No. 1.

ORGANIZATION

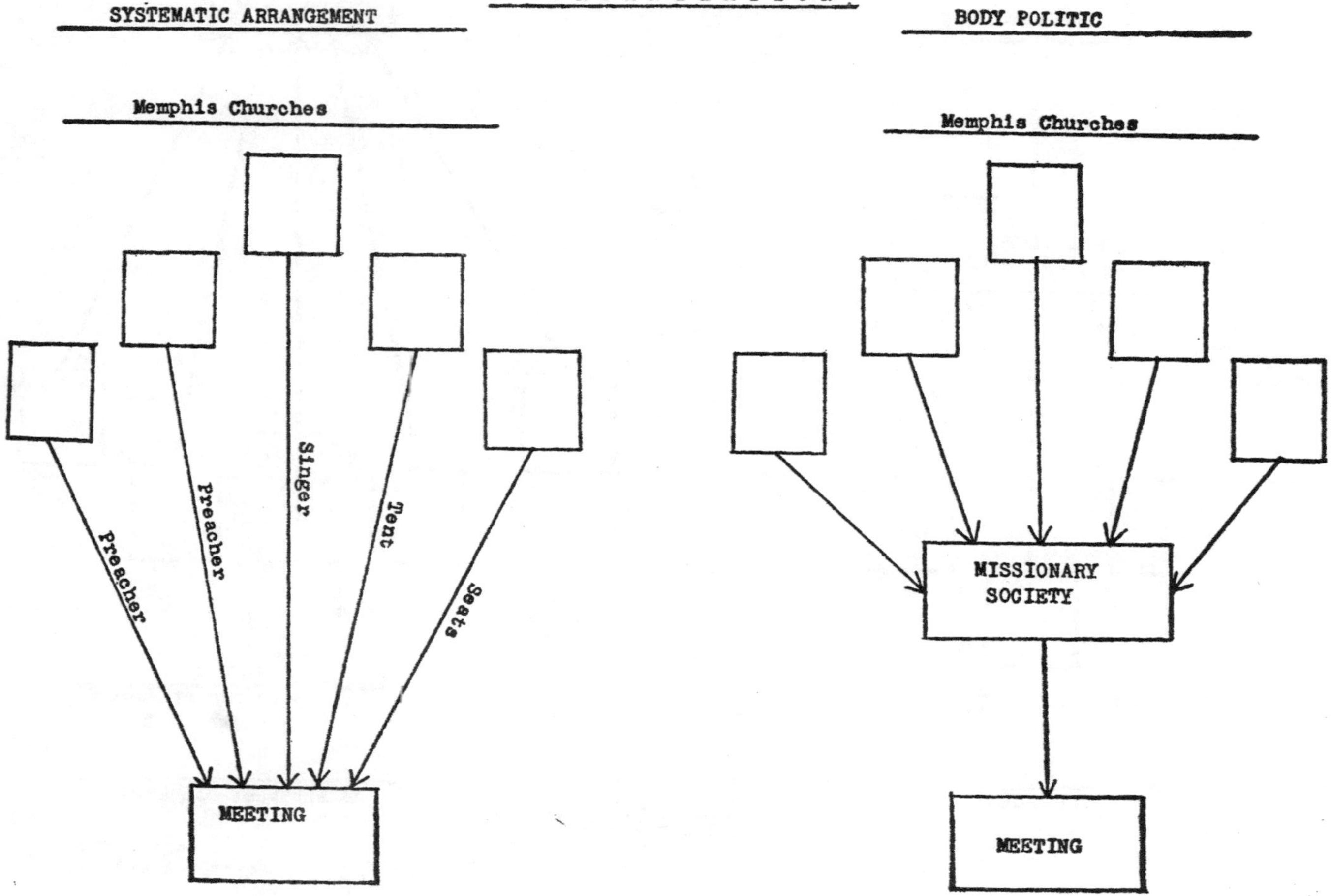

SYSTEMATIC ARRANGEMENT

Memphis Churches

Preacher
Preacher
Singer
Tent
Seats

MEETING

BODY POLITIC

Memphis Churches

MISSIONARY SOCIETY

MEETING

Porter's Projector
Chart No. 2.

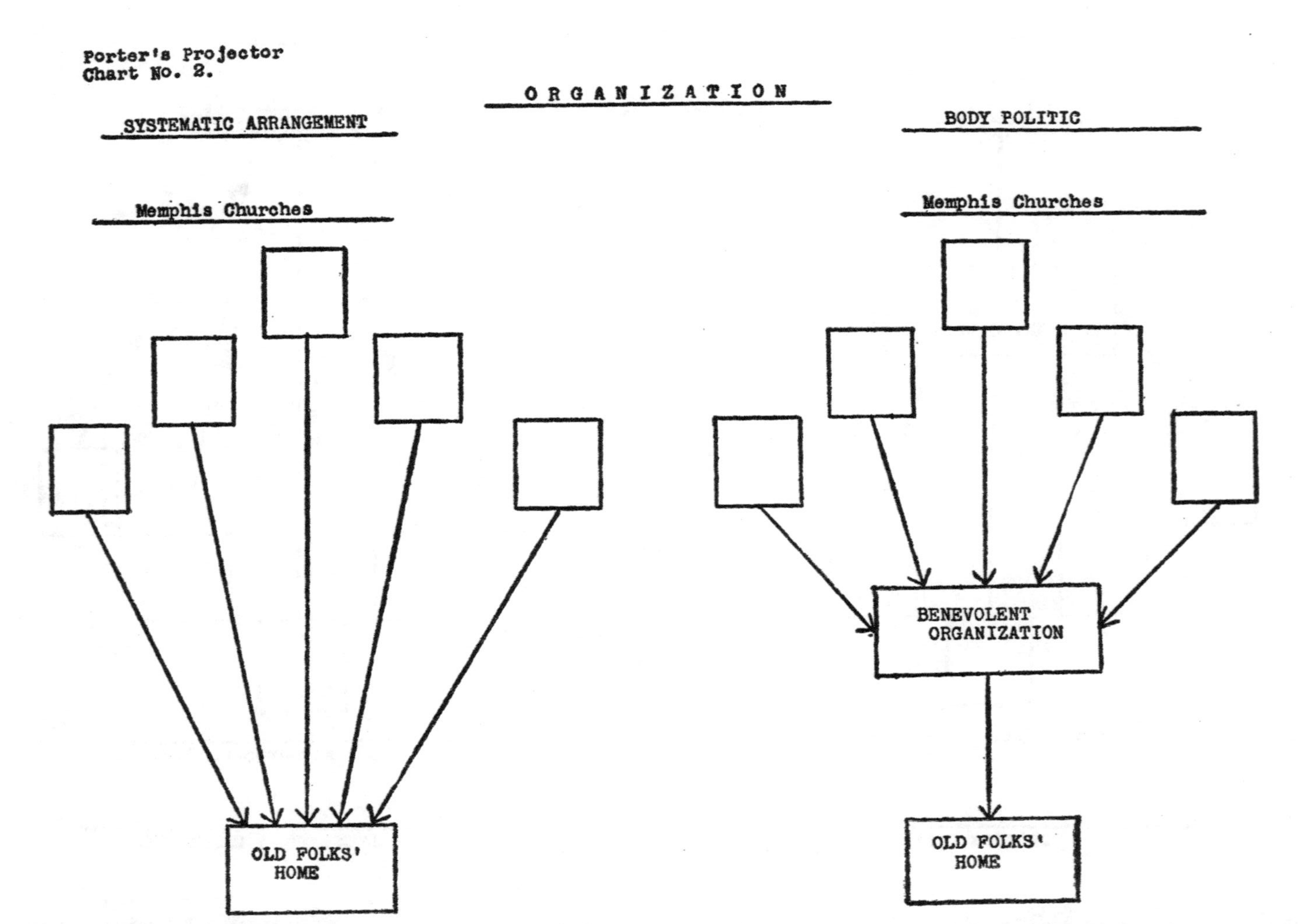

own responsibility. That is "a systematic arrangement"; and *that is one way, that's a how by which churches can care for the needy.* I am asking you again, Brother Woods, will you endorse that as a scriptural arrangement, as a systematic arrangement, that is not contrary to the scriptures? Put it down and tell me. Will you? Are you nodding your head that you mean you will? Brother Woods nodded his head. I don't know whether he meant to be nodding to me or whether he did it unconsciously. Anyway, he will tell us in his next speech whether he will endorse that as a scriptural arrangement, a systematic action, by which a home can be maintained. But here is what he is defending: The word "organization" in the sense of "a body politic and corporate"—a benevolent organization, a body politic and corporate. Comparable to a Missionary Society from that standpoint. It is a body politic and corporate. And the contributions are sent to that benevolent organization which takes charge of them and then does the work of benevolence out here. And, consequently, it is in no way parallel to this whatsoever. There is the body politic and corporate that I oppose. *I oppose* that *kind of organization,* and *I am in favor of a systematic arrangement.*

Then, we might get the next one—number three, just now, and then I'll go to other matters. I forgot to check my time, though I believe I have it right. How much do I have?

BROTHER DOUTHITT: "About six minutes."

Six minutes. Well, thank you.

Porter's Projector
Chart No. 3

THE "HOW" VERSUS "ORGANIZATION"

MAT. 28:19 - TEACH - HOW - ORGANIZATION { CHURCH / MISSIONARY SOCIETY }

1 TIM. 5:16 - RELIEVE - HOW - ORGANIZATION { CHURCH / BENEVOLENT ORGANIZATION }

Here is the matter of the chart on *the how.* Matt. 28: 19 said, "Go ye therefore and teach all nations." Well, the Christian Church came up with the question: How? Those who were in favor of the Missionary Society said, "How are you going to do it? How are you going to teach? The Book doesn't *detail the how;* therefore, we have a right to organize the Missionary Society as a part of *the how* and do the work through that." But *we insisted* that the church was God's *sufficient organization;* you didn't need the Missionary Society, a separate body, set up.

Here (pointing to chart) we have 1 Tim. 5: 16—the matter of relieving the widows. Brother Woods comes up with the same question: "How?" And he makes *that how* to include *the organization.* But last night he came along and surrendered the whole thing by saying, "After you got *the organization* you still had *the how."* Therefore, he admitted that *the how* and *the organization* are different things. And so he has an organization of a benevolent society, just as the Christian Church had the Missionary Society; and *we are still insisting* that the church is *God's all-sufficient organization.* We don't need anything beyond that. Each church, acting in its own local capacity, can take care of its own, can take care of its needy, and it can also preach the gospel, without setting up any kind of "boards or conclaves unknown to the New Testament," using Brother Woods' own phraseology. Thank you.

Now then, we glance through here for some notes and see something that he said. He said, "Brother Porter believes it is all right for an individual to send contributions to a corporation." He brought up the *Gospel Guardian,* in that connection, as a corporation; and since I think it is all right for brethren to help the *Gospel Guardian,* that means I should help the Missionary Society. Well, Brother Woods believes it is all right to help a Christian school individually; and upon the same basis, he believes it is all right to help the Missionary Society individually, because he admits that they are both corporations. Thank you, Brother Woods.

Then, on this chart number three, which we have just used a while ago, he said in this the teaching is not the thing involved. Besides, he said the reason we can't have a Missionary Society in the teaching program is because the Missionary Society does not *inhere in the command to teach.* Now, get that. A Missionary Society does not inhere in the command to teach. Why? Why, Brother Woods? Will you tell me? You said it doesn't. Now, I want to know why. Why doesn't a Missionary Society inhere in the command to teach? The Lord did *not detail the how*. The Lord said *teach*. He didn't say *how to teach*. Why doesn't the Missionary Society inhere in the word "teach"? Why doesn't it, Brother Woods? You won't forget it, will you? We'd like to know. Just tell me *why*. Then, he turned right around and said, "But our benevolent organizations *do inhere* in the *command to relieve*." Now, I want to know *why?* If one command, "to teach," would not include the Missionary Society, why would the other command, "to relieve the afflicted," require or authorize the benevolent organization? In other words, if the Missionary Society *does not inhere* in the command *to teach*, I want to know why the benevolent society *inheres* in the command *to relieve the widows*. *Why*, Brother Woods? *Why?* I wonder if echo will answer, Why?

Then the matter of his parallel charts over here.

The church and the home are parallel. There is an axiom in geometry, I believe, that lines that are parallel to the same line are parallel to each other. Brother Woods says here that the orphan home is running a parallel line with the church. The orphan home is running—Is it the orphan home? I can't see that. "Church and the home are parallel." All right. So we have the orphan home and the church parallel, but the Missionary Society is parallel to the church. He argued that the other night; that it is wrong because it is parallel to the church, doing the work of the church. They are parallel; therefore, the orphan home is parallel to the Missionary Society. So he gets right back on that. If parallel lines, if lines that are parallel to one line, are parallel to each other, then, he makes the Missionary Society and the orphan home parallel to each other in the chart that he is using now.

He wants to know: "Does the *Gospel Guardian* do *a work* of the church?" The *Gospel Guardian* is an individual enterprise. No churches are contributing to the *Gospel Guardian*. Just as the Abilene Christian College down in Texas, set up under the same sort of incorporating laws, is also an organization teaching the Bible, which Brother Woods believes may be done as individuals, because he has argued

THE CHURCH and the HOME MOVE ON PARALLEL LINES

(Woods' Chart #18)

there are certain duties that run parallel. That is, there are some duties which the home may perform which may be performed also by the church. There are some duties of an individual; there are other duties of a church. They may overlap. The same thing is true with respect to this. And I will take his statement. If he wants me to read it, I will read it for him in my next speech along that particular line. Now, then, to this over here, if I have time.

BROTHER DOUTHITT: "You have a half a minute."

Half a minute? We will just note how utterly helpless he seemed to be on this situation.

He wanted to know: "Where is Porter on this?" Well, suppose I say Porter is a part of the Christian Baptizing Association up here. Suppose I would say that takes in Porter. He is one of those fellows who organized that. And so you just notify us when you have some baptizing to do, and we will send our Association over there, some members of our Association, to do the baptizing for you. Now, I want to know, Brother Woods—I am demanding that you tell us—why you put this one, the Christian Benevolent Corporation, over in the realm of incidentals and rule out all the others. (Time Called.)

Thank you very kindly.

Woods' Second Negative

Brethren Moderators, Brother Porter, and Ladies and Gentlemen:

Brother Porter told us that he could say that I had made a feeble effort, but he wouldn't; and he didn't. And the reason he didn't is that Brother Porter is a truthful man! He doesn't want to get up here and say things that are not so, and I was glad to see his veracity manifested here on this occasion.

He says that I mustn't squirm now and try to get around the idea that the home is an additional thing. Why I should want to get out of that I don't know, because if I hadn't said it, I would turn right around and say it. I illustrated it just as plainly and clearly as I could, that it is the function of the church to preach the word; and, the Missionary Society is not inherent in the work of the church; but the

Porter's Roll
Chart No. 2.

LAW AND EXPEDIENCY

To Be Expedient - Must Be Lawful. 1 Cor. 6:12.

COMMANDS	INCLUSIONS	PERVERSIONS	INCIDENTALS	ADDITIONS
Build Ark Gen. 6:14-16	Gopher Wood Three Stories	Cottonwood Ten Stories	Tools - Size Transportation	Another Building
Teach Mat. 28:19	Whole Counsel Truth	Human Traditions Doctrines of Men	Blackboard - Radio Charts - Press	Christian Missionary Society
Baptize Mat. 28:19	Water - Believers Burial	Wine - Infants Sprinkling	Ocean - River Pool - Baptistry	Christian Baptizing Association
Sing Eph. 5:19	Spiritual Songs Melody in Heart	Worldly Songs Melody on Harp	Books - Tuning Fork Voice Parts - Notes	Singing Saints Society
Partake Lord's Supper 1 Cor.11;Acts 20:7.	First Day - Bread Fruit of Vine	Midweek - Beef Buttermilk	Plates - Cups Place - Hour	Christian Communion Confederation
Pray Phil. 4:6; Jas. 1: 6.	To God In Faith	To Virgin Mary In Pretense	Length of Prayer Posture	Christian Praying League
Give 1 Cor. 16:1,2; 2 Cor. 9:6, 7.	As Prospered Cheerfully	Sparingly Grudgingly	Collection Plates Envelopes	Christian Fellowship Federation
Visit Orphans Jas. 1:27.	Food - Clothes Shelter	Oppress - Vex Neglect	House - Tent City - Country	Christian Benevolent Corporation

church is not an orphan home. Brother Porter says that the church has an obligation to care for orphans. Then, if the church is *not* an orphan home, and the church is obligated to care for orphans, then the church has got to supply *some kind* of an orphan home. Now, a fellow who *can't see that* is in need of more instruction than I would be able to give on this occasion! I do not see why Brother Porter doesn't recognize that fact.

He admits that he is still in the negative on this, but said he couldn't get any other kind of proposition. I am amazed at that statement, literally amazed. In the first place, I submitted propositions to Brother Porter which he turned down and, in their place, sent the two that we are debating; and I signed them just exactly like he sent them. *The reason that we have these propositions is that Brother W. Curtis Porter wrote them both!* And yet, he said we couldn't get any other kind. Now, why couldn't we have any other kind? Because he can't affirm a positive approach in this matter of taking care of orphans. He told the truth on that matter!

He says we admit that children can be cared for in private homes. That's not the church doing it. And so it hasn't answered my demand. But he says, "Now, I submitted the Memphis arrangement; and that is a situation in which children can be cared for; and, therefore, there is an example of the churches doing it." I deny it, as he has pictured it here. I want his chart number one, I believe; his Memphis chart. I want you to see that this does not parallel what he said. What did he say in the letter? He believes that the Memphis churches can establish an old folks home.

Now, watch what he is doing here: He says here is the picture of it (pointing to the chart). Here is one church supplying the preaching, and another the singing, another the tent, another the seats. That is a temporary arrangement. What we are talking about is a permanent arrangement. Old people don't get younger. In the next place, observe this: This is not a parallel to his proposition. *These churches do not all sustain the same relation to that meeting.* One church alone does the preaching, another church does the singing, another church supplies the tent, and another one the seats. He said the churches could cooperate in *one*

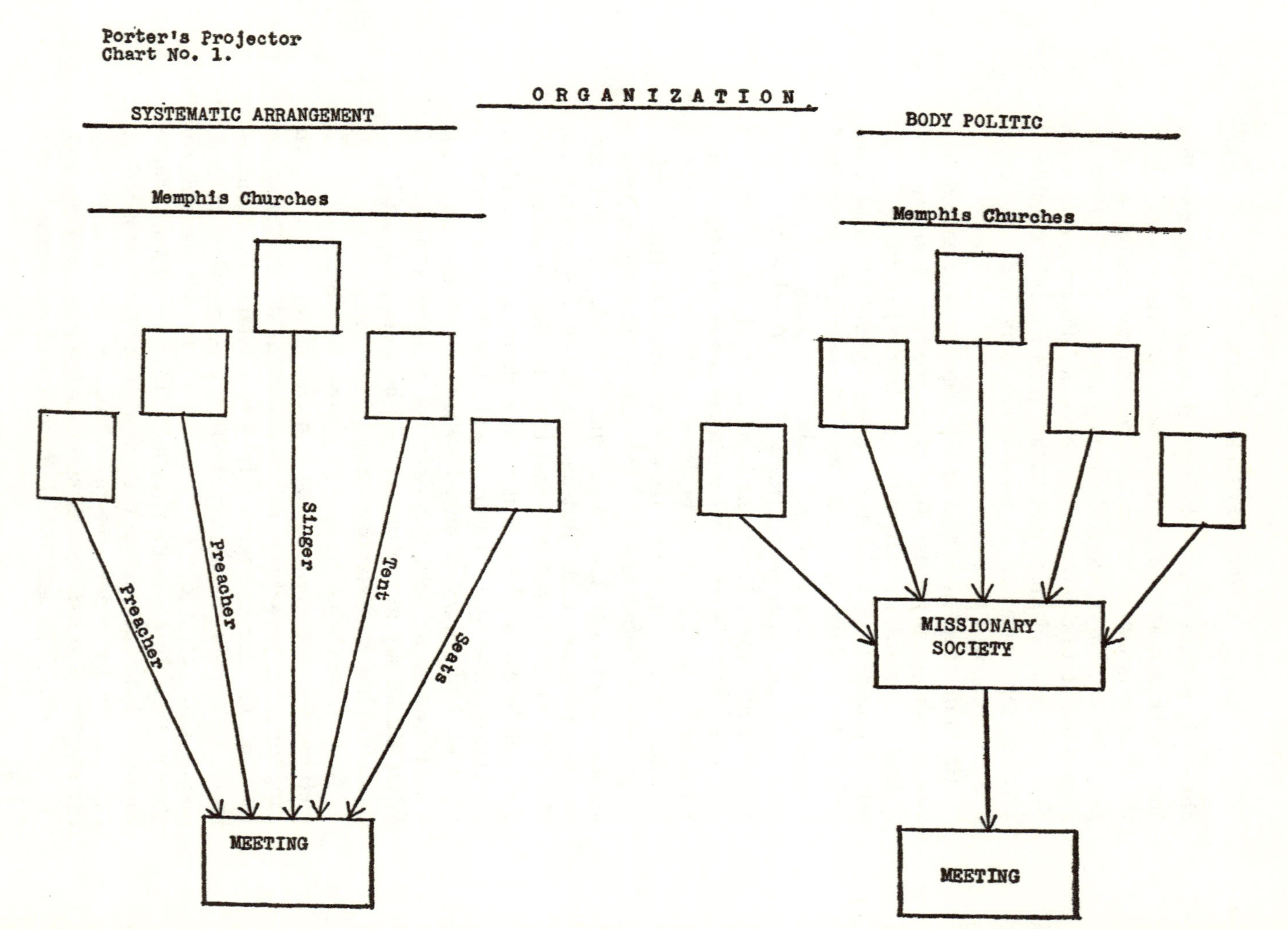
Porter's Projector
Chart No. 1.
ORGANIZATION
SYSTEMATIC ARRANGEMENT
BODY POLITIC
Memphis Churches
Preacher
Preacher
Singer
Tent
Seats
MEETING
Memphis Churches
MISSIONARY SOCIETY
MEETING

phase of church activity. He has several different phases of it here. That, friends, is not a parallel to the situation that he has set up. Now, according to this, one church could do *all* the praying, another one *all* the singing, another one *all* the preaching. And therefore, why couldn't one church take care of *all the orphans in Memphis?* If one church can turn over to the other churches the singing; if the group can turn over to another church the preaching, and another the praying, why can't they turn over to another church the care of the orphans? If his parallel has any application at all, that's it. And down it goes, world without end. There isn't anybody who knows that better than W. Curtis Porter! Now, Brother Porter, *you haven't told us how the churches can cooperate in the care of children!* You haven't done it. This is not it, because this is just one church doing one phase of activity. This is just the way one church can do it. Instead of having churches cooperating in it, you have one church doing the whole work in its phase of it. Your moderator has said that there are a *dozen ways* in which the church can do it. I will settle for six. Tell him *six* of them, Brother Douthitt! Now, let him get busy on that. And remember this: One church here is the preaching church, another is the praying church, another one the singing church. Why not, then, another one *the orphan home church?* Brother Porter, you will never get out of that difficulty. Ah, no, you haven't met the issue. It still remains.

Let us have chart number fifteen. It still remains that he has taken a position here that is in flat contradiction to his proposition with reference to the Memphis churches.

What has he said in his letter? This is not one church performing one function and another, another. This is all the churches in Memphis, twenty-eight of them, performing just one function; and that is to establish a home for the aged. He said, "That's right." Get busy, Brother Porter, and meet the issue and quit quibbling. That, friends will suffice for that.

He asks if I will accept this Memphis situation. No, because it is an impossibility. It can't exist. The situation of going out here and establishing a home and putting a group of people out there, and not having any sort of supervision,

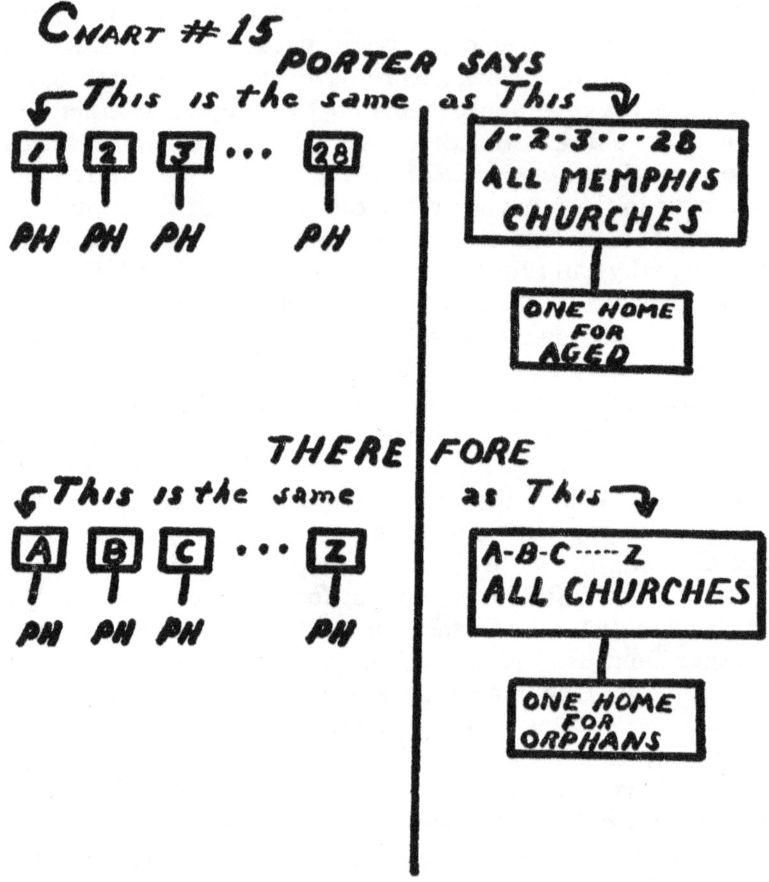

no organization of *any kind,* is a physical impossibility. He has described something that can't exist. Brother Porter, have you folks started one of these arrangements like that? If so, where is the location, and in what city? Evidently, if *this* is the right way, you have some around over the country. Where are they? Give me the names and addresses of two locations where that is being done. You will do it, won't you? You won't forget that, will you? Brother Porter, you forgot some of the things I asked you. You won't forget that, will you? Now, don't!

Let us have his chart number four. Again, friends, we are on the question of what I regard as an irresistible argu-

Pörter's Projector
Chart No. 4

WOODS SAID ABOUT CHART NO. 11:

"HERE IS ANOTHER ARGUMENT. I CONSIDER THIS, FRIENDS, ONE OF THE FINEST ARGUMENTS THAT I HAVE, IN 25 YEARS OF CONTROVERSY AND IN 100 DEBATES, APPROXIMATELY, I HAVE EVER SEEN. . . BUT I CONSIDER THIS ABSOLUTELY UNANSWERABLE AND IRRESISTIBLE."

- WOODS - From Tape.

CHART NO. 11

AXIOM: "The WHOLE of anything is the SUM of its parts"

•

PROOF MY PROP. REQUIRES:
- • Care Of Orph. & Aged
- • Ch. Support " " " "
- • Ch. Cooperation in the Support of " " "

(a) This we have already done.
(b) Porter concedes foregoing anyway.

•

Syllogism:
(1.) All situations, the component parts of which are scriptural, are scriptural situations.
(2.) The component parts of the whole work involved in my prop. are scriptural.
(3.) ∴ the whole work involved in prop. is scriptural.

•

PORTER'S ALTERNATIVE:
(a) Deny the major premise.
(b) Repudiate Public Statements.

ment. I think I could quit on this one. He says that I said it was the finest I had ever seen. I told him I didn't say that, and this (his chart) shows I didn't. I said it was one of the finest; and it is. Now then, let us have my chart number eleven.

Here it is, the axiom: The whole of anything is the sum of its parts. I am obligated (or was the first two nights) to show you that it is right for churches to cooperate in the care of the orphan children. And here is what my proposition requires: First, the care of the orphans and needy; church support of orphans and aged; church cooperation in the support of such. I cited Eph. 4: 28, James 1: 27, and so on. Church support of it, Acts 11. Church cooperation, 2 Cor. 8: 9. Brother Porter conceded all of those. Now, the argument was that since all of that is scriptural, and he admits that, therefore, the conclusion follows that the whole work involved in my proposition is scriptural. Let us see what my proposition requires. You can't care for the orphans and aged, you can't have church support for such care, you can't have cooperation, church cooperation, in such care, without having *somewhere* to care for them.

Let us have chart number nine. Here is what it takes to care for the needy. And this will indicate why I say to you that my proposition stands. Paul said, "remember the poor," Gal. 2: 10. This requires for the orphan: a place, food, clothing, education, supervision, medical care. For the aged: shelter, food, clothing, and medical care. I said that you can't provide that without having *some place* to provide it. Now, that establishes the place. I established the fact of church participation. He admits it. Then the conclusion follows that my proposition stands proven.

Let us have his chart number five on the Missionary Society. I was absolutely amazed at his efforts here. I tell you I was. I do not believe that I have ever seen a more wretched or miserable failure than characterized this effort.

I want you to see it here: In an effort to defeat my argument, he has here "a deadly parallel" to Woods' chart: Axiom: The whole of anything is the sum of its parts. Now look what he says proof for the Missionary Society requires: (1) An obligation to preach the gospel; (2) obligation for the

CHART No. 9

"REMEMBER THE POOR"

Gal. 2:10

THIS REQUIRES

FOR THE ORPHAN:

- A Place
- Food
- Clothing
- Education
- Supervision
- Medical Care

FOR THE AGED:

- Shelter
- Food
- Clothing
- Medical Care

Porter's Projector
Chart No. 5.

A "DEADLY PARALLEL" TO WOODS' CHART NO. 11

AXIOM: "The WHOLE of anything is the SUM of it's parts."

PROOF FOR MISSIONARY SOCIETY REQUIRES:
1. Obligation to preach the gospel.
2. Obligation of church to support preaching of gospel.
3. Church cooperation in supporting preaching of gospel.
(a) This has already been done.
(b) Woods concedes foregoing anyway.

SYLLOGISM:
(1) All situations, the component parts of which are Scriptural, are Scriptural situations.
(2) The component parts of the whole work involved in Missionary Society are Scriptural.
(3) The whole work involved in Missionary Society is Scriptural.

WOODS' ALTERNATIVES:
(1) Endorse Missionary Society.
(2) Repudiate best argument of 25 years and 100 debates.
(3) Repudiate proposition and admit defeat.

church to support the preaching of the gospel; (3) church cooperation in supporting the preaching of the gospel. Now, Brother Porter says that those three points lead irresistibly to the Missionary Society. I didn't know that the obligation to preach, the obligation of the church to support preaching, and church cooperation in that made a Missionary Society! W. Curtis Porter thinks it does. Now, friends, that's the way he meets my argument. Is that the Missionary Society? The very idea! That is the most absolutely ridiculous effort I ever saw put forth in my life! Now, get it, please. Here is the difference: You can't have care for the orphans, you can't have church care for the orphans, you can't have church cooperation in the support of orphans without having *some kind of an orphan home.* You may not call it an orphan home; but it is some kind of a home for orphans. But, you can preach, the churches can support the preaching, and the churches can cooperate in the support of such, *without* a Missionary Society. Brother Porter, down goes your effort. It still remains that my argument is absolutely irresistible. Now, I want to see some more on it. I want you to do some more with it. You haven't met the argument, and a silly grin won't suffice for it. I tell you that! (Laughter.)

Now, let's have his chart number one. I want you to note, please, that this is, as I pointed out a moment ago, a temporary situation. Now, let us make it parallel. Remember, please, these are the Memphis churches. This, instead of the meeting, is an orphan home, or at least, the care of the needy. But now, let us make the application to a permanent thing. Let us change this from a gospel meeting to a church that was established out there. That would be your parallel. It is not a parallel truly, but that's your parallel of it. Now then, Brother Porter, change that to a group of brethren cooperating out there every Lord's day. Then, do you still say that this situation would hold here? If it does, then which one of these congregations exercises supervision of it? Which one? Ah, friends, he hasn't met the parallel. He still remembers that Brother W. Curtis Porter says that churches in Memphis can combine their energies and support an old folks home. But if they can do it in Memphis, why can't they do it in Indianapolis? If they can do it in Memphis, why can't they do it in Tennessee, in Indiana, and Arkansas, or wherever it may be? Why can't they?

I predict that this is the last time that Brother W. Curtis Porter will be asked to represent the *Guardian* position on this question. I am making another prophecy!

Next, he says the church can preach without any other organization. If it can, then why does the *Gospel Guardian* exist? Brother Porter comes along and says there isn't any need of another organization because the church is all-sufficient. Well, one of two things is true. He doesn't believe in the all-sufficiency of the church, or else he has an extra organization, because he has an organization that's incorporated for the purpose of preaching the gospel. Again, the question is: What does the word "organization" mean? If it means something apart from the church, and a rival to it, then I say it is wrong; and it would be wrong if the *Gospel Guardian,* or any other paper, falls into that category. But then, that is not the sense in which we speak of "an organization." We mean simply *a means* by way of which the church accomplishes *its* work.

Porter's Projector
Chart No. 1.

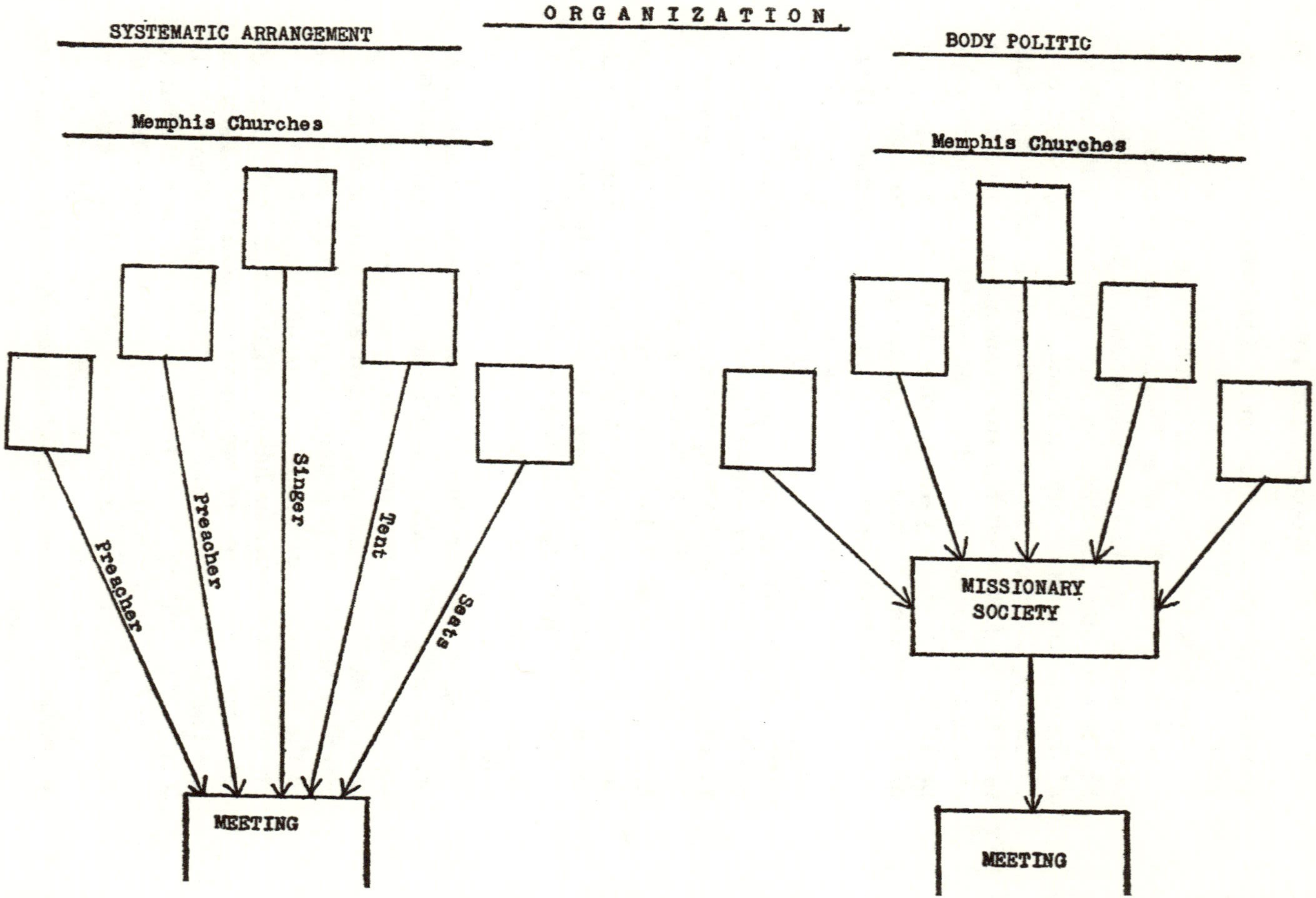

ORGANIZATION

SYSTEMATIC ARRANGEMENT

Memphis Churches

Preacher

Preacher

Singer

Tent

Seats

MEETING

BODY POLITIC

Memphis Churches

MISSIONARY SOCIETY

MEETING

He wants to know if the Missionary Society inheres in the word "teach." No, just as I explained to you. It is not there. I want to answer and give more attention to his chart; and in so doing, I would like to have my chart number twelve.

One of the questions that Brother Porter conveniently forgot to answer was this: *Where are you* on this chart, Brother Porter? You will forget to answer it the next time. Observe that right over here under inclusions, on the matter of visiting the orphans, you have all of the elements of the orphan home right there. There is the orphan home on his chart. If he puts the private home there, then I will put the orphan home there, because that is what the orphan home is. But if he says the orphan home is not there, then his private home is not there, because that is what the orphan home is, whether it has one orphan or a hundred! But if he says that that's not where it is, then his home is not there. And I asked him to place his home on that chart. You think he will answer that? You wait and see if Brother Porter tells us where the private home is on that chart.

Here is the parallel. Brother Porter believes that the ark is the thing commanded; the gopher wood, the essential; the incidental: the tools, the size and so on. But it would be wrong to have a little ark over there; and, therefore, he parallels that with the orphanage. Now, it would be wrong to attach anything to the ark because it would be another building. But Brother Porter believes it would be all right for Noah's sons to build them *a few little boats (if they didn't attach them to that ark) and start paddling around on the outside!* One of them could be named the *American Christian Review;* and another, *Bible Talk;* and here comes the last saying, "Me too, the *Gospel Guardian,*" paddling along right at the last! (Laughter.) He doesn't object to little arks, just so those little arks are not tied on to the big ark, just so you keep them out in the water a ways. Now, anybody ought to be able to see that, especially Curtis Porter.

These men (Brother Porter and his group) have identified themselves with the anti-Sunday school position. I want to show you how true that is. Let me call your attention,

Porter's Roll
Chart No. 2.

LAW AND EXPEDIENCY

To Be Expedient - Must Be Lawful. 1 Cor. 6:12.

COMMANDS	INCLUSIONS	PERVERSIONS	INCIDENTALS	ADDITIONS
Build Ark Gen. 6:14-16	Gopher Wood Three Stories	Cottonwood Ten Stories	Tools - Size Transportation	Another Building
Teach Mat. 28:19	Whole Counsel Truth	Human Traditions Doctrines of Men	Blackboard - Radio Charts - Press	Christian Missionary Society
Baptize Mat. 28:19	Water - Believers Burial	Wine - Infants Sprinkling	Ocean - River Pool - Baptistry	Christian Baptizing Association
Sing Eph. 5:19	Spiritual Songs Melody in Heart	Worldly Songs Melody on Harp	Books - Tuning Fork Voice Parts - Notes	Singing Saints Society
Partake Lord's Supper 1 Cor.11;Acts 20:7.	First Day - Bread Fruit of Vine	Midweek - Beef Buttermilk	Plates - Cups Place - Hour	Christian Communion Confederation
Pray Phil. 4:6; Jas. 1: 6.	To God In Faith	To Virgin Mary In Pretense	Length of Prayer Posture	Christian Praying League
Give 1 Cor. 16:1,2; 2 Cor. 9:6, 7.	As Prospered Cheerfully	Sparingly Grudgingly	Collection Plates Envelopes	Christian Fellowship Federation
Visit Orphans Jas. 1:27.	Food - Clothes Shelter	Oppress - Vex Neglect	House - Tent City - Country	Christian Benevolent Corporation

CHART NO. 12

ITEM	ESSENTIAL	INCIDENTAL	ADDITION
Ark	Gopher Wood	Tools, Size of Trees, etc.	Little Ark
Benevolence	Doing Good	Money, Food, Clothes	Orphanages, Homes for Aged
Teaching	Truth	Oral, Written Radio, Tracts	Sunday School
Preaching	Gospel	Pulpit, Radio, Bldg.	Gospel Guardian!
	(1)	(2)	(3)

Where is the Private Home?

1. ________ ?
2. ________ ?
3. ________ ?

please, to chart number five. Chart number five is our next one.

Here is an exact parallel between these two here. On this side I have the *Guardian*. On this side I have the home, the orphan home. The masthead of the *Guardian* says it is to "propagate and defend New Testament Christianity"; that is the aim of it. The aim of the home is to visit the fatherless and widows. In an article in the August 4, 1955, issue of the *Gospel Guardian*, it is said the organization of it is exactly the same as the orphan homes. In character, they are both nonprofit. In their manner of support, the orphan home receives money from churches and individuals, and the *Gospel Guardian* gets money from churches and individuals. I know they deny that they get money from churches, but I shall prove it if he demands the proof, and I will be glad to produce it. I hope that he calls upon me tonight, or before this debate is over, to prove that they get money out of the church treasury, and that it is supported—it receives money—in that fashion. Now then, what is the difference, friends? What is the difference? He says this (the orphan home) is wrong because it is another organization. Well, is this (the *Guardian*) the same organization as the church, or is it *another*? It is another organization. He says this (the orphan home) is wrong because it is doing a work of the church. Well, isn't this (the *Guardian*) doing a work of the church? I tell you every argument that this man has made against the orphan home can be made against a religious paper; and as long as these brethren, who are sometimes popularly styled Ketchersideites, or Sommerites, or Guardianites, adhere to the practice of publishing papers, they have a millstone around their necks.

Let us look further. Turn to chart number three. I want you to note that in every field of activity we have this antiism.

It is the same in principle as the anti-Sunday school position. In the field of edification, benevolence, evangelism, and worship, we have it. In the field of edification we have the anti-Sunday school hobbyists. Their opposition is that the Sunday school is an unscriptural organization. They demand that we show identity with 1 Cor. 14. And, of

CHART No. 5

The Guardian		The Home
1. "Propagate and Defend N.T. Christianity"	←AIM→	1. "Visit the fatherless and widow"
2. "Same"	←Organization→	2. "Same" (G.G., Aug. 4, '55)
3. Individual Business Enterprize (Non-Profit)	←Character→	3. Home (Non-Profit)
4. Receives Money from Churches And Individuals	←Support→	4. Receives Money from Churches and Individuals

WHAT IS THE DIFFERENCE?

Chart No. 3—HOBBYISM IN THE CHURCH

Church Activity	
1. Edification	1. Edification: Anti-Sunday School Hobbyist Objection: S.S. an unscriptural Organization. Demand: Show Identity with I Cor. 14.
2. Benevolence	2. Benevolence: Anti-Orphan Home Factionists Objection: Institutionalism Demand: Show identity with 2 Cor. 8:13.
3. Evangelism	3. Evangelism: Anti-Cooperation Groups. Objection: Centralized Control Demand: Give detailed Pattern
4. Worship	4. Worship: One Cup Advocates Objection: Individual Cups. Demand: Produce Example

course, they reject the idea of any implication of *a method of procedure* in the word "teach." In the field of benevolence, Brother Porter and other anti-orphan home factionists object on the ground that the home is institutionalism. And they demand, some of them, at least, that we show identity with 2 Cor. 8: 13. In the field of evangelism, the anti-cooperation groups object on the grounds that such cooperation is centralized control; and they demand that we give a detailed pattern. In the field of worship, there are the one-cup advocates. Their objection is to individual cups; and they demand an example. The opposition is the same in principle from beginning to end; and, therefore, to espouse it is simply to espouse the cause of anti-ism.

Now, turn to chart number one. My time is up? I thank you.

Porter's Third Affirmative

Brethren Moderators, Brother Woods, Ladies and Gentlemen:

I appear before you at this time for my closing speech in this session of the debate. During this speech I want to pay my attention to the things that have been said by Brother Woods, who has just preceded me.

I wonder if Brother Woods forgot something. How about those written questions I handed to you, Brother Woods? Did you forget them?

BROTHER WOODS: "Yes."

Well, then. Brother Woods forgot all the written questions, and yet he reprimanded me because I missed one or two of his oral questions. I gave him a list of eight written questions, and he forgot *every single one of them.*

BROTHER WOODS: "Brother Porter, may I say this?"

BROTHER PORTER: "All right."

BROTHER WOODS: "I will be mighty glad if you would allow me to answer them and give you the additional time in order that you may do it. I just simply overlooked them and did not come to them in my notes, and I will be glad to do that; and then you can take up the extra time that I use in answering the questions in addition to your speech."

BROTHER PORTER: "Well, any way. It doesn't matter to me. Or you can answer them tomorrow night."

BROTHER DOUTHITT: "Brother Porter, I believe, since the arrangements have been made for twenty minutes each and since Brother Woods has twenty minutes yet, I believe it would be best just to go ahead with your twenty minutes, and let him answer tomorrow night."

Well, probably so, because it will mess up the tape recorders in their recordings; and so it will be all right for you to answer them in your next speech. All right. I lost some time there; so keep track of it.

One thing that he mentioned in the speech preceding this one, that I overlooked, was a statement he made that the church is God's Missionary Society. He said that's where a difference comes in. The church is God's Missionary Society, but that the church is not God's Orphan Home or Benevolent Society. So there is a difference between the orphan home and the Missionary Society. The church is God's Missionary Society, but it is not God's Benevolent Organization. I want to read to you a statement made by Brother Woods back in 1946, in the *Annual Lesson Commentary,* on page 340. Brother Woods says:

"In line with the fact that our lesson today deals with the autonomy of the church, we point out that the contribution here alluded to was raised wholly without the high pressure organizational methods characteristic of today. There was *no organization at all;* the churches, in their own capacity, raised the funds, and they were gathered by brethren specially appointed for the purpose. This is the Lord's method of raising money, and it will suffice in any case. *There is no place for charitable organizations in the work of the New Testament church.* It"—that is, referring to the church—"It is the only charitable organization that the Lord authorizes or that is needed to do the work that the Lord expects his people to do today."

Now Brother Woods says the church is God's Missionary Society, but it is not God's Charitable Organization. Right here in this he said *it is God's Charitable Organization,* and it is God's *only* Charitable Organization. The church is. Brother Woods said it is. And there is *no place for any other organization.* "No place for a Charitable Organization," he says, "in the work the Lord expects the church to do." *No place for it.* He has made room for it, though, since 1946. There wasn't any place for it then. He has many places for it now.

Now, that little play that he made about "Sommerites" and "Ketchersideites" and so on. When brethren begin to shout "Sommerites!" and "Ketchersideites!" they are doing it for the very same purpose that D. N. Jackson and other Baptist preachers have in mind when they begin to shout "Campbellites"!

From the audience: "Amen."

And if you don't have any idea what that is, you just study a while and see if you can't figure just what it is that Baptist preachers have in mind, when we meet them in debate, when they begin to shout, "Campbellism! Campbellism! *Campbellism!*" That is evidently the same purpose that Brother Woods has in mind in shouting, "Sommerism! Ketchersideism!" I don't have to tell you what the purpose is. You can draw your own conclusions.

Regarding the orphan home being a separate body, he said, "Why, certainly; and if I didn't say it, I would say it now. *It is an additional body.* If I hadn't already said it, I would say it now." He says, "I believe it is. And so I will say it now." All right, we are going to see some more about this matter. In the debate that Brother Woods had with Leroy Garrett in March of 1954—that is less than two years ago—Brother Woods made this statement:

"Brother Garrett says he objects to our position in the matter because it sets aside the divine function of the church, in that he maintains that it establishes two bodies, whereas the Lord established but one. Now, may I say, friends, in reply to that, that it is a complete misapprehension of my position, and that of my brethren, to allege that we do defend two bodies. I am just as much opposed to the idea of two bodies as Brother Garrett is. My position, and that of my brethren, and that which I am defending tonight as scriptural, is that we do not have two bodies—that what we do is the church functioning through the only divine body in existence that is ordained for that purpose."

That statement was made in the first negative of the Woods-Garrett debate on the orphan home question held in

Stockton, California, on March 20, 1954, and has been copied from the tape recordings. Less than two years ago Brother Woods said, "I *deny* it is a *separate body;* it is *not a separate body;* it is the church functioning through the *only divine body* that God has authorized." Now Brother Woods says that it is *two bodies.* "I admit that it is a *separate body;* and if I hadn't already admitted it, *I would say it now.*" Well, he has found more places, and he has found more bodies to go in the places now.

"There must be a home of some kind," he said. "We have to have a home of some kind." And Porter wasn't dealing fairly in this matter because he was on the negative of the thing. He said, "The fact is, that Porter wrote these propositions." Why, certainly, after we had negotiated for weeks and weeks and weeks and could not get a proposition that would allow me to take an affirmative position. But even the propositions that he sent to me were negative propositions, and even committed me to the idea of denying church cooperation. And when *nothing else could be obtained,* then I wrote these, and he accepted them, because nothing else was possible to obtain. All right; so much for that.

On the matter of the charts—oh yes, I want to get back to chart number eleven, Brother Woods' chart number eleven, on the Warren Argument. We want to take a look at that for just a little bit. Brother Woods said concerning this, it was the most miserable, wretched, feeble effort that he ever saw in his life. If it had been any better, I don't know what Brother Woods would have done. I don't know what would have happened to him if it had not been such a feeble, miserable, wretched effort that Porter made. Now, here is his argument, friends: that "the *whole* of anything is the *sum* of its parts." And "proof of my proposition requires: the care of the orphans and the aged; and church support of the orphans and aged; and church cooperation in the support of the orphans and aged. This we agree is already true, and Porter concedes the foregoing, anyway." Then his "Syllogism": that "all situations, the component parts of which are scriptural, are scriptural situations. Second, the component parts of the whole work involved in my proposition are scriptural. And third, the whole work involved in my proposition is scriptural." Then he said "Porter's alternative" is to "*deny the major premise,* or *repudiate his public statements.*" Now, that, he says, is an *irresistible argument.* Up here are the three things that his proposition demanded, and he implied that was all it demanded. Why, those things were agreed to before this debate ever started, so far as that goes. That doesn't even touch top, edge, side, nor bottom of the proposition. But that's his *irresistible* and *unanswerable* argument. And I gave you a deadly parallel. Let us have now my chart number five as a deadly parallel to that and see how wretched, poor, and miserable the thing really is. I am certain of the fact that people in the audience are able to get a better grasp of it than Brother Woods seems to have had. We want you to look at it again, because I am just certain of the fact that it is going to stand—that Brother Woods will not touch it. It will stand just as it is.

Now, then, A Deadly Parallel To Brother Woods' Chart Number Eleven. "*The axiom:* the *whole* of anything is the

Porter's Projector
Chart No. 5.

A "DEADLY PARALLEL" TO WOODS' CHART NO. 11

AXIOM:"The WHOLE of anything is the SUM of it's parts."

PROOF FOR MISSIONARY SOCIETY REQUIRES:
1. Obligation to preach the gospel.
2. Obligation of church to support preaching of gospel.
3. Church cooperation in supporting preaching of gospel.
(a) This has already been done.
(b) Woods concedes foregoing anyway.

SYLLOGISM:
(1) All situations, the component parts of which are Scriptural, are Scriptural situations.
(2) The component parts of the whole work involved in Missionary Society are Scriptural.
(3) The whole work involved in Missionary Society is Scriptural.

WOODS' ALTERNATIVES:
(1) Endorse Missionary Society.
(2) Repudiate best argument of 25 years and 100 debates.
(3) Repudiate proposition and admit defeat.

sum of its parts." Now, that's exactly what his chart said concerning the matter. "Second, proof for the Missionary Society requires: first, obligation to preach the gospel; second, the obligation of the church to support the preaching of the gospel; and third, church cooperation in supporting the preaching of the gospel. This has already been done, or shown, and Woods concedes the foregoing anyway." The "*Syllogism:* all situations, the component parts of which are scriptural, are scriptural situations; second, the component parts of the whole work involved in the Missionary Society is scriptural; therefore, the whole work involved in the Missionary Society is scriptural. *Woods' alternatives:* he must *endorse the Missionary Society,* or *repudiate one of the best arguments* in twenty-five years and one hundred debates, or *repudiate his proposition and admit defeat.*" What did Brother Woods do? He talked about what a *wretched, miserable, poor effort* Porter made. I wonder why he didn't show from the chart how wretched and miserable and poor it was instead of just asserting it and trying to make you believe it was without actually dealing with it. Now, what did he say? He said, "Here are three things, and Porter says these things *lead irresistibly* to the Missionary Society. Therefore, Porter endorses the Missionary Society." Now, *Porter didn't say any such thing.* I am simply giving you *Woods' chart in parallel.* I don't believe it at all. There is not a thing on earth to it; nor his, either. I am simply showing that, *according to his chart,* these *three things lead irresistibly to the Missionary Society.* I don't believe it. But Woods must believe it, because that is the very basis on which he made his argument for the benevolent organizations. And if his chart sustains the benevolent organization, then this chart sustains the Missionary Society. They are exactly parallel. *One is the deadly parallel of the other.* And Brother Woods hasn't touched the matter, top, edge, side, nor bottom. And regardless of how feeble the effort may be, and regardless of what he may say about it, it stands untouched; and I *challenge* him to come back up and deal with it and show us something more about it. Now, those three things do not lead irresistibly to the Missionary Society, because there is a *fourth component part that is lacking.* We all agree on an obligation to preach the gospel. We all agree that the obligation of the church is to support preaching the gospel. We all believe the church may cooperate in the support of preaching the gospel. We all believe that. But we do not believe that leads irresistibly to the Missionary Society. Why? Because there is a *fourth component part missing.* That is, that such cooperation may be rendered through a human organization set up by the wisdom of men. And that's the one element missing in that; and that's what makes the chart wrong. And that *same element* is *missing* in his. His proposition doesn't say that churches may care for the needy, they may support the needy, and they may cooperate in the care for the needy. That's not it. But his proposition says "churches may build and maintain benevolent organizations." And the fourth component part of his chart is missing. We agree that churches may care for the needy—the aged and the orphans. We agree that there is an obligation. We agree that churches may cooperate in such care. But the fourth component part of his chart is missing, that that cooperation may be rendered through human organizations set up by men, separate, corporate bodies politic. And so the element is missing that would make it necessary, and one falls upon the very same basis as the other. I don't believe either of them. But if Brother Woods believes the other is irresistible, if he believes that chart he has made leads irresistibly to the establishment of the orphan homes, the benevolent organizations, then he must believe these same three points, stated in exactly the same three ways, lead irresistibly to the organization of a Missionary Society through which to do the preaching of the gospel.

Now, then, he came to my chart number one, and he said, "Now, that's not the same thing at all, because we have here a meeting that is only a temporary arrangement, and not permanent."

Here one church is doing all the preaching, another church is doing the singing, another church is doing this, and another church is doing that. So he said that isn't the parallel at all.

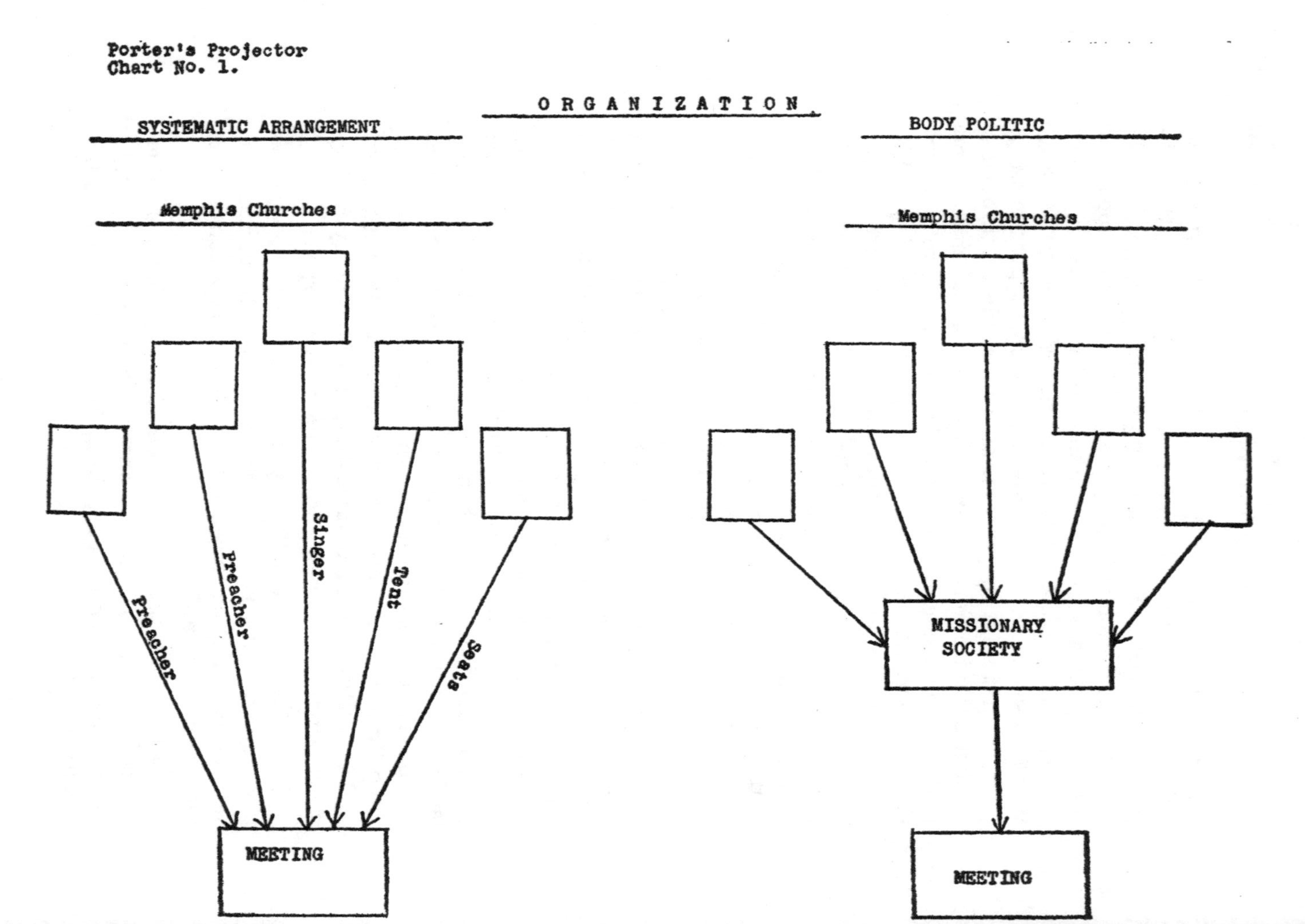
Porter's Projector
Chart No. 1.
ORGANIZATION
SYSTEMATIC ARRANGEMENT
Memphis Churches
Preacher
Preacher
Singer
Tent
Seats
MEETING
BODY POLITIC
Memphis Churches
MISSIONARY SOCIETY
MEETING

Porter's Projector
Chart No. 2.

O R G A N I Z A T I O N

SYSTEMATIC ARRANGEMENT | BODY POLITIC

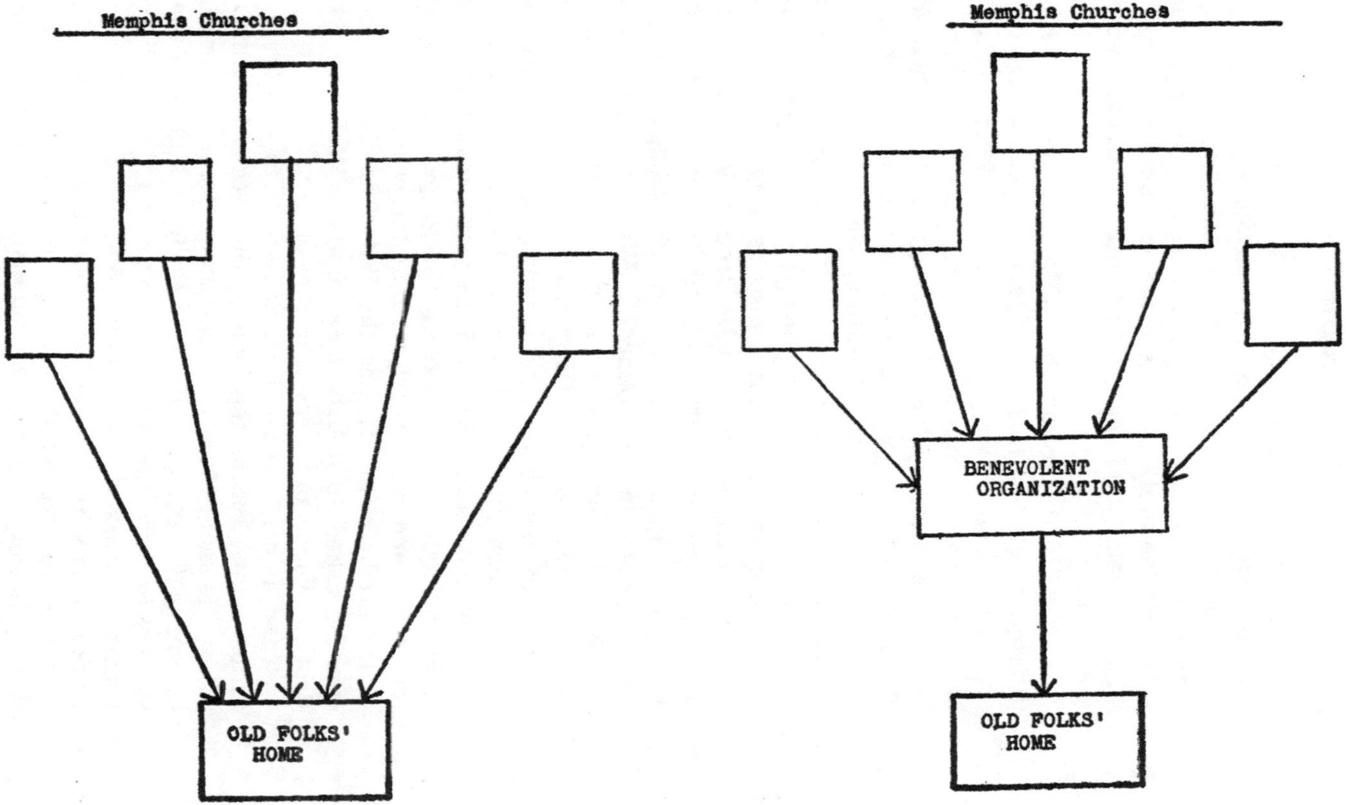

But he missed completely chart number two where I had the Memphis home set up in which there was one function being performed, the caring for the aged, and all the churches cooperating in it, and each church sustaining the same relation to it. He missed the one completely that dealt with the home, and dealt with the one that had to do with the meeting.

But we have here another difference, he said. Another difference between this is this fact: you can't have care for orphans without having a home of some kind. There must be a systematic arrangement if you care for orphans. Nobody is opposing systematic arrangement, Brother Woods. Nobody is even opposing a home in which children may be cared for. Not a bit. The thing we are opposing is that human organization you have set up through which to do it. And just as there must be a systematic arrangement in the care of orphans, there must also be a systematic arrangement in preaching the gospel. Brother Woods, do you believe in a systematic arrangement in preaching the gospel? The Missionary Society advocates come along and say, "Here is our systematic arrangement." Will you take it, Brother Woods? They have a systematic arrangement. And if you have to have a benevolent organization, a benevolent society, in order to have a systematic arrangement to care for the orphans, then there is no reason why the Christian Church shouldn't have a Missionary Society as a systematic arrangement through which to preach the gospel. One is just as reasonable and just as scriptural as the other.

He predicts that this is the last time that Porter will ever be asked to debate these issues. Well, we will let Brother Woods' prophecy take care of itself.

Then he came to some charts here. He says the *organization* simply means the *way* or the *means* by which it is done. He said, "Does the Missionary Society inhere in the command?" And he said, "No. Porter asked me if the Missionary Society inheres in the command. No." Well, that wasn't all I asked you, Brother Woods. I asked you *why*. I asked him why. If the benevolent society inheres in the command to care for the needy, then why doesn't the Missionary Society inhere in the command to teach? You didn't touch it. I asked you *why*. Tell us *why*, Brother Woods. Why does it inhere in one command and doesn't inhere in the other? Will he tell us?

Porter forgot to tell him where he is on the chart. He just completely forgot that. I wonder if Brother Woods was asleep. I said, regarding that, "Well, suppose we put Porter right here in the Christian Baptizing Association—make him a part of that. I am one of the fellows that sets up the Christian Baptizing Association. So you notify us if you have some baptizing to do, and we will send a delegation from our Association to do it." Brother Woods hasn't told us why he will put *this one* (pointing to Christian Benevolent Corporation) over here in the realm of expediencey and keep these out. Upon what basis will you do it, Brother Woods? We have here the *Commands* in one column; we have the *Inclusions* in another; the *Perversions* in another—ways in which the command may be violated or changed; *Incidentals* involved in another. And over here we have *Additions*. Then, he brought up his chart in parallel to this about Noah's ark and the little ark, and he said, "Now, Brother Porter would not object to it if we have a bunch of other little boats floating around here, just so you don't tie them to the ark." Brother Woods says, "Well, the boats are all right; let us tie them to the ark." Brother Woods says they are all right; we will just tie them to the ark and they are still all right. Yes, sir, Brother Woods ties them to the ark, you see. I am still wanting to know why you keep these out and put this one in—the Christian Benevolent Corporation? It is a *separate body*. You have said it is. It is a *body politic and corporate*. You have said it is. It is an additional body. You have said it is. And so are these. The Missionary Society is an additional body; and so is the Baptizing Association, the Singing Saints Society, and the Christian Communion Confederation, the Christian Praying League, the Christian Fellowship Federation. They are all extra bodies. Brother Woods says, "I will take this one and put it in the realm of incidentals, but I will keep all the others out." How will you do it, Brother Woods? Let us see you try. You haven't tried yet. You talk about a feeble effort. I wonder what you folk think about what he has

Porter's Roll
Chart No. 2.

LAW AND EXPEDIENCY

To Be Expedient - Must Be Lawful. 1 Cor. 6:12.

COMMANDS	INCLUSIONS	PERVERSIONS	INCIDENTALS	ADDITIONS
Build Ark Gen. 6:14-16	Gopher Wood Three Stories	Cottonwood Ten Stories	Tools - Size Transportation	Another Building
Teach Mat. 28:19	Whole Counsel Truth	Human Traditions Doctrines of Men	Blackboard - Radio Charts - Press	Christian Missionary Society
Baptize Mat. 28:19	Water - Believers Burial	Wine - Infants Sprinkling	Ocean - River Pool - Baptistry	Christian Baptizing Association
Sing Eph. 5:19	Spiritual Songs Melody in Heart	Worldly Songs Melody on Harp	Books - Tuning Fork Voice Parts - Notes	Singing Saints Society
Partake Lord's Supper 1 Cor.11;Acts 20:7.	First Day - Bread Fruit of Vine	Midweek - Beef Buttermilk	Plates - Cups Place - Hour	Christian Communion Confederation
Pray Phil. 4:6; Jas. 1: 6.	To God In Faith	To Virgin Mary In Pretense	Length of Prayer Posture	Christian Praying League
Give 1 Cor. 16:1,2; 2 Cor. 9:6, 7.	As Prospered Cheerfully	Sparingly Grudgingly	Collection Plates Envelopes	Christian Fellowship Federation
Visit Orphans Jas. 1:27.	Food - Clothes Shelter	Oppress - Vex Neglect	House - Tent City - Country	Christian Benevolent Corporation

CHART No. 5

The Guardian		The Home
1. "Propagate and Defend N.T. Christianity"	← AIM →	1. "Visit the fatherless and widow"
2. "Same"	← Organization →	2. "Same" (G.G., Aug. 4, '55)
3. Individual Business Enterprize (Non-Profit)	← Character →	3. Home (Non-Profit)
4. Receives Money from Churches And Individuals	← Support →	4. Receives Money from Churches and Individuals

WHAT IS THE DIFFERENCE?

done in dealing with that chart. I just wonder what you think of it.

He said that the *Gospel Guardian* gets money from the churches. I don't know what he intended to mean by that. Did you mean, Brother Woods that the churches are *contributing* to the *Gospel Guardian?* Is that what you meant? I just wonder what you meant by that statement. You may clarify it for us if you wish.

Then on his chart number five, when he paralleled The Guardian and The Home, he had some on one side and some on the other side. He came along to that. Let's see, that was chart number five. I wonder if we might see that chart.

Woods' chart number five. Here he showed the parallel between *The Guardian* and *The Home. The Home* on one side; *The Guardian* on the other side of the chart. The aim and the character and the support and so on. And here he has the one, the *Gospel Guardian,* receiving money from churches (or church support) and individuals; and over here (pointing to "The Home") it receives money from churches and individuals. Suppose, Brother Woods, that you put on this side (pointing to "The *Guardian*") the *Abilene Christian College.* Will you make it parallel with the other? They get individual support and maybe some support from churches. Will you do it? Will you say that is the same thing as the Home that you are contending for, and that the church can support it? You have the church supporting this (pointing to "The Home"); therefore, you must have the church supporting this (pointing to A.C.C. to replace "The *Guardian*") if you make them parallel, according to your position. He says the church can support this (the Home). Brother Woods, can the church support this (Abilene Christian College)? I want to know now. You tell us. Thank you.

Woods' chart number nine. If I have time, I want to look at that. Woods' chart number nine. Here is when he draws the contrast on the aged and the orphans. Chart number nine—"Remember the Poor"—Gal. 2: 10.

CHART NO. 9

"REMEMBER THE POOR"

Gal. 2:10

THIS REQUIRES

FOR THE ORPHAN:

- A Place
- Food
- Clothing
- Education
- Supervision
- Medical Care

FOR THE AGED:

- Shelter
- Food
- Clothing
- Medical Care

And this requires for the orphan, a *place,* and *food,* and *clothing,* and *education,* and *supervision,* and *medical care;* and for the aged, *shelter,* and *food,* and *clothing,* and *medical care.* Now, then, Brother Woods says this is impossible in the Memphis situation—that the churches, putting their aged in one building, and each church supporting its own responsibility, its own aged there, cannot provide for them shelter, cannot provide food for them, cannot provide clothing for them, cannot provide medical care for them. He said it is a *physical impossibility.* I wonder if that's wretched and feeble. Yes, sir, it is a *physical impossibility,* upon the basis of the Memphis churches placing the aged in one building, and each caring for its own. They cannot provide shelter; they cannot provide food; they cannot provide clothing; they cannot provide medical care. He said that is a physical impossibility in that sort of setup. That's sufficient. It may be that I have missed a chart somewhere. If I have, I would be glad to get back to it and pay attention to it. (Time Called.)

I thank you.

Woods' Third Negative

Brethren Moderators, Brother Porter, Ladies and Gentlemen:

I regret that in the heat of controversy I overlooked the questions Brother Porter handed me. Evidently, it is all right for him to pass up argument after argument and overlook a number of these matters presented; but if I fail to answer a question, even inadvertently, that's bad; I am going to make this proposition to him: Tomorrow night, I shall not ask you any questions; and you may present questions that will take the place of the questions now. I want to be fair with you. In order that there may be no advantage taken of Brother Porter, I will not submit any written questions tomorrow evening; and he may submit questions as he likes.

The questions are these: "Do churches have a scriptural right to contribute funds to the needy in private homes that are denominational?" I do not believe so, if such contributions would, in any fashion, support denominational teaching. "Do churches have a scriptural right to contribute funds to the Buckner Orphan Home, of Dallas, Texas?" That's answered in question number one. Number three: "Do we need benevolent organizations to care for orphans because not enough private homes are willing to take orphans into them for care?" Yes. Number four: "If it is impossible for the needy to be cared for except in some such organization as Tipton Home, were the churches unable to do the work of benevolence for nearly nineteen hundred years of its existence?" That's on a par with saying that if it is impossible for the truth to be preached except in some organization as the *Gospel Guardian,* were the churches unable to do the work of teaching the gospel for nearly nineteen hundred years before its existence?" That, friends, is asked for prejudicial purposes. That's all. Number five: "If they were unable to do such work, where is the New Testament record of any such organization?" The record is in the fact that the needy were provided for and there must have been *some method* by which to provide for them. Six: "Did you endorse any such organizations as Boles Home in 1939?" Yes. Seven: "If you did not, what New Testament teaching caused you to oppose them?" I did not oppose orphan homes in 1939. *Neither did Brother Porter!* "If you did endorse such organizations at that time, as Boles Home, then what is the name of one of the organizations that brethren formed for the care of orphans that you opposed?" The Woman's Board of Missions of the Christian Church formed at least seven different orphan homes in the past, and I could give you example after example of organizations that are wrong in that respect. And that, friends, covers his questions. I hope now that Brother Porter will feel I have dealt fairly with him along that line by not asking any questions tomorrow night.

He says that I have shouted "Sommerite" and "Ketchersideite" for the same purpose the Baptists call us Campbellites. Well, I haven't done that. I said that it was a movement popularly styled that. I know that Brother Daniel Sommer did not claim to originate this, and I know that his son resents and rejects any such suggestion along that line. And, it wasn't for the purpose of creating any prejudice or reflecting upon them. But, they were known for their advocacy of these views long before Brother Porter and these brethren with him espoused them. It is only in the last five or six years that the *Guardian* movement espoused the views that Daniel Sommer taught *all these years;* and, therefore, in order to identify the views, I simply mentioned that. That's the reason. I do not mean that Daniel Sommer originated this idea, or, at least, that he claimed to. He didn't claim to. He claimed that the New Testament taught it, just as you brethren claim it. But the point is, you are stealing Daniel Sommer's thunder and refusing to admit it. Isn't that right, Brother Allen Sommer? Say *amen.*

BROTHER SOMMER: "Amen."

That's right. That's right. (Laughter.) And I would admit it. I wouldn't repudiate it. I wouldn't refuse it. Brother Porter thinks it is prejudicial for me to make statements of that type, but it is all right for Brother Porter to *call us* digressives; to say that we are leading the church *into apostasy;* to say that we are apostates, and have *the same thing* as the Missionary Society! That's not prejudicial. Oh, no! I wonder just how far Brother Porter likes to go in these matters, anyway. Sometimes he likes to place the stamp on others. I have here, an article that he wrote for the *Gospel Advocate* in 1945, dated November 22, and the title of it is, "Another Heretic." You listen to what Brother Porter said: "We wish to call the attention of the brotherhood to a new form of heresy that is now threatening the peace of the church. It is the theory that there is no judgment after death or at the second coming of Christ. This theory is being advocated by a number of preachers who seem determined to wreck the church if possible. The following men have been actively engaged"; and he mentions the names which I shall pass over. "Brethren, let me warn you against using these false teachers." *That sounds like a quarantine, doesn't it?* "By the preaching of their new heresy, they are sowing discord among brethren. They are causing division contrary to the doctrine preached by the apostles, and should be marked and avoided according to Paul's instructions in Rom. 16: 17. If you wish to save the church in your community from discord, dissension, and division, you should take no chance in using any of these men for any preaching service, meetings, or otherwise. If you call them to preach, you are inviting trouble. Why take a chance of destroying the church in your community when you can use men who are loyal to the truth of the New Testament." Who wrote that? W. Curtis Porter. Brother Porter, those who live in glass houses ought not to throw stones.

He says that in the Garrett debate (conducted in Stockton, California) I said there is one body. That's right. Brother Garrett was charging that I was teaching two bodies in defending the orphan homes. Obviously, I rejected such an idea. Certainly there is but *one* divine body. But that one divine body acts, or uses means by which to carry out its obligations. Brother Porter admitted that the church can run a home; and that home is something aside from, and independent of, the church. And, that's exactly what I mean by another body; and he knew it. I am certain that it is not necessary for me to direct attention again to chart number eleven. The difference between the essential or the component parts of the two charts is this: You can preach, you can support the preaching of the gospel, and you can have church cooperation in the support of the gospel without *anything* that resembles the Missionary Society. But you can't supply care for the orphans, and church care for the orphans, and cooperation of churches in the care of the orphans without *some place to do it!* You can't do it. So the two are not parallel. Yet, that is the best Brother Porter can produce in reply to my argument. I still say that my chart number eleven is absolutely irresistible; and I would be willing to rest my case on it alone.

He said that I missed the chart or diagram that dealt with the home in Memphis. I dealt with the one he said illustrated it. Look at this now, friends. Brother Porter's position with reference to the Memphis home, as he tries to explain it, is that each of these churches is independent of the rest of them; you put the old person or the old people in the home, and each church takes care of its own old people there. That is his position. But I asked him this question: "Brother Porter, if the churches in Memphis can build an old folks home for the aged, cannot these same churches also build a home of the same type you endorse for homeless children?" He answered, "Yes." An unqualified *yes*. All right, then, we change it from an old folks home to an orphan home; and each one of them is taking care of its own orphans out there in that home *without any kind of organization*. Of course, if this church sent a baby out here, and that baby needed a little attention, and another person out there is taking care of another church's baby, he couldn't do anything for that baby there, because he would have to let the person taking care of the baby from that church take care of it! Isn't that silly and ridiculous? The babies would be in bad shape if you didn't keep each church's supervisor out there to take care of each church's babies! *I would be ashamed if I couldn't produce a better argument than that.* I would indeed. We agree that these churches can help. We agree that they can cooperate in such; that they can pool their resources. But he says that you can't have *any kind* of an arrangement that is of an *organizational nature*, because if you do, you have *a separate organization*. What has he got to do? He has to let this church take care of its babies, and this church take care of its babies, and so on and on, and you couldn't let them switch babies at all, because that would make it wrong because then you have got one church doing the work of another church! Isn't that silly? Again I say, Brother Porter, I would be ashamed if I couldn't produce a better argument than that.

I then asked the question: In whose title should the property of such a home as you have in mind for old folks in Memphis rest? "Well," he said, "in the man who owned the property." I then asked him this question: Will the churches or the home take legal custody or guardianship of those to be provided for in this home? He said those who sent the people to the home. In other words, this church sends an orphan baby down here; and this one, another. Now, each church has supervision over its own baby; therefore, the supervisors for these babies couldn't spank the babies over here if they got out of order! *They would have to call the supervisor from this church.* Wouldn't they? Again I ask: How ridiculous and silly can a fellow get?

I then asked him the question: In the case of the home for the homeless children, who will administer discipline? He said each one of them could take care of its own. All right, then, if this child over here got unruly and got one of the other church's children down, they couldn't pull the first child off. They would have to yell for his own supervisor to come and get him. (Great laughter.) Again I ask: *How silly can a fellow get?* Brother Porter, I have seen you stand before great audiences and, with the power of a genius, blast out Baptist doctrine. It is a pitiful situation when a man of your caliber descends to such a position as you have here tonight. I say it with grief and with sorrow. I do, indeed. I entertain the hope that you will repudiate such a ridiculous position as you occupy tonight and come back to the position of appreciation and respect with which you have been held by the brotherhood. I hope that day will soon come.

I want you to get this. I want a chart here to illustrate this. Let us have chart number seven. I want you to see some things about this. Now, watch, friends, chart number seven. We will have it in just a moment.

Brother Porter believes, and those who are associated with him, that it is right to have a church building. All agree the brethren can meet in a comfortable building, sit on comfortable seats in an air-conditioned building, or one that is properly heated. They believe it is right to supply the preacher and his family with a home; and so do I. They believe that it is right to provide support for such a home. And tonight, every thread that I have on was supplied me by the brotherhood. And that is characteristic of the other preachers, or most of them, who are in this audience. These preachers are not only supporting themselves in such fashion, they are supporting their families, feeding their own children, educating their own children, with money that comes out of the Lord's treasury; living in a home that the church provides for them, living off of the fat of the land, driving good automobiles, wearing splendid clothes, taking vacations, buying hunting and fishing equipment, and enjoying the luxuries of life; and at the same time some of them are trying to get churches *to quit* sending ten dollars a month

CHART NO. 7

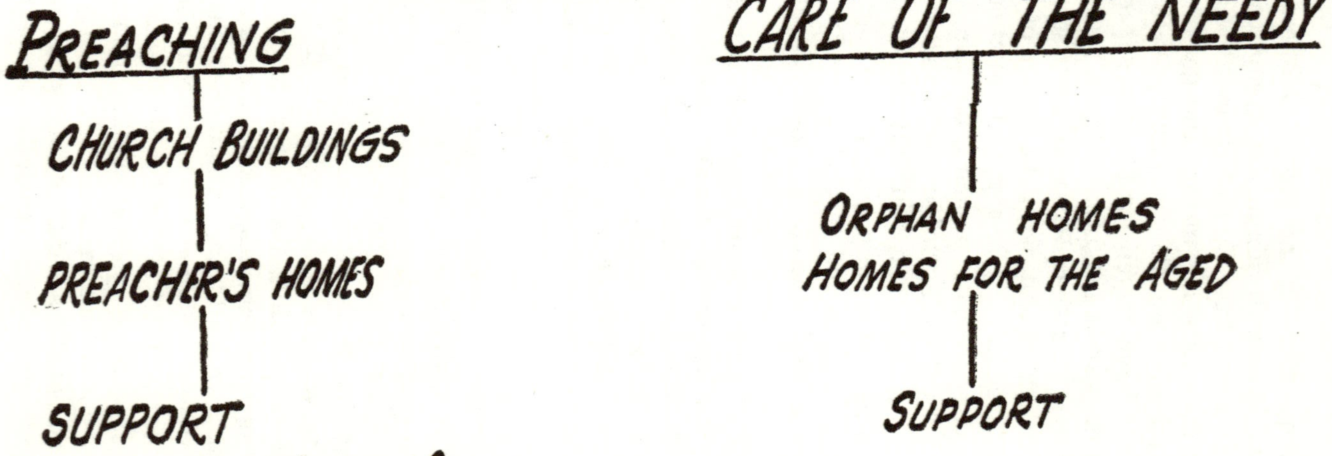

PREACHING	CARE OF THE NEEDY
CHURCH BUILDINGS	ORPHAN HOMES
PREACHER'S HOMES	HOMES FOR THE AGED
SUPPORT	SUPPORT

Cite Scripture for:

1. CHURCH BUILDINGS ____________
2. BUILDING COMMITTEES, FINANCE COMMITTEES ____________
3. Church-OWNED PREACHER'S HOMES ____________
4. INCORPORATED CHURCHES ____________
5. CHURCH TRUSTEES ____________

to an orphan home to take care of children that haven't got any dad or mother, or whose dad and mother ran off and left them! I tell you, ladies and gentlemen, before I do a thing like that, I hope my right arm loses its cunning, and I hope that my tongue cleaves to the roof of my mouth. I would be ashamed of such a thing as that. I surely would. The same argument that justifies the preacher's home justifies the home for the aged. The same argument that justifies the church building, a place for the church to meet, justifies an orphan home. There is a command to assemble; the command to assemble implies a place to meet; hence, the church building. There is an obligation to care for the needy, the orphans and the aged. The command to care for the aged or the homeless and fatherless implies *a place* for such; and, therefore, the same argument that justifies this justifies that. These brethren believe in justifying *this,* but they fight *that.* Again I say I would be ashamed of such.

He asked, "Why is the Missionary Society not inherent in the command to teach?" Because you don't have to have a Missionary Society to teach, but you must have *some place* to take care of the needy. You have to! I don't care what you call it. I have stated that over and over. And, up until this moment Brother Porter has not replied to it. I showed you this: The church is its own Missionary Society; hence, it doesn't need another. But, the church is not its own orphan home; therefore, unless it can supply a home, then it cannot provide for the needy, because it is not an orphan home. The church is not an orphan home. But Brother Porter admits that the church has an obligation to take care of the needy. All right, *how* can you take care of them? Well, you can supply that which the needy lack. What is that? A home. What happened to their original home? It is gone. Is the orphan home in competition with the church? No. It is not doing the work of the church. What is it doing? It is doing the work of a home. Is it in competition with the church? No, because it is not doing the work of the church. Is it in competition with the home? No, because the home is gone. What is the orphan home? It is the restoration of that which the child had but lost, and

Porter's Roll
Chart No. 2.

LAW AND EXPEDIENCY

To Be Expedient - Must Be Lawful. 1 Cor. 6:12.

COMMANDS	INCLUSIONS	PERVERSIONS	INCIDENTALS	ADDITIONS
Build Ark Gen. 6:14-16	Gopher Wood Three Stories	Cottonwood Ten Stories	Tools - Size Transportation	Another Building
Teach Mat. 28:19	Whole Counsel Truth	Human Traditions Doctrines of Men	Blackboard - Radio Charts - Press	Christian Missionary Society
Baptize Mat. 28:19	Water - Believers Burial	Wine - Infants Sprinkling	Ocean - River Pool - Baptistry	Christian Baptizing Association
Sing Eph. 5:19	Spiritual Songs Melody in Heart	Worldly Songs Melody on Harp	Books - Tuning Fork Voice Parts - Notes	Singing Saints Society
Partake Lord's Supper 1 Cor.11;Acts 20:7.	First Day - Bread Fruit of Vine	Midweek - Beef Buttermilk	Plates - Cups Place - Hour	Christian Communion Confederation
Pray Phil. 4:6; Jas. 1: 6.	To God In Faith	To Virgin Mary In Pretense	Length of Prayer Posture	Christian Praying League
Give 1 Cor. 16:1,2; 2 Cor. 9:6, 7.	As Prospered Cheerfully	Sparingly Grudgingly	Collection Plates Envelopes	Christian Fellowship Federation
Visit Orphans Jas. 1:27.	Food - Clothes Shelter	Oppress - Vex Neglect	House - Tent City - Country	Christian Benevolent Corporation

which the church supplies, James 1: 27. That, friends, is the truth on it.

He says I believe it to be all right to tie on a bunch of little arks. I don't believe in tying them on. I don't believe in little arks to start with! But Brother Porter does. He is the fellow who believes in the little arks. And, have you ever identified him on this chart yet? I asked him two or three times to tell us, "Brother Porter, where are *you* on this chart?" He said, "Well, suppose that I am over here in this Baptizing Association." Is that where he really is? Does he want us to believe that that's where he is? I don't think that's where he thinks he is, but he must be somewhere on this thing, and I have been trying to find out where he is. I have asked him repeatedly this question: Where is the private home on this chart? He says the private home can take in a child. I haven't found out where *it* is.

He said my effort was so feeble. Brother Porter thinks that if you tell people this, that means they wouldn't know it, unless you told them. It is strange that he chides me so much for saying that, and then comes right back and says the same thing, isn't it? Well, he is a nice fellow. He can't do anything with this proposition because he is on the wrong side of the fence. That's what is the matter with him.

Now then, chart number five. He says, "Let us just suppose that instead of the *Guardian* here it is the school." A school cannot take the place of the *Guardian* because it is not the sole function of a school to "propagate and defend New Testament Christianity." It is not parallel to that. It is not parallel in that it is not an individual business enterprise in the same sense the paper is. In the next place, it wasn't organized for the purpose of propagating and defending New Testament Christianity exclusively. Therefore there is no parallel between the two. But there is an exact parallel between the *Guardian* and the home. And he didn't meet that. He said, "Well, what about something else?" It is not something else that you were supposed to answer. It is this. Now, that, friends, is not the way to debate. Why doesn't he meet the issue? He wants to change my argument and then answer my argument that he changed. That's not meeting the issue.

CHART No. 5

The Guardian		The Home
1. "Propagate and Defend N.T. Christianity"	←AIM→	1. "Visit the fatherless and widow"
2. "Same"	←Organization→	2. "Same" (G.G., Aug. 4, '55)
3. Individual Business Enterprize (Non-Profit)	←Character→	3. Home (Non-Profit)
4. Receives Money from Churches And Individuals	←Support→	4. Receives Money from Churches and Individuals

WHAT IS THE DIFFERENCE?

He says that I have said that the Memphis situation is an impossibility. It is. Absolutely it is. And I want to show you why it is an impossibility. Let us have his chart number two.

I will show you why this is an absolute impossibility. He said that we could change it from an old folks home to an orphan home; that it would be all right. Here is the picture: He said this could be not only an old folks home, but an orphan home. Now, it is an orphan home, but it hasn't *any sort* of supervision whatever. It is an impossibility, friends, to take care of orphans—children—to maintain a home without having a supervisor, a superintendent or *somebody over* them. Whatever you call it, whether a parent, or a matron, or superintendent, or a president, or something, you must have some sort of supervision for that home. He has shifted ground on us, anyway. Here, he has these churches acting individually. Now, Brother Porter, to make it fit your letter, you must draw a circle around that, put all those children together and let the churches put their funds together, and support it, and then you will have it. (Time called.)

I thank you.

Porter's Fourth Affirmative

Brethren Moderators, Brother Woods, Ladies and Gentlemen:

At this time I continue my affirmation of the proposition which Brother Douthitt has just read; that "it is contrary to the scriptures for churches to build and maintain benevolent organizations for the care of the needy." And then the type of benevolent organizations concerned in the matter is mentioned by designating some of those organizations, such as Boles Home, Tipton Home, and other homes for orphans or homes for the aged of like nature. This question, this issue, that we have for discussion is not a matter of whether or not it is contrary to the scriptures, or in harmony with the scriptures, for churches to take care of orphans. That certainly is not the issue involved whatsoever. The issue involved is whether or not churches have the scriptural right to build and maintain benevolent organizations through

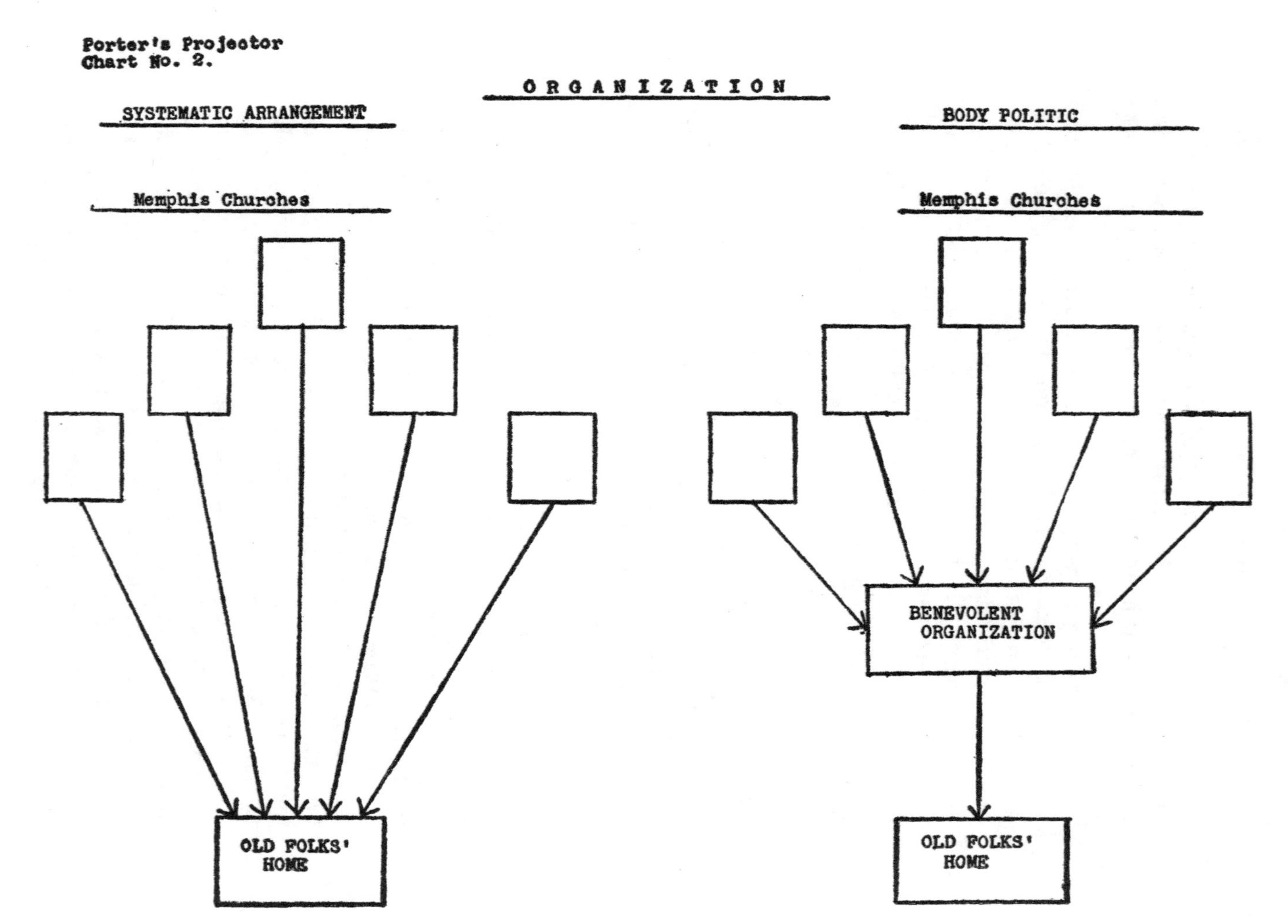
Porter's Projector
Chart No. 2.
O R G A N I Z A T I O N
SYSTEMATIC ARRANGEMENT
Memphis Churches
OLD FOLKS' HOME
BODY POLITIC
Memphis Churches
BENEVOLENT ORGANIZATION
OLD FOLKS' HOME

which to do that work of benevolence; and the whole question is one of organization, and not merely one of method, or means, or mode, or anything of that nature, or whether there is an obligation or anything like that: but it is simply a question of organizations. Does the church have the right to build and maintain benevolent organizations, such as these mentioned, for the purpose of caring for the needy?

Now, last night Brother Woods said he would, in view of the fact that he had overlooked my questions, not ask me any tonight; and, in harmony with that gesture, I will be lenient toward him. I have only two questions for him tonight; and I will give these at the beginning before I go on to other things.

1st. Do you believe that individuals have a right to publish religious papers, such as the *Gospel Advocate, Firm Foundation,* and others?

2nd. Is the operation of such a private enterprise parallel to another ark that might have been built by Noah in addition to the other one that God authorized?

Next I want to call your attention to some further affirmative arguments. Not that such is needed, because the one I have on this chart here has scarcely been referred to; and it stands untouched and unharmed, and will stand thus when the debate comes to a close. But for your consideration I do want to call your attention to one or two other things, and then back to this chart, and then to some things said by Brother Woods in the closing speech last night.

In the letter of the apostle Paul to the Philippian brethren, in the fourth chapter and the ninth verse, Paul said, "Those things that you have learned, and received, and heard, and seen in me, do; and the God of peace shall be with you." Thus Paul calls upon the Philippian brethren to observe the things which he had done and follow along the same line. The things they had seen and heard in him, to do those things. Then, over in the twentieth chapter of the Acts of the apostles, and verse 35, addressing the elders of the church at Ephesus, the same apostle said, "I have showed you all things, how that laboring you ought to support the weak, and to remember the words of the Lord Jesus, how he said, It is more blessed to give than to receive." He had told the Philippian brethren to observe or to do the things which they had learned from him and had seen in him. He tells the brethren at Ephesus that he "had showed them all things," how that "they ought to labor and support the weak," and to "remember the words of the Lord Jesus" that "it is more blessed to give than to receive." And, of course, other statements made by other inspired men would be in perfect harmony with the statements made by the apostle Paul; and there would be no conflict between what he did and what others did along that line, and what others said and what he said, or what others said and what he did. There would be perfect harmony between them all. And in James 1: 27, when James said, "Pure and undefiled religion before God and the Father is this, To visit the fatherless and the widows in their affliction, and to keep himself unspotted from the world," we are shown, at least, how individuals may care for orphans and widows. And certainly that obligation we recognize well; and, oftentimes, that is carried out in the care of those who are in need. Then, in the sixth chapter of the Acts of the apostles, we have revealed to us a case in which there was relief administered to those who were in need by the church in Jerusalem when certain widows were neglected in the daily ministration. There arose a complaint about the matter; and in taking care of the situation, we find the church acting in its congregational capacity. The need was relieved. There was *no organization formed.* There was no separate body built nor maintained in order that the work might be done; but the congregation, acting in its congregational capacity, took care of the widows upon that occasion. I am sure the same thing can be done in the same way now. And that is one of *the hows* by which we can proceed in caring for those who are in need today. We do not need to set up an organization, either within the church or without the church, a body corporate and politic, or anything of that kind; but simply the church in its congregational capacity did the work then; and it certainly can also do the work now.

Then, in the next place, I call your attention to the fact that the church of the Lord Jesus Christ is an all-sufficient institution. I do not mean by that that the church is sufficient to do everything that might be done in the world and everything that man might undertake to do; but the church is sufficient to do all that God has assigned the church to do. And I think perhaps Brother Woods will agree with me on that. At least I know he has in days gone by.

And in support of that, I call to your attention, in the first place, that the church of the Lord Jesus Christ, in its congregational capacity, was able to do the work of evangelism among the lost. In 1 Tim. 3: 15 Paul referred to the church as "the pillar and ground of the truth." And in 1 Thess. 1: 8 Paul declared that from the Thessalonian brethren "had sounded out the word not only in Macedonia and Achaia, but in every place their faith toward God has spread abroad." The work of preaching the gospel, therefore, had been done by the church without any other organization involved, as something to be built and maintained by such congregations. But they acted in their congregational capacity, and the work was done. From them the word of the Lord was sounded out. And there was no need of anything else through which the church was to operate as an organization to do that work. In other words, there was no place for a Missionary Society to carry on that work of evangelism. They did not have it in those days. Nothing of that kind was organized, but the church acting in its congregational capacity did it.

The same thing is true with respect to the work of edification. We have in the mission of the church, of course, three parts: evangelism of the lost, and edification of the members, and the work of benevolence for the needy. And so in the edification of the body we find that the church was sufficient as a congregation to do that work. In Eph. 4; 16 Paul declared that "the body fitly joined together and compacted by that which every joint supplieth, according to the effectual working in the measure of every part, maketh increase of the body unto the edifying of itself in love." And there was no need of setting up some kind of Sunday School Corporation, or anything of that kind, through which the church would do the work of edifying. But the congregation did the edifying. It was sufficient to accomplish the work that God had assigned it to do.

Then, in the third place, in the work of benevolence, we find the same thing to be true. In Acts 6: 1-6, which I gave a while ago, the example of caring for the needy widows in the city of Jerusalem in the church there. Then in Acts 11: 27-30, when the church at Antioch sent relief unto the brethren which dwelt in Judea, we find the same thing in operation. There was *no Board* of any kind set up. There was no human organization of any kind established. But the congregation, acting in the congregational capacity, was able to accomplish the work, and I am sure that it can be done *that way now.* And so these examples show to us *how* the work was carried on. Just as the church could do its work of evangelism without building and maintaining a Missionary Society, and just as the church could do the work of edification without building or maintaining Sunday School Organizations, so the church could do the work of benevolence without building and maintaining benevolent organizations such as Brother Woods is trying to defend during this discussion. Well, so much for that.

Now, briefly, I call your attention over here again to this chart on Law and Expediency.

I have shown a number of *commandments* there that God has given. I have shown various other things regarding it. The *command* to build the ark; and certain things were to be *included;* they may be *perverted* in certain ways; and there are certain *incidentals;* but another building constructed by Noah would be an *addition* and, therefore, contrary to the divine authority. And so in *teaching,* the same thing is true. There are certain things *included*; there are certain ways in which it can be *perverted;* there are certain *incidentals* involved; but at the same time, to set up another body, another building, a Christian Missionary Society, would be an *addition* that would not go in the realm of incidentals, and that this Christian Missionary Society would be contrary to the teaching of the New Testament, just as the other building that might be erected by Noah would be contrary to the authority that God gave him to build an ark. And in the matter of *baptizing,* the same thing is true. While certain things may be involved as *incidentals,* and so on; yet to organize a Christian Baptizing Association, another

Porter's Roll
Chart No. 2.

LAW AND EXPEDIENCY

To Be Expedient - Must Be Lawful. 1 Cor. 6:12.

COMMANDS	INCLUSIONS	PERVERSIONS	INCIDENTALS	ADDITIONS
Build Ark Gen. 6:14-16	Gopher Wood Three Stories	Cottonwood Ten Stories	Tools - Size Transportation	Another Building
Teach Mat. 28:19	Whole Counsel Truth	Human Traditions Doctrines of Men	Blackboard - Radio Charts - Press	Christian Missionary Society
Baptize Mat. 28:19	Water - Believers Burial	Wine - Infants Sprinkling	Ocean - River Pool - Baptistry	Christian Baptizing Association
Sing Eph. 5:19	Spiritual Songs Melody in Heart	Worldly Songs Melody on Harp	Books - Tuning Fork Voice Parts - Notes	Singing Saints Society
Partake Lord's Supper 1 Cor.11;Acts 20:7.	First Day - Bread Fruit of Vine	Midweek - Beef Buttermilk	Plates - Cups Place - Hour	Christian Communion Confederation
Pray Phil. 4:6; Jas. 1: 6.	To God In Faith	To Virgin Mary In Pretense	Length of Prayer Posture	Christian Praying League
Give 1 Cor. 16:1,2; 2 Cor. 9:6, 7.	As Prospered Cheerfully	Sparingly Grudgingly	Collection Plates Envelopes	Christian Fellowship Federation
Visit Orphans Jas. 1:27.	Food - Clothes Shelter	Oppress - Vex Neglect	House - Tent City - Country	Christian Benevolent Corporation

corporate body politic, and set that up to do the work of baptizing would be an *addition* and, therefore, contrary to the divine authority. And the same with respect to *singing* if we should organize a Singing Saints Society. The same with respect to *partaking of the Lord's supper* if we should organize a Christian Communion Confederation. Or in the matter of *prayer* if we should organize a Christian Praying League. And in the matter of *giving* if we should organize a Christian Fellowship Federation. All of these would be contrary to the New Testament teaching, to New Testament authority, because they are *additions*. And in exactly the same way, to set up Christian Benevolent Corporations to care for the needy is an *addition* and is, therefore, contrary to the teaching of the New Testament. Upon this I am sure that I am safe to stand; and my opponent, Brother Woods, has done but very little with it. He has paid but very little attention to it. He has asked me, "Where is Brother Porter on that chart?" Well, actually Brother Porter is a part of that divine institution over there to whom the command to teach and baptize and sing and partake of the Lord's supper, and things of that kind, have been given. But we want to know by what authority he can move the Christian Benevolent Corporation over in the realm of incidentals and leave the others out? Why all of these are contrary to the New Testament teaching, but this one is in perfect harmony with it? We want him to tell us about that tonight; and so far, he has made no effort to tell us anything about it.

Now, then, I want to return and note some things regarding his speech last night. And if I don't get to all of them, I have two other speeches following, and I hope to get to everything before we come to a close tonight.

Concerning the questions which I asked him last night, one was: Do we need benevolent organizations because private homes are not available for orphans? Or are private homes not willing to take orphans into their care? He said, "Yes, that's why we need them." But, actually, I am sure that there are many more private homes desiring children today than there are children that are available. And, upon that basis, certainly, he is entirely wrong about it. A short time ago, over in Kentucky there was a family, a lady, who requested somebody to take her children. She was dying of a rare lung malady, and she had five children ranging in ages, I believe, from five to twelve, or something like that. An appeal was made for somebody to take these into the private home. And I have this statement by the man who made the appeal:

"To whom it may concern: This is to certify that in response to the one editorial in the December 15, 1955, issue of the *Gospel Guardian* regarding finding Christian homes for the five Richardson children of Irving, Kentucky, that ten letters were received requesting all five of the children. Six letters requested two or more and five requested one or more.

"In addition to this, there were two telephone calls requesting all five of the children, one requesting two or more, and four requesting one or more.

"Altogether eighty-three children could have been placed in Christian homes as a result of this one notice.

"In witness whereof I set my hand this second day of January, 1956. Houston Gately, Route 1, Box 85, Irving, Kentucky. Signed in the presence of Howard I. See, 577 Clermont Drive, Lexington, Kentucky."

And so there eighty-three children could have been placed in private homes. They were not little two-day-old babies with blue eyes and brown, curly hair. Just were not that kind at all. And yet numbers were willing to take all of these children in a group into their homes, into private homes, and take care of them. I say that if this one way were given the proper leeway, we wouldn't need any other way by which to care for our orphans.

Then, regarding another of the questions, he said that he endorsed Boles Home in 1939—that he endorsed Boles Orphan Home in 1939. I want to read you a statement made by Brother Woods about that in the Abilene Christian College Lectures of 1939, and on page 54. He said:

"In this connection it is a pleasure to commend to the brotherhood Tipton Orphans Home, Tipton, Oklahoma. The work there is entirely scriptural, being managed and conducted by the elders of the church in Tipton, Oklahoma, aided by funds sent to them by the elders of other congregations round about. *We here and now declare our protest against any other method or arrangement for accomplishing this work.*"

Brother Woods said in 1939 that he was against *any other arrangement* for accomplishing this work, except as the Tipton Orphan Home, with the work placed under the elders. And Boles Home was not organized that way. Boles Home wasn't set up that way. And Boles Home is not that way today. And yet he said that was the *only arrangement* that *he would endorse in 1939.* Yet he tells us last night that he endorsed Boles Home in 1939. Well, make your own decision about the matter.

Again, I asked him what organizations for the care of orphans did he oppose in 1939. He said he opposed the Woman's Board of Missions which organized orphan homes to care for orphans. Well, why did you do that, Brother Woods? You say that's the only way *we* can do it. If it is the only way *we* could do it, it is the only way *they* could do it; so they couldn't help it. If that's the only way *we* can do it, why, that would be the only way *they* can do it. Why did you criticize that? Why did you object to that? And, besides, let us see if that was all Brother Woods was talking about. Now, Brother Woods, there wasn't any need for you to be quibbling about this. You just as well come on and shell down the corn about the matter—that you did not have in mind at all any such thing as the Christian Church, with the Women's Board of Missions, setting up benevolent organizations. Here is what Brother Woods said about it: "This writer has ever been unable to appreciate the logic of those who affect to see grave danger in Missionary Societies, but scruple not to form a similar organization for the purpose of caring for orphans." Now, then, who were these? Who were these who were forming a similar organization to care for orphans? He said the Women's Board of Missions—that they were the ones he was opposing. Well, now, this statement says *the very ones* that *were forming those organizations* were *the ones* who *saw grave danger in the Missionary Societies.* Now, did the Christian Church Board of Missions see grave danger in the Missionary Societies? Did it? Well, that was a Christian Church organization. They were going along one hundred per cent with the Missionary Societies. And they were not the ones at all who saw grave danger in Missionary Societies. But the ones that you said were forming similar organizations were those who saw grave danger in Missionary Societies. And, Brother Woods, we know, and you know, that you had *no reference* to members of the Christian Church. You were referring to *our own brethren.* Now, we want you to come up and face it and tell us what those organizations were. Not organizations the Christian Church formed, because they did not see grave danger in the Missionary Societies. These organizations were being formed by people who saw grave danger in the Missionary Societies. And you said you opposed that. Now, I want to know what those organizations were, formed by brethren who saw grave danger in Missionary Societies.

I asked him, since he claimed it was impossible for us to take care of orphans except through some organization such as he had designated, how the church managed to do work of benevolence for nearly nineteen hundred years. He said, "Well, it is on a par with its being impossible to preach the gospel in any other way except through the *Gospel Guardian.*" Now, I wonder who ever said it is impossible to preach the gospel except through the *Gospel Guardian.* I never said anything like that. I don't know of anybody else who did. But you said, Brother Woods, it is impossible to do it any other way except through these benevolent organizations; so you don't have any par at all. You are far below par.

Concerning the matter of organizations, and I want to get to this. He is confusing *organization* with *place.* And I want chart number six if I have time to use it just here. My chart number six. He says there must be a place to care for orphans. Who said there must not be a place? He is confusing *place* with *organization.*

Now, friends, look at this. Here (pointing to left side of chart) is *place* over here, and the house in which you have it is the *location.* That is the *place,* certainly. But think of *place versus human organizations* in the work of benevolence. Over here (pointing to right side of chart) we have

Porter's Projector
Chart No. 6

PLACE Versus HUMAN ORGANIZATION

LOCATION

BENEVOLENCE

HUMAN SYSTEM

HOUSE

HOUSE

INSTITUTIONAL ORPHAN HOMES

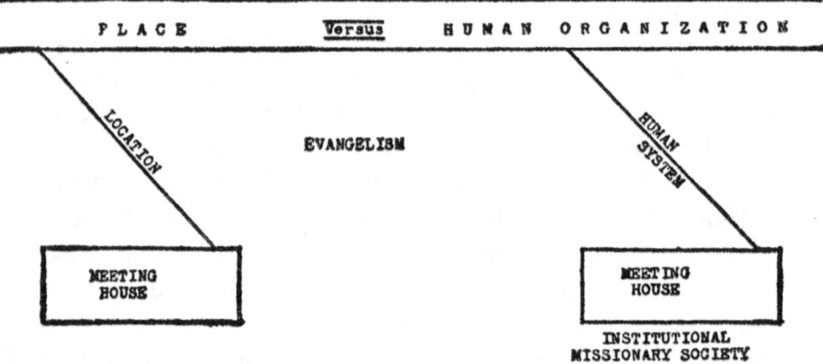

a *human system,* and that human system is the Benevolent Organization, the Institutional Orphan Home. And, of course, here is a *house* over here too. But notice the fact that over here is an organization, and *they have a house.* Here is a *place,* or *location,* over here. But the *place is one thing,* and the *organization is something else.* Just as in this case (pointing to lower half of chart). You take the place, or location, of a meetinghouse; and you take evangelism; you take a human organization or Human System, the Institutional Missionary Society. It also must have a *place;* but the *place is not the organization.* The organization is not the place. The place is one thing; the organization is something else. The place up here (pointing to top half of chart) is one thing; the organization is something else. Certainly, you must have a *place*. (Time Called.)

Thank you.

Woods' Fourth Negative

Brethren Moderators, Brother Porter, Ladies and Gentlemen:

I should like to say in the very outset of the debate tonight that, in view of the fact this is the final session of the discussion, I am most grateful to my brethren for the invitation and for the confidence imposed in me in placing into my hands the defense of what we believe to be the truth. I have never been associated with a finer congregation than the Garfield Heights church, nor have I ever been treated more royally in a discussion or a meeting than in this. I have enjoyed every moment of it, and it is my sincere conviction that such discussions can but result in much good.

And, I am very happy that Brother Porter has, at last, in this the final session of the debate, attempted to prove his position by the Bible. Tonight is the *first time* he has introduced a passage of scripture, and quoted it, and made an argument upon it. True it is he has some references on the board, or on the chart; and, he put Matt. 28: 18-20 on the board the other night. But, three nights have passed, and up until this moment, or until this hour, we had heard nothing from the scriptures regarding this matter.

He says it is not a question of whether it is right for churches to care for orphans. He admits that. But, he says it is a question of organization. Well, that's right. The difference between us is that I say it is *organized* care; he thinks it is *disorganized* care. That became very obvious last evening in the ridiculous and silly picture he drew of the old folks home. But more about that a little later. *Much more* about it a little later!

First, his questions: "Do you believe that individuals have a right to publish religious papers, such as the *Gospel Advocate*, the *Firm Foundation* and others?" Yes. But, the difference between Brother Porter and me is this: He has made an argument that *any kind* of an organization that does the work of the church is sinful. I showed last evening that the *Gospel Guardian* is organized under the laws of the state of Texas as a religious corporation; and, therefore, if an organization is wrong simply because it is incorporated, and is doing a work of the church, that would make our religious papers wrong! Brother Porter can't consistently believe in such papers and hold to his position in this debate.

"Is the operation of such a private enterprise parallel to another ark that might have been built by Noah in addition to the one God authorized?" Not from my point of view, but from yours it is. Now, that is the difference.

First, he introduced Phil. 4: 9, "Those things, which ye have both learned, and received, and heard, and seen in me, do: and the God of peace shall be with you." He made no argument upon it. In about twenty debates that I have had with anti-Sunday school people, they have cited that and said, "You never saw Paul engage in a Sunday school in your life; therefore, *the Sunday school is wrong!*" The same type of argument exactly as that which Brother Porter makes tonight.

Acts 20: 35 says we are to support the weak. I introduced that the first night in the first moment of my speech. That doesn't designate the method.

In James 1: 27 he says tonight that this teaches the care of the needy, but that such is individual care. And in the *Gospel Guardian* of some time past (March 5, 1954), the quotation of which I shall be glad to present if he wants it, and give him the issue, Brother Porter quoted that passage *to show that it is the church's obligation!* Has he changed his position on it? I ask him the question. Answer it, Brother Porter, in your next speech.

Acts the sixth chapter, the case of the widows neglected in the daily ministration. He said there was no organization there. It depends entirely on what you mean by the word "organization." I would like for you to spend just a moment or two in considering this matter. The church, at that time, numbered no less than fifteen thousand members. I think I am safe in saying that. Some estimate it as high as forty thousand. But, to be on the conservative side of it, I shall say there were fifteen thousand people. Now, there were seven men who were selected to take care of that business. Besides that, they had a treasury. All of those fifteen thousand people participated in it, because not a one of them said that the things that he had were his own. They had all things common. Do you mean to tell me *seven men* took care of *fifteen thousand people's needs?* They were appointed over the business. I ask Brother Porter to make a clear statement if he thinks those seven men did all of the administration characteristic of this affair on that occasion. I await comment until we have it. Now, that, ladies and gentlemen, is the crux of this matter.

What am I contending for here tonight? An organization in competition with the church? No. Let us have chart number one.

Here exactly, friends, is what we are contending for. The Federal Government has an obligation to distribute mail; and in so doing, it has the Post Office Department. Now, it might have *some other* kind of department. We wouldn't have to call it the Post Office Department. It might do it some other way, but it has to do it in *some* way. Whatever that way is, that is the way essential to that particular purpose. The State Government has an obligation to provide roads. There might not be a Highway Department, but there has to be *some kind* of department. In like fashion, the Masonic Lodge takes care of the aged. They might have some other method, but there has to be some method. In like fashion, the Catholic Church has its orphanages. There might be a number of ways in which they could perform this, but there must be *some* way. In like fashion, friends, Brother Porter and I agree that the church of Christ sustains an obligation to the needy. I don't care whether you call them orphanages, homes for the aged, benevolent organizations, houses for the poor; it doesn't make any difference what you call them, you must have something! I maintain that this is what they had in Acts 6. I ask Brother Porter to answer when he comes back. All right.

His next statement is that the church is sufficient. He gave us 1 Tim. 3: 15, the church "the pillar and ground of the truth"; and 1 Thess. 1 and 8, the "word sounded out." He said they had no Missionary Society. That's right. But, they had a church house. They might not have called it that. They had *some* place to meet. And, the very fact that

Chart No. 1

Organizations in Different Categories

Fed. Gov't.----Post Office Dept.
State Gov't.---Highway Dept.
Masonic Lodge---Homes for Aged.
Catholic Church---Orphanages.
Church of Christ---Orphanages & Homes for Aged

Rival These?
Do These

they were commanded to and did assemble implies that they had some place to assemble. In like fashion, friends, the church sustains an obligation to those whose home is gone. You may not call it an orphan home. But whatever it is, it is *that*. Whatever means it takes to accomplish the care that the church owes to such people, that's what it *is*. Now, the difference between Brother Porter and me is not, as he well said, over whether we are to care for the needy. It is not even over whether the church is to do it. We agree on that. It is whether or not it takes any sort of an organization besides the elders of the church to take care of the needy. That is the sole issue. I'd like for you in a moment to examine it a little further.

In the field of edification, Eph. 4: 16, the "body is fitly framed together." He doesn't scruple to organize classes in which the Bible is taught, made up of people who are members of the church and those who are not members. There is an organization, an organization apart from that which characterizes the elders and deacons—the organizational setup of the church in its worship. He doesn't oppose that. He defended it in a debate with Brother Waters, and successfully argued that this is not the Missionary Society. But yet, when in the field of benevolence we insist on the *same sort* of systematic procedure, Brother Porter objects. The difference between us is: I maintain there must be an organized, systematic approach. His method is the most disorganized system that you've ever seen, as you will in a few moments note.

Acts 11: 27-30, the contribution sent from Antioch to Jerusalem. That doesn't state the method by which it was accomplished. Brother Porter hasn't the slightest concept from that verse as to what was done.

Now, we come to his chart on law and expediency. He said I had said virtually nothing about it. I answered it every time it has been before us. Every time I have been up here I have answered it.

In the first place, observe this: Brother Porter won't tell us *where* the private home is on that chart. That is the first thing I have asked him. I have asked it repeatedly; and, up to now, I have no answer. In the second place, I pointed out to him that the orphan home is right here (where the needs of orphans are designated); not over here (where Brother Porter has the benevolent corporation). Now, if it were over here, it would be wrong; it would be an addition. If this is what it is, it would be wrong. But that's not what it is. Where is it? It is right here, except you need two or three other points there. You ought to have supervision; you ought to have discipline in there. If you had these, right there is where it would be. Right there. That's all I am contending for. But, now watch: To have it there, you must have an organization. You must have it in order to be legal.

Porter's Roll
Chart No. 2.

LAW AND EXPEDIENCY

To Be Expedient - Must Be Lawful. 1 Cor. 6:12.

COMMANDS	INCLUSIONS	PERVERSIONS	INCIDENTALS	ADDITIONS
Build Ark Gen. 6:14-16	Gopher Wood Three Stories	Cottonwood Ten Stories	Tools - Size Transportation	Another Building
Teach Mat. 28:19	Whole Counsel Truth	Human Traditions Doctrines of Men	Blackboard - Radio Charts - Press	Christian Missionary Society
Baptize Mat. 28:19	Water - Believers Burial	Wine - Infants Sprinkling	Ocean - River Pool - Baptistry	Christian Baptizing Association
Sing Eph. 5:19	Spiritual Songs Melody in Heart	Worldly Songs Melody on Harp	Books - Tuning Fork Voice Parts - Notes	Singing Saints Society
Partake Lord's Supper 1 Cor.11;Acts 20:7.	First Day - Bread Fruit of Vine	Midweek - Beef Buttermilk	Plates - Cups Place - Hour	Christian Communion Confederation
Pray Phil. 4:6; Jas. 1: 6.	To God In Faith	To Virgin Mary In Pretense	Length of Prayer Posture	Christian Praying League
Give 1 Cor. 16:1,2; 2 Cor. 9:6, 7.	As Prospered Cheerfully	Sparingly Grudgingly	Collection Plates Envelopes	Christian Fellowship Federation
Visit Orphans Jas. 1:27.	Food - Clothes Shelter	Oppress - Vex Neglect	House - Tent City - Country	Christian Benevolent Corporation

The state requires it. And so, if you will just put down supervision and education, and the organization necessary to meet the demands of the state, I will accept that right there as the picture, because that's what it is. In order that this may become crystal clear to us, I have prepared a chart or two that will suggest it. I am going to ask now that first of all we have chart number seventeen.

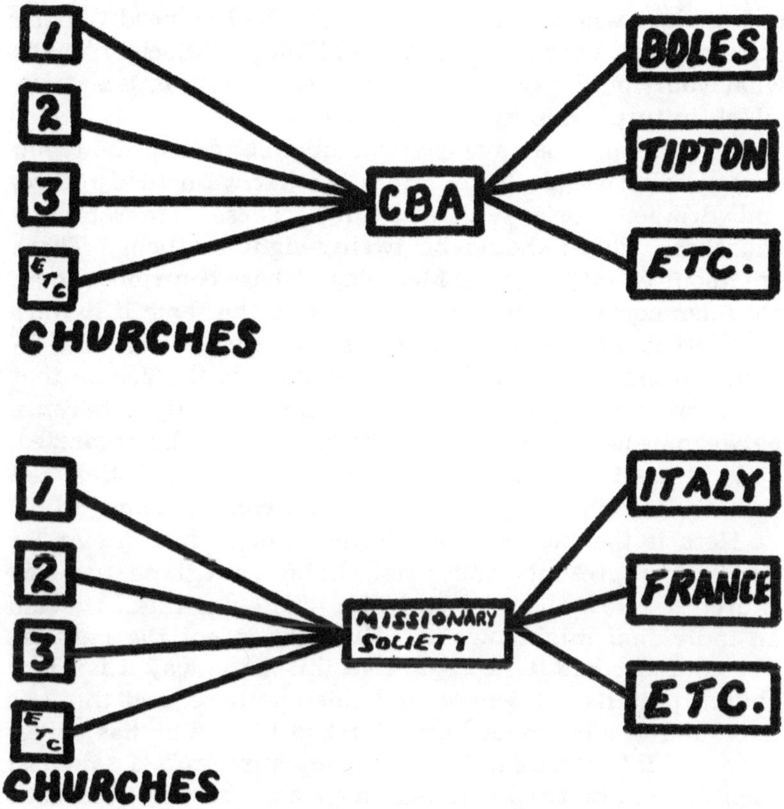

Chart number seventeen. This, friends, is going to suggest to you exactly why Brother Porter is in error here. Here is the picture he is trying to draw of it. He is trying to make it appear that the orphan home is parallel to the Missionary Society. Christian Benevolent Corporation. I have Christian Benevolent Association. I thought he had Association here, but it won't make any difference. Now, let this represent the churches: one, two, three, and on and on, a group of churches here. Here is the picture of the situation: The churches contribute to this organization (Christian Benevolent Association); and they, in turn, establish Boles and Tipton and other orphan homes. There is the parallel to the Missionary Society. Let these represent the churches, as such, and this the Missionary Society. The money is sent to the Missionary Society, then it is *sent on to the place* where it is applied to the field of need. If the orphan home were parallel to the Missionary Society, that's what you would have. The money sent *to an organization* which in turn establishes orphanages.

Now then, let us have chart number sixteen to show you exactly what we do have. Here is what we actually have, and Brother Porter endorses this. These represent the churches. There should be twenty-eight of them. There are about twenty-eight in Memphis. These contribute to an old folks home (and he said it would be the same if it were a children's home); not through some organization, but directly to the home, and I might even say to the people that are characteristic of that home. And, the only difference between us is, he says that this home must *not* be organized. I say it has to be. Now, let us examine that a little. Let us have Brother Porter's chart of the Memphis home.

Here is the picture that Brother Porter has drawn for us: This represents the home here, and these are the churches. Now then, I asked him who owns this. He said an individual might own it. But that is not the parallel. The churches had it. He said that this is the way it is: This church puts its folks here, and this one here, and this one here, and this one over here. I asked him: Who has supervision of it? He said, "Each of the churches." I said last night, if that be true, you must have a supervisor from *each* church for *each* group of children. And I mentioned that if a child from one group got another child from another group down, the supervisor for the second child couldn't pull the first child off, but would yell for the supervisor from the other church to come and get him off of his kid! Look what

Chart # 16

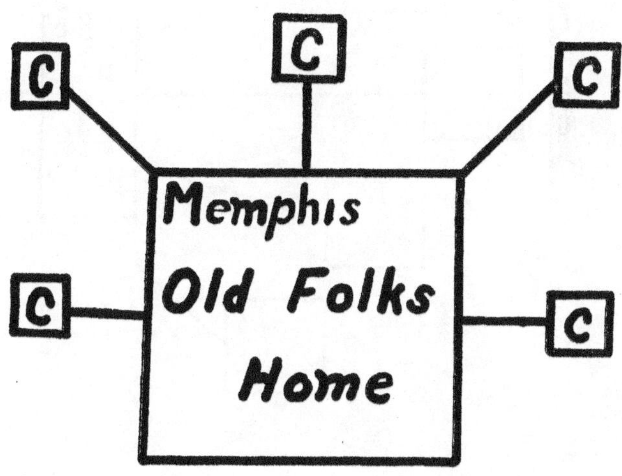

Pooling of Funds –
Cooperation

else it would take. It would take twenty-eight different *matrons*, a matron from each church! You would have to have twenty-eight different *cooks* cooking for each group of them. You would have to have twenty-eight *piles of coal!* You would have to have twenty-eight *furnaces* to warm those children! You would have to have twenty-eight *tables* for the children to eat on! You would have to have twenty-eight *bathrooms* for the children to bathe! And then, you would have twenty-eight *elderships* overseeing that home! Isn't that a conglomeration? Now, that, ladies and

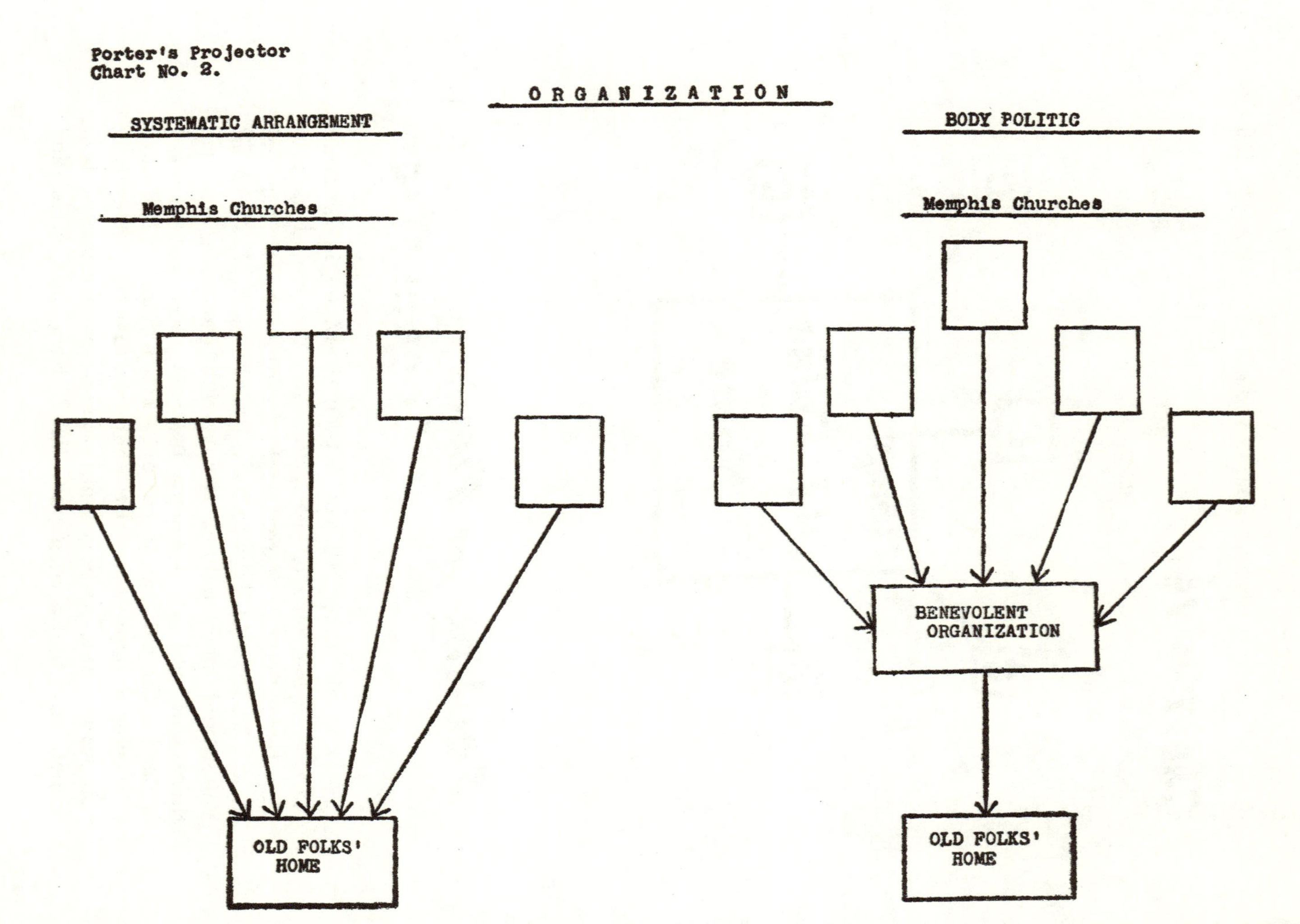
Porter's Projector
Chart No. 2.
O R G A N I Z A T I O N
SYSTEMATIC ARRANGEMENT
Memphis Churches
OLD FOLKS' HOME
BODY POLITIC
Memphis Churches
BENEVOLENT ORGANIZATION
OLD FOLKS' HOME

gentlemen, is his picture. Thank you. Ah, no, Brother Porter has not met the proposition.

He says that as a result of the *Guardian* notice (of a family of children available for adoption) they received enough letters with reference to the children to take eighty-three of them. Wonder what the *Guardian* is doing in the business of placing children? I saw in the charter that it is a *charitable* institution, organization; organized as a *charitable organization*. Does it have a license for placing children? If not, didn't it violate the law of the state of Texas when they published that issue, since the state of Texas requires one to have a license in order to place children in that state? Are they violating the law in what they are doing? He said there wouldn't be any need for the orphan homes if the homes would open up and let the children go into private homes. Well, then, the church couldn't do its duty! *You said it is the church's duty to do it.* According to Brother Porter, now it is not; the church could be deprived of its responsibility in that respect. But, is he telling us correctly on this? I have here a letter that appeared in the *Chicago Tribune* of a recent issue. "Dear Mrs. Starr: We would like to take a child into our home. In other words, we want to be foster parents to a small child. How do we go about doing it?" Listen to the answer: *"There are seventeen agencies which use child placement of foster homes for children. Most of them are prompt in responding to a request for a child, since they are desperately in need of homes with a healthy environment."* Desperately in need of homes. "Write or call the Community Referral Service, 123 West Madison Street, Randolph 60363." That says they are *desperately* in need of homes. And, another thing, it has occurred to me that if there is such a demand for children, why is it that some of those folks who want children are never around when the home gets them? It is a good thing the home was there, because the people who are supposed to be wanting them so badly, it seems, *are never around* when the home was there. It's a good thing the home was there!

I have here a letter from Brother John B. White, superintendent of the children's home at Lubbock, Texas. He tells me that they have a number of children down there they would like to put in homes, but they can't find anybody to take them. Brother John B. White, superintendent of the children's home at Lubbock, Texas. Maybe you can help them place those, too!

Brother Porter again cites the Abilene lecture in 1939. He finds it a whole lot easier to meet me in 1939 than 1956. He can't meet me in 1956; so he meets me in 1939! That is evidently an easier task. Now, suppose he could prove me to be inconsistent. I have explained repeatedly the sense in which I was using those terms. But, just suppose he succeeds in that; that doesn't meet the issue here tonight. And, Brother Porter, an appeal to such matters is evidence of the failure that is characteristic of your effort here this evening. (Time called.)

I thank you.

Porter's Fifth Affirmative

Brethren Moderators, Brother Woods, Ladies and Gentlemen:

I am grateful for the opportunity of returning to the stand and continuing my part of this investigation of the issue before us tonight. I want to take up the things that were said by Brother Woods during the speech to which you have just listened. But before doing so, I had just a few other notes on the other speech that I want to get to; and since some of them have been repeated in this speech, of course, that will take care of them in that part of the speech to which you have just listened when I come to that part.

I was discussing the matter of organization when my time was called, and I was showing you the difference between a place and an organization. Brother Woods seems terribly confused about this matter, and he doesn't know the difference between *a locality* and *a corporation;* or between *a place* and *an organization.* He doesn't know the difference. He thinks they are all the same thing. I wonder if you folks think that—that an organization is a place, or a place is an organization. That's what he is contending for, and he comes up over and over and over and says you can't take care of orphans without a *place.* Who ever said you could? Who ever entertained such an absurd idea, anyway, Brother Woods? I didn't. You eliminate the place, and you eliminate the orphans, and us too. If there is no place here, then we are all gone. So it is not a matter of place, Brother Woods; it is a matter of organization—not place at all. Certainly, you must have a place. Whatever that place is where they are kept, that becomes a home, just like the *place* where the preacher stays becomes a *home* for the preacher; but that's not an organization. It is an organization that he is supposed to defend, and not a place. If it is just a matter of place, we had just as well shake hands and go home, because I am certainly in favor of a place. But I am not in favor of a benevolent organization. There is a difference between a place and an organization. And I showed you on that chart a while ago that, with respect to the work of

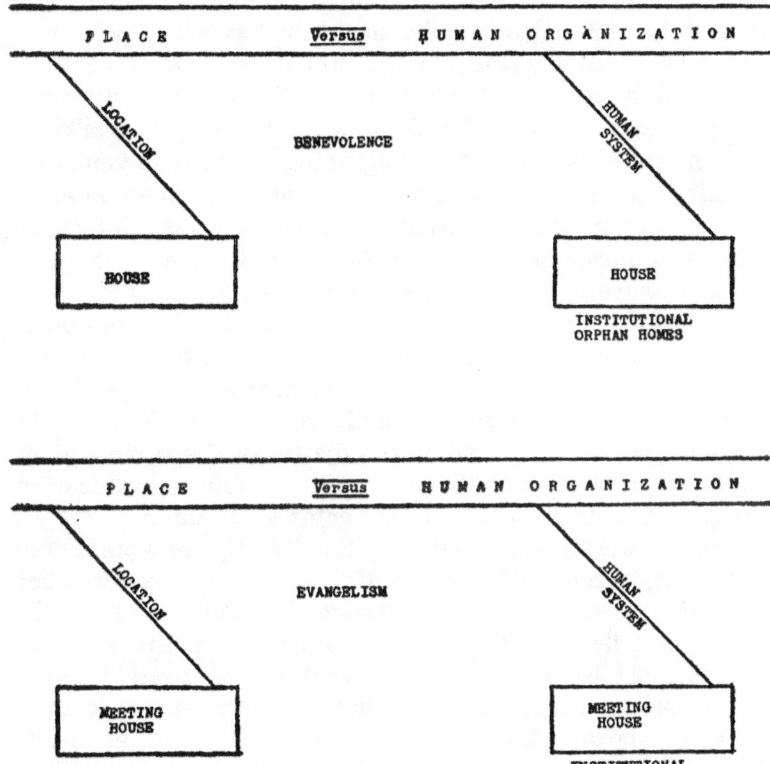

benevolence, there must be a place, or a locality, or a house where they are kept.

But in addition to that, you have an organization over here known as the Benevolent Organization or the Benevolent Society. And the same thing is true in preaching the gospel. You can't preach the gospel without a place, Brother Woods. Since you say we can't take care of orphans without a place; and, therefore, we must have an organization, then since we can't preach the gospel without a place, we have to have an organization through which to preach it besides the church. If not, why not? If, because a place is required to take care of orphans authorizes an organization separate from the church, or in the church, or wherever you may put it, then on the same basis, since you must have a place in which to preach the gospel, then that authorizes a Missionary organization. And if not, why not? Tell these people. Explain it to them, Brother Woods. You haven't done it yet. You talk about a thing being a millstone around a man's neck, this Missionary Society is a millstone around yours; and you will never get from under it. And you can't explain it, and this audience is beginning to see that you can't explain it, I am afraid; and so we are going to keep on after you on that particular ground. There is a vast difference between a place and an organization. They are not the same, and I am sure that you can see they are not the same.

Then again he said about this—he made this statement last night, and he made it again tonight—that it is either *organized* or it is *disorganized.* I have heard the anti-Sunday school brethren say that over and over, Brother Woods. In our debates with them, when the matter of the Bible classes comes up, and we say that it is not a human organization like that that is maintained by Sectarian Denominations of the earth, they come back and say, "Well, are your Bible classes *organized* or *disorganized?*" Which are they, Brother Woods? *Organized* or *disorganized?* And you say this thing has to be organized or disorganized; and if it is organized, it must be a *corporation.* If it is organized, it must be a separate body. And if it is not a separate body, if it is not a corporation, then it is *disorganized.* Well, good-bye Brother Woods, when you meet Ervin Waters again, or Van

Bonneau, or some of those brethren among the anti-class group, because they will remind you of your statement that if you don't have a corporation, it is *disorganized.* If you don't have a separate body, it is *disorganized.* And when you claim that your Bible classes are not a separate body, when you claim they are not a separate group, that it is not a corporation, they are going to show you, then, according to your argument, that you will have a *disorganized* thing there. Well, that's another thing concerning the homes that he mentioned last night; and some of it came up a while ago.

He said a lot of these preachers are in favor of having preachers' homes, and they believe in living on the fat of the land, and they even can buy fishing tackle and hunting equipment and things of that kind, and have a glorious, hilarious time on the great salary they are getting; but, at the same time, they oppose giving ten dollars to poor little orphans. Now, that's simply an appeal to prejudice and emotionalism. That has no part in this debate, Brother Woods. We are discussing this from the standpoint of New Testament teaching, and not from the standpoint of prejudice and emotionalism. And, certainly, that has no place in it whatsoever, because I know of nobody who opposes giving ten dollars to poor, little, helpless orphans. We are not opposing orphans. We are not opposing caring for orphans in some place or in some home. The things we are opposing are the benevolent organizations you set up in which to do it. That is the same old argument made by the Christian Church preachers: that you are opposing evangelism if you oppose the Missionary Society. Willing to have the good things of life and let the poor heathen go to hell because you won't use our Missionary Society through which to get the gospel to them.

Now, he said the same argument that justifies the preacher's home justifies the orphan home. Well, then, upon the same basis, Brother Woods, the same argument that justifies a benevolent organization for the orphans justifies a ministerial organization for the preachers. If not, why not? Is that the way the preachers' homes are maintained? Do you have the preacher's home like that you are providing for the preacher? Do you have an organization set up? Do you have it chartered? Do you have it placed under a Board of Directors? Do you have it set up as a separate body or *corporation* to maintain the home for the preacher? Is that what you have? That is what you are contending for for the orphans. And if you have them parallel, then you have got to have the same thing for the preachers; and until you get them that way, you don't have any parallel, Brother Woods.

And on the Memphis home he said it is impossible for each church to care for its aged in the same building with others. He went on in that case—and brought it up a while ago—about the impossibility of having a thing of that kind, and about spanking the babies if you converted it into a children's home—spanking the babies and feeding the babies. You would have to have twenty-eight different spanking machines, and, of course, twenty-eight different spankers, and twenty-eight different tables, and twenty-eight different cooks, and so on, because you have twenty-eight congregations having the aged, or the orphans, in that particular location. Now, that's Brother Woods. And he wondered how silly a man could get, and he talked about the "silly grin" and things of that kind. Now, Brother Woods, I consider that beneath the dignity of a man of your ability. I do. I really do, Brother Woods. To get up and talk about that thing that way—about a "silly grin." I have had Baptist preachers talk to me that way. I wonder if you are talking to me that way for the same reason. (Laughter.)

I showed in that Memphis setup that you can have a house out there. It may belong to the family that lives there. And a number of congregations may have a needy person to be placed in that home to be cared for, and each congregation hires that family to take care of that particular person. If it happens to be an aged person or an orphan, it doesn't change the situation at all. And if any cooking is to be done, the same family can cook for all of them, because each church pays the part of that necessary to take care of the one which it has there. If there is any spanking to be done, I suppose they could do the spanking too, Brother Woods. But according to Brother Woods, in order to get any spanking done, they would have to set up a *Spanking*

Corporation, and charter it under the laws of the state, get it under a Board of Directors, and then get the spanking done. (Laughter.) Well, I can spank preachers without any corporation. (Laughter.) "How ridiculous," he said, "can a man get?"

Now, then, I am just as grateful to the brethren who called me for this work in this discussion as Brother Woods is to the Garfield Heights church. I have appreciated the privilege of coming and helping you in this discussion, trying to get before you the teaching of the New Testament as we believe it to be. And, of course, we want you to consider these things fairly, and prayerfully, and conscientiously, and make your decision upon what you find recorded in the Book of God.

Now, he said, "Brother Porter has at last attempted to prove his proposition by the Bible." Well, that's more than Brother Woods ever got to. He spent his two nights without ever getting that far; so I have made more progress than he did, because he never did give us a single passage that set up any such organization that he is contending for during this debate. So I have made progress far beyond my opponent.

He mentions the question of organization, but he wants to know if it is organized or disorganized. And that has already been taken care of. And he said, "The difference is that Porter argues that *any kind* of organization that does the work of the church is wrong." I showed you the other night that Brother Woods had made the statement that there are certain duties that run parallel. There are some duties that are individual duties; there are some that are church duties. They may overlap. They run parallel. He has made that statement in debate. And because an individual may do a thing that is parallel with some work that the church is doing, that doesn't mean that it is the work of the church. Is the church contributing its funds to that? Is the church working through that? Is the church building and maintaining that? If so, then the church is doing its work through that organization.

I asked him: "Do you believe individuals have the right to publish papers, such as the *Gospel Advocate, Firm Foun-*

dation, and others?" And he said he did. "Is the operation of such enterprise parallel to another ark that might have been built by Noah in addition to the one God authorized?" And he said, "Not from my viewpoint; but from yours, it is." Well, we will just let that go for what you may think it is worth. "Not from my viewpoint; but from yours, it is."

Now, we come to the passages which I introduced. Phil. 4: 9, about the things that you "have heard, and learned, and seen in me, do." Brother Woods said the anti-Sunday school brethren have used that for years and have come up with the idea, "Where did you ever see a Sunday school in Paul's teaching and practice? Where did Paul ever do anything or practice anything like that?" What did you tell them, Brother Woods? What did you tell them when they asked you that question? We are just curious to know what Brother Woods told them. If you will tell us, we might find out just where you stand on that. What did you tell them, Brother Woods?

On Acts 20 and 35 he said, "I gave that the other night." Well, he did; but there is not a word in it that indicates any sort of an organization such as he is contending for.

And James 1: 27 and Acts 6. He says we admit there is an obligation; but he said the whole thing depends on the meaning of the word "organization." But Porter says there is no organization there. He said the whole thing depends on the meaning of "organization." Well, I showed that "organization" has two meanings: one is systematic arrangement, and another is a separate body, a body politic and corporate. Now, which of these is Brother Woods defending. I asked him the first night of the debate, in my very first question: What is the meaning of the word "Corporation"? He said, "It means a body politic." All right, the things he is defending are set up as Corporations—every one of them. I have over here some sixteen charters of incorporated institutions, set up as corporations; and he said that means a body politic. That's the *kind of organization* that *he is contending for*. Now, can he find *that kind of organization* in Acts 6? I *challenge* him to make the effort. The trouble is, he is confusing "organization" with "an organization." "Organization" may simply mean a systematic arrangement.

But when you talk about "an organization," then you are talking about *a separate body.* You are talking about a corporation, a body politic. And my opponent is contending, not merely for "organization" in the sense of *systematic arrangement;* he is contending for "an organization." And "an organization," Brother Woods, means the same thing with respect to benevolence that it does with respect to Bible class teaching. Tell us: Are your Bible classes *"organization,"* or are they *"an organization"?* Which? When you teach a Bible class on Sunday morning, is that *organization* in the sense of *systematic arrangement?* Or is it *an organization?* Now, don't forget to tell us about that, because you are trying to defend, during this debate, not merely *organization,* but you are trying to defend *an organization.* In fact, "organizations" in the plural.

How much time do I have? I forgot to check my time when I started.

BROTHER DOUTHITT: "About five and a half minutes."

Thank you. He said now on this matter of Acts 6 there were fifteen thousand members there, approximately, and seven men were selected and placed over this, and they had a treasurer. And he asked, "Did seven men take care of the needs of fifteen thousand members?" Were those members all widows, Brother Woods? Here were seven men set up to look after the daily ministration of the *widows.* And according to Brother Woods, there were approximately fifteen thousand widows in that congregation; and he wanted to know if they took care of the needs of the fifteen thousand members. Fifteen thousand widows over there. Must have been a pretty good sized war around there somewhere that eliminated the men. (Laughter.) Now, then. Yes, there were seven men placed over that business; and they had money to use, of course, and a treasurer. But at the same time, it was the church in operation. It wasn't an organization or a corporation set up under some other kind of Board. Not at all. It was simply the congregation working in its congregational capacity without any other corporation, without any other body. It was the divine body, the body of the Lord, the one body the Bible talks about, that did the work.

Then he came to chart number one—Woods' chart number one. We want to look at that again just a moment, please, if you have it.

Chart No. 1

Organizations in Different Categories

Fed. Gov't. ----Post Office Dept.
State Gov't.---Highway Dept.
Masonic Lodge---Homes for Aged.
Catholic Church---Orphanages.
Church of Christ---Orphanages & Homes for Aged

Rival These?
Do These

This chart concerns the Federal Government. And he keeps coming back to this, and we want to take a look at it, because there are people in the audience tonight, perhaps, who haven't been here before. And he argued tonight that since the Federal Government could maintain a Post Office Department, which is an organization within an organization, without that Department becoming a rival to the Federal Government; and the State Government could maintain a Highway Department without that organization becoming a rival of the State Government; and the Masonic Lodge could maintain Homes for the Aged without the Homes for the Aged becoming rivals of the Masonic Lodge; and the Catholic Church has Orphanages without those Orphanages becoming rivals of the Catholic Church; then upon the same basis, the church of Christ can have Orphanages and Homes for the Aged without those becoming rivals of the church of Christ. And I showed why these were not rivals. The Federal Government has a legislative branch that can authorize a law, or can enact a law, to authorize a Post Office Department. And the State Government has a legislative department that can authorize the existence of a Highway Department. And the Masonic Lodge can make its rules and regulations; and so can the Catholic Church. But in the church of Christ we have no legislative body; and since God did not set up another organization through which the church can work, then nobody in the church has the right to do it; and, therefore, these would become rivals, whereas those would not, since we have the authority in those institutions back of them to set them up. I also called attention to the fact that not only does the Catholic Church have orphanages that don't rival the Catholic Church, but it also has Missionary Societies that don't rival the Church. And upon the same basis that he has justified this, we can have Missionary Societies in the church. What has he ever said about it? He has been "as dumb as an oyster" from the time it has been mentioned until now. He has not even mentioned that particular point that I have alleged against it. Brother Woods, why don't you do something about it? Tell us why the Catholic Church can have Missionary Societies that don't rival the Catholic Church, and yet the church of Christ cannot have them. Tell us why. You haven't, Brother Woods. You know you haven't touched that particular point. So in your next speech tell us something about it. We want to know.

Regarding the church being all-sufficient, he said, "Yes, it is all-sufficient in evangelism." But he said in the work of benevolence we have to have a house. "Have to have a house." Yes, certainly. Yes, and in the work of evangelism we have to have a house. He said so do the orphans have to have a house. Yes, certainly so. But *the house is not the organization,* Brother Woods. Can you distinguish between a house and an organization? The Missionary Society is an organization; the house is merely a location where the organization may operate. The benevolent organization is the corporation—that is the separate body. The *house* is merely a *place* where it may *operate.* There is a *vast difference* between *the organization* and *the house.* But Brother Woods doesn't seem to be able to get a conception of a house meaning anything except an organization, or an organization meaning anything except a house.

On the work of edification he said, "Now, Porter organizes classes." Well, I have asked him already about that. Are these classes, Brother Woods, set up after the manner of your benevolent organizations? Don't forget to tell us now. It is almost time for you to speak. And please tell us when you first get on the floor: Are these classes set up after the same pattern as your benevolent organizations? Are the Bible classes in which you have taught in churches throughout the land set up after the same manner, after the same order, the same type of arrangement, that you have in your benevolent organizations? We want to know. (Time Called.)

Thank you very kindly.

Woods' Fifth Negative

Brethren Moderators, Brother Porter, Ladies and Gentlemen:

I am happy to be before you for the second negative speech of the evening, and the first thing I want to notice is Brother Porter's statement that I do not know the difference between a locality and an organization. He says that I am confusing the house, or the place, with the organization; that an organization is not a house or a place. I am well aware of that fact. But what I am unable to understand is *how* it is possible for the work, that Brother Porter says is necessary to be done, to be done in a house that has no organization! That's what I am trying to get over. Do you know what picture this man has presented to you tonight? *Twenty-eight churches take a group of orphans and dump them into a house and leave them there without any kind of supervision, any kind of oversight, any kind of discipline, any kind of teaching, any kind of instruction.* That's the picture. Brother Porter, look up here a minute. Just one minute. I want to know *who* is to take care of those children in that home? You have beat around the bush on that enough now! We have talked and talked and talked about this. We are going to get down now to the crux of this matter. I want to know what kind of situation is going to be maintained in that home for these twenty-eight churches and their children. What are you going to call the fellow who has charge of it? In the first place, *who* has charge of it? You may decide you are going to have a spanking machine anyway, whether he is chartered or unchartered, whether he is incorporated or unincorporated! There has *got to be* some kind of supervision for that home. Now describe it in your next speech.

What are we agreed upon, friends? There is an obligation to the orphans. The church has that obligation. The churches may cooperate in meeting that obligation. They may even establish a place to do it, but that's as far as we get. When we start trying to find out *how* we are going to conduct the place, we are told there can't be any kind of organization there. Now that, friends, is Brother Porter's position in this debate tonight. He says, "Of course, you can't take care of children without a place. That's right. I agree that that's right." You can't take care of babies without *somebody* to take care of them, either! Now, what are you going to call those who take care of them? *Is that the work of the elders?* And I want to know this: You presented us a picture of cooperative work in the Memphis old folks home. I want the name and address of one of those works that is going on today. And, in the second place, I want the pattern, the New Testament pattern, that justifies the picture that you have drawn. What verses do you present that justify that situation? Now, friends, that's the issue; and let him meet it!

He says, "Why, of course, it is right for the church to have a preacher's home; but," he said, "a preacher's home is not an organization." It isn't? I thought it was. I thought a private home is an organization. Is it? Brother Porter, you said that the preacher's home is not an organization. You said it isn't. I want to know if Brother Porter thinks that there is no organization characteristic of a private home.

He says that the Missionary Society is a millstone around my neck; that I can't explain my position in the light of the Missionary Society. I have explained it repeatedly; and until this very moment, Brother Porter ignores it. What is the difference between the church and the Missionary Society? Here it is: The Missionary Society is *a machine* that *uses means* to accomplish that which the church ought to be doing, and would be doing but for the Missionary Society; whereas, the orphan home is simply the church doing its own work, *the means* by which the work is done. Now, get the difference, please: The church is its own Missionary Society, but the church is not its own orphan home; therefore, it must supply the orphan home. I am going over this one more time, and I am going to insist that Brother Porter do what he hasn't even remotely done up to this moment; that is, to notice it: The orphan home is not in conflict with the church because the orphan home is not the church. The orphan home is not in conflict with the private home because the private home is gone. What is the orphan home? It is the effort on the part of the church to restore that which the child had, but has lost. And, it takes some sort of supervision. Now then, here is the place. What is the supervision? That which is characteristic of the superintendent and his assistants. Why the incorporation? Because the state law requires it. That's the reason. Because you can't operate without state supervision. The same reason that the *Gospel Guardian* is incorporated. That's exactly the reason.

He says, "You say the Missionary Society is not in the word 'teach.' All right, then, why do you say it isn't essential?" Here is the reason: It is true that the word "teach" doesn't imply the Missionary Society. The church does the teaching. But I pointed out to you that the church is not a home. Therefore, in the command to care for the needy there is the orphan home implied. Brother Porter put some words into my mouth; and I want to correct him on that. He did that two or three times. He said that I said the church was God's Missionary Society, but the church wasn't God's benevolent society. I did not say that. That's putting an interpretation on what I said. I said that the church is not an orphan home. It is a benevolent society. It is also a Missionary Society. But it is not a gospel meeting; so it arranges a gospel meeting. The church is not an orphan home; so it arranges an orphan home! Again I say, friends, people who cannot see that are pitifully deluded and blinded.

Let me suggest further. The children the *Guardian* advertised for were not cared for *by the church*. They were cared for by the *Gospel Guardian* and the private home that took them. Now, the question is: *How does the church do it?* You haven't told us *how* the church does it. That's not a picture of it, because that's done in another way. If the church is all-sufficient, I want to know why the *Guardian* charitable organization was participating in it. It looks to me like you were doing the very thing there you are now opposing. What have we got? We have an organization. What is it called? The Gospel Guardian Company. What was it organized for? As a *charitable* institution. That's part of it. What did it do? It was engaging in the care of orphans. Now, such was very temporary, I admit; but, it was care just the same! Therefore, there, if you please, is exactly what Brother Porter is opposing here. Exactly that.

He said on last evening I talked about the preachers receiving support and then turned around and said some of them opposed sending ten dollars to orphans. I didn't say that. Again, Brother Porter misrepresented what I said. I said they would oppose *a church's* sending ten dollars to an orphan home. That's what I said. And that's what you oppose, isn't it? Look up here, Brother Porter. That's what you oppose, isn't it? Isn't it? Isn't it, Brother Porter?

BROTHER PORTER: "You want me to answer?"

No, Brother Douthitt won't let you. (Laughter.) (Brother Cecil Douthitt, Brother Porter's moderator, had ruled that no one was to speak from the floor or the audience after

Brother Allen Sommer, Editor of *The American Christian Review* had uttered an "Amen," during one of the speeches.)

It seems that Brother Porter did not appreciate my reference to a silly grin. Well, I will just leave off the word "grin." (Laughter.) I hope that this will help him. He said that this sounded like a Baptist preacher's statement. Well, I might say the only time that I ever see such a grin is when I am looking at Baptist preachers under similar circumstances! (Laughter.) Brother Porter, two can play at this game. I suggest that we stay with the argument. Maybe he thinks that he can do a better job at this.

He wants to know where the Sunday school is. It is in the word "teach." That's the argument I have always made. That's the argument you've made. And, in your debate with Waters, when Waters charged that the Sunday school is on a par with or parallel to the Missionary Society, you said, "No." You argued that the word "teach" suggests the idea of an organization, method, or procedure; but, that the word "teach" does not necessitate the Missionary Society. You said exactly the same thing I am saying here tonight. Exactly. In fact, the position that you hold on this question tonight is, *in principle,* that of the anti-Sunday school people!

He talks about the homes being incorporated. He said I am defending an incorporated home. Certainly, I am, because you have to operate according to the laws of the state. The churches in California have to be incorporated to exist. Now, Brother Cogdill, quit shaking your head. I know that's right. There isn't any use for you to shake your head. I have been out there. I know the law. I know you can't operate in California without having the church incorporated. That's the law on it.

BROTHER COGDILL: "Just to own property, Brother Woods."

BROTHER WOODS: "Well, all right, you have to have property."

BROTHER DOUTHITT: "I believe, brethren, that it would be better for us just to go on with the speech and—"

BROTHER WOODS: "Well, Brother Cogdill back there was trying to shake his head at me."

BROTHER DOUTHITT: "I don't think that—"

BROTHER WOODS: "I want to ease his pain a little bit."

BROTHER DOUTHITT: "Sometimes a man can be mistaken, Brother Woods. I don't believe I would personate a man that has no opportunity whatever to answer."

BROTHER WOODS: "Well, I didn't mean any reflection on Brother Cogdill."

BROTHER DOUTHITT: "If you want to meet Brother Cogdill in debate, he would be glad to take you on."

BROTHER WOODS: "Well, fine. I just would be—"

BROTHER DOUTHITT: "But don't address him that way."

BROTHER WOODS: "It will be a very good thing to do, Brother Douthitt. I will just be happy to do that."

BROTHER TOTTY: "Just a minute, Brother Woods. Brother Douthitt has shown partiality from the beginning."

BROTHER WOODS: "Count my time, please."

BROTHER TOTTY: "Just as long as there is an "amen" to them, it is perfectly all right; but the first time it started this way, it was all wrong. Now, if Brother Cogdill didn't want to be personated, he should not have shaken his head at Brother Woods. (Laughter and clapping of hands.) If Brother Cogdill wants any debates, brother, he can get them by the baker's dozens. I wrote him seven letters about a debate, and he never answered one."

BROTHER DOUTHITT: "Let's go on. Let's go on with the debate, and immediately after this over, let these men sign up."

BROTHER TOTTY: "All right."

BROTHER WOODS: "Now, everybody is in a good humor. We are all happy here. (Laughter.) We are all happy."

It is impossible for the churches of Christ to function in their present circumstances, in California at least, to have places to meet and to own property without having some sort of corporation. I think we'll agree on that. And, we also agree that it is right to conform to the law under those circumstances. And, in *any* state you must have trustees; and there isn't anything in the New Testament about trustees; therefore, you must have a legal setup, or arrangement, in any state; in this state, Texas, Tennessee, or anywhere else. What this man is opposed to is what the law of the land requires! What are we agreed upon? You can take care of the orphan; you can have a place to do it; but it must be done illegally. That's exactly the basic position this man is holding tonight.

He wants to know if the Bible classes are organized. Are they an organization? Is it possible that Brother Porter could ask such a question as this? Anything that is organized constitutes an organization. The very fact that it is organized makes it an organization. The word "organization" is the noun form of the verb "organize." The difference between a verb and a noun. Is it possible this man didn't know that? Now, of course, the Bible school is an organization. It isn't an organization separate and apart from the church in the sense that it operates as a rival to, or in competition with, the church. But, it is an organization that is *not* the church. If he thinks it is, I want to know this: Just what is the status of those children and those individuals in the Sunday school who are not members of the church? If it is exactly the same as the church, these individuals that are enrolled in the Bible school and are not members of the church, don't forget to tell us what they are and what their status is. Will you, Brother Porter? Get busy on that when you come up here.

He says that there is no authority for us to set up a body politic. Where is the authority for *individuals* to set up a body politic? You have an organized affair in the paper, and I do not object to that. Neither does Brother Porter object to it; but it is an organization, and it is a corporation, and it is a corporation that is owned by individuals. Where is the authority for *individuals* to form a corporation to "defend and propagate New Testament Christianity"? I ask him for the authority for it.

He said, "There must have been a lot of widows in that Jerusalem church!" Well, probably so. He doesn't know how many there were. But, it doesn't follow that the widows were the only ones who received care. Does Brother Porter think they were the only ones who received care? Now, Brother Porter, I am surprised at this exhibition of a lack of information about that incident you have manifested here tonight. The text says that not one of them said the things that he possessed were his own, but they had all things common; they sold their possessions and took the money and laid it at the apostles' feet. What was that money used for? *It was used for all of them.* You know what he tried to do tonight? He tried to leave the impression that the money was used only for the widows. Ah, yes, that's what he did; and you know he did. Exactly that. I would be ashamed to pervert the scriptures in that fashion. All the money was brought and laid at the apostles' feet, and they distributed it to everyone as they had need. *That was every one of them.* You just don't know what the New Testament teaches on that, Brother Porter. I am surprised, very surprised.

Now then, to my chart number one. How much time do I have, please?

BROTHER WATSON: "You have five and a half minutes."

Thanks. Friends, repeatedly I have sought to get Brother Porter to reply to the original argument made on this chart. Here was the argument as originally made: The Federal Government exists as an organization apart from the Post Office Department, but the Post Office Department is not in conflict with it. I introduced this to show that these do not rival these. When he replies he never meets the argument I have introduced. He says, "Well, the Catholic Church has a Missionary Society; therefore, it is right for the church today to have a Missionary Society." I might reason like this: The Catholic Church has a pope today; therefore, it is right for the church of Christ to have a pope, and be just as pertinent as his argument is. Now, isn't that ridiculous? That's the basis of his argument here. The Catholic orphanage does not rival the Catholic Church. All right. "It has a Missionary Society"; therefore, the Missionary Society does not rival the church. Well, look now, in like fashion, the Catholic Church has a pope; the church of Christ has elders; therefore, on the basis of that, it would be the same thing as saying that the elders are equal to the pope in the Catholic Church. It would be on the same basis. Brother Porter has never seen the argument; never has met the issue here.

Chart No. 1

Organizations in Different Categories

Fed. Gov't.----Post Office Dept.
State Gov't.---Highway Dept.
Masonic Lodge---Homes for Aged.
Catholic Church---Orphanages.
Church of Christ---Orphanages & Homes for Aged

Rival These? Do These

The issue is not: Does the Catholic Church *have* other organizations? Certainly it does. Does it have organizations that are unscriptural? Of course, it does. A great many things about it are unscriptural. A great many things are unscriptural about other matters here. But the point is not that; the point is this: Are these organizations (on the right side) that rival the existence of these (on the left side)? That's the point. Now, it doesn't mean that there are not other matters that would be wrong. Indeed so. And look at another difference here. The "Missionary Society" that the Catholic Church operates, also operates orphanages. In addition to operating missions, it operates orphanages. Well, the parallel would be exactly what I presented a while ago. And, to this very minute, Brother Porter hasn't answered it.

Now, friends, that covers his speech, item by item, statement by statement, argument by argument.

I would like to have my chart number twelve, please. His argument is that the Lord commanded the ark. The essential is gopher wood. The incidental is the tools, the size and so on. This is exactly what he has here, only simplified in a fashion that makes it clearer. And the addition would be a little ark. Then, his parallel is that the item is benevolence; the essential is doing good; the incidental, the money the food and the clothes; and the addition, orphanages and homes for the aged. Now, look at my parallel, according to his argument: The item would be teaching. The essential would be truth, that which is to be taught. The incidental, the manner in which you go about it: oral, written, radio, or tracts. And the anti-Sunday school men would say that the addition is the Sunday school; and Brother Porter has virtually admitted that by claiming that the Sunday school is an organization. Look further: Under preaching here, the item; the essential would be the gospel; the incidental would be the method or means through which it is done: the pulpit, the radio, or the building; and, if his argument possesses any merit at all, the religious paper would be the addition. Now, I do not say that it is an addition, because I do not accept his conclusion or the argument that he draws upon it. But, that is his position. Here is a question that up to this moment I have not been able to get him to answer. I have asked it about five times already. Brother Porter, *where is the private home that takes the orphan* on your chart, or on mine? Now, where is it? It does seem you would be able to place it *somewhere!* It must be on there, somewhere. Now, will you locate it for us? We want you to do that. Please do that in your very next speech, because if you don't, you won't have any chance to do it.

Now, hurriedly, I want to introduce some matters. Chart number four, please. This, friends, has not yet been introduced; and I hurry to get it in, in order that Brother Porter

CHART NO. 12

ITEM	ESSENTIAL	INCIDENTAL	ADDITION
Ark	Gopher Wood	Tools, Size of Trees, etc.	Little Ark
Benevolence	Doing Good	Money, Food, Clothes	Orphanages, Homes for Aged
Teaching	Truth	Oral, Written Radio, Tracts	Sunday School
Preaching	Gospel	Pulpit, Radio, Bldg.	Gospel Guardian!
	(1)	(2)	(3)

Where is the Private Home?

1. _________ ?
2. _________ ?
3. _________ ?

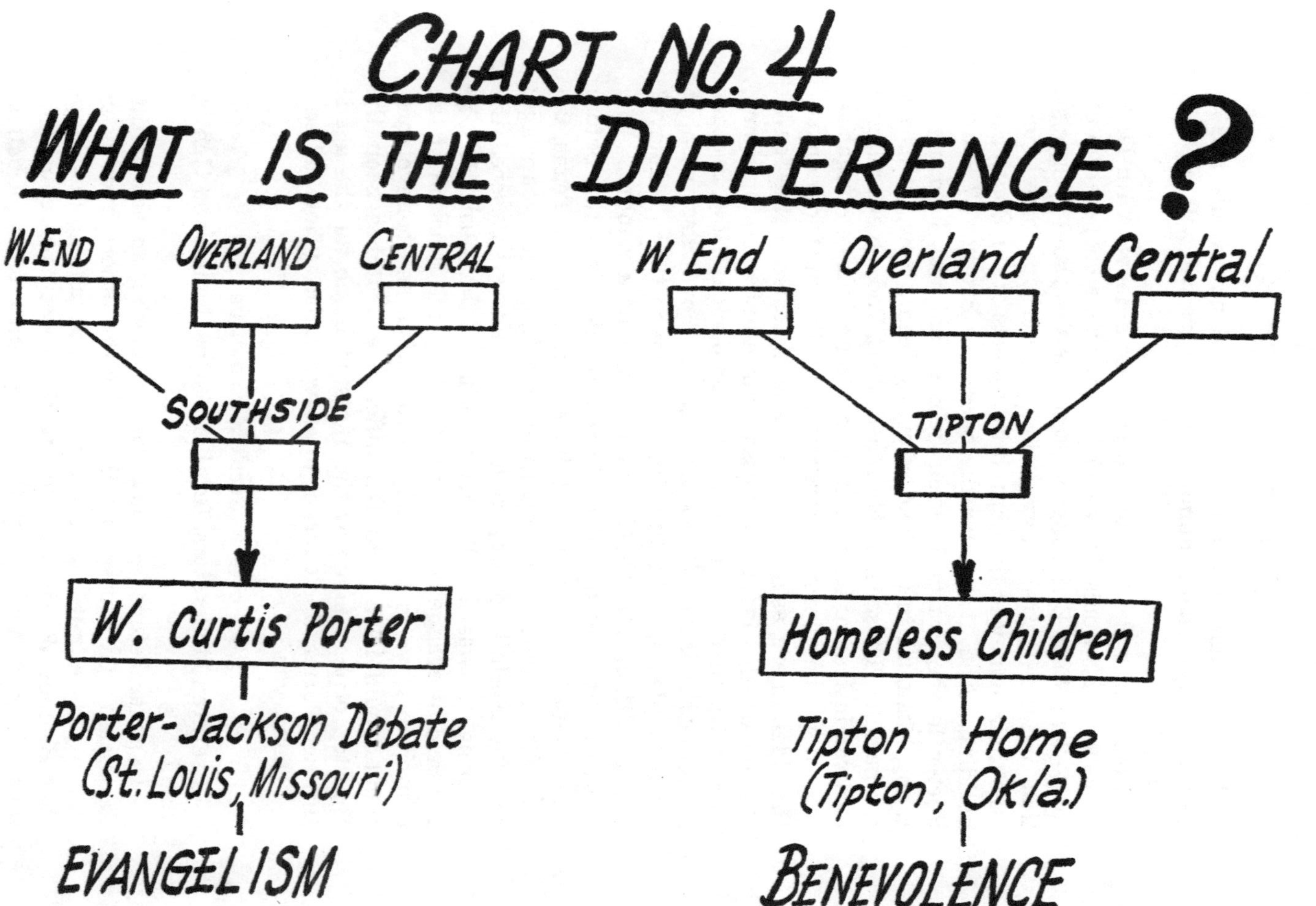

CHART NO. 4
WHAT IS THE DIFFERENCE?
W.END
OVERLAND
CENTRAL
SOUTHSIDE
W. Curtis Porter
Porter-Jackson Debate
(St. Louis, Missouri)
EVANGELISM
W. End
Overland
Central
TIPTON
Homeless Children
Tipton Home
(Tipton, Okla.)
BENEVOLENCE

will have a chance to reply to it. And now while this is before us, get chart number thirteen so we will have it quickly.

Some years ago Brother Porter held a debate with D. N. Jackson in St. Louis, Missouri; and it was a cooperative effort. The West End congregation, the Overland congregation, and the Central congregation, and perhaps some others, sent their money to the church that meets at the South Side building. And, it was for the benefit of Brother W. Curtis Porter in the Porter-Jackson debate that was held at St. Louis, Missouri, in the field of evangelism. Now, let us see the parallel: These same churches, West End, Overland, and Central, instead of sending it to the South Side congregation, send it to the Tipton congregation in Tipton, Oklahoma,—the elders there, as in this case,—and instead of being for W. Curtis Porter, it is for homeless children in the Tipton Home, Tipton, Oklahoma, in the field of benevolence. Now, Brother Porter, *what is the difference?* Let us have chart number thirteen, please, right quickly. How much time do I have?

BROTHER WATSON: "You have half a minute."

All right. Let us get this one quickly to get this before you. Here is chart number thirteen. In Houston, Texas, the churches conducted a cooperative meeting some years ago; and the Norhill congregation and its elders sponsored the meeting. It was the Wallace meeting in the Music Hall, in the field of evangelism. Now, it is both the function of the church to serve in the field of evangelism and benevolence. What would have been the difference if it has been the Houston orphan home or the Houston home for the aged? Brother Porter, don't forget to answer this! (Time called.)

Thank you.

Porter's Sixth Affirmative

Brethren Moderators, Brother Woods, Ladies and Gentlemen:

I appear before you now for my closing speech of this discussion. Of course, it will be, as the others have been, just twenty minutes long. And I want to take up the things that Brother Woods said during the speech preceding and take a look at those things that he has introduced. I believe

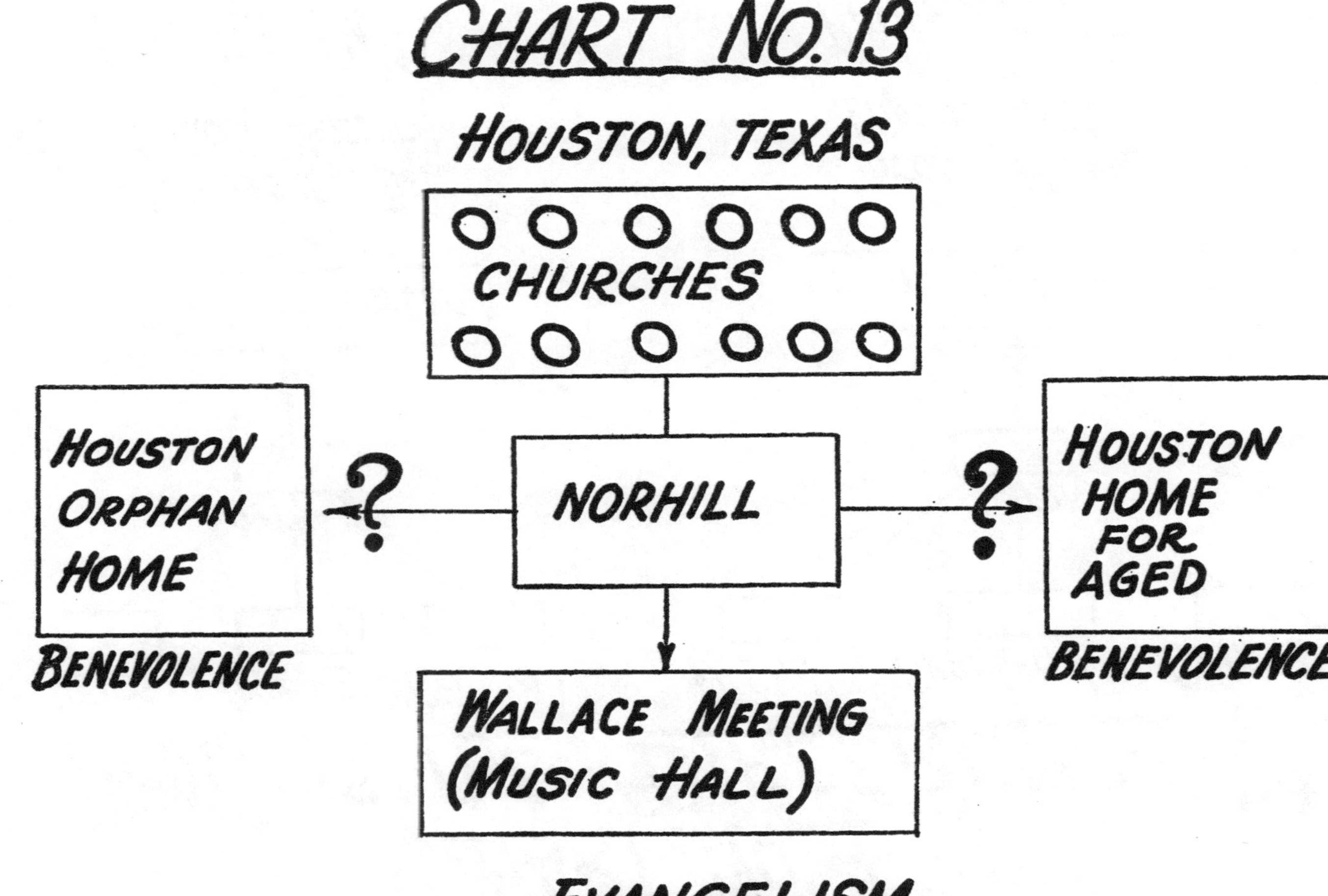
CHART NO. 13
HOUSTON, TEXAS
CHURCHES
HOUSTON ORPHAN HOME
BENEVOLENCE
?
NORHILL
?
HOUSTON HOME FOR AGED
BENEVOLENCE
WALLACE MEETING (MUSIC HALL)
EVANGELISM

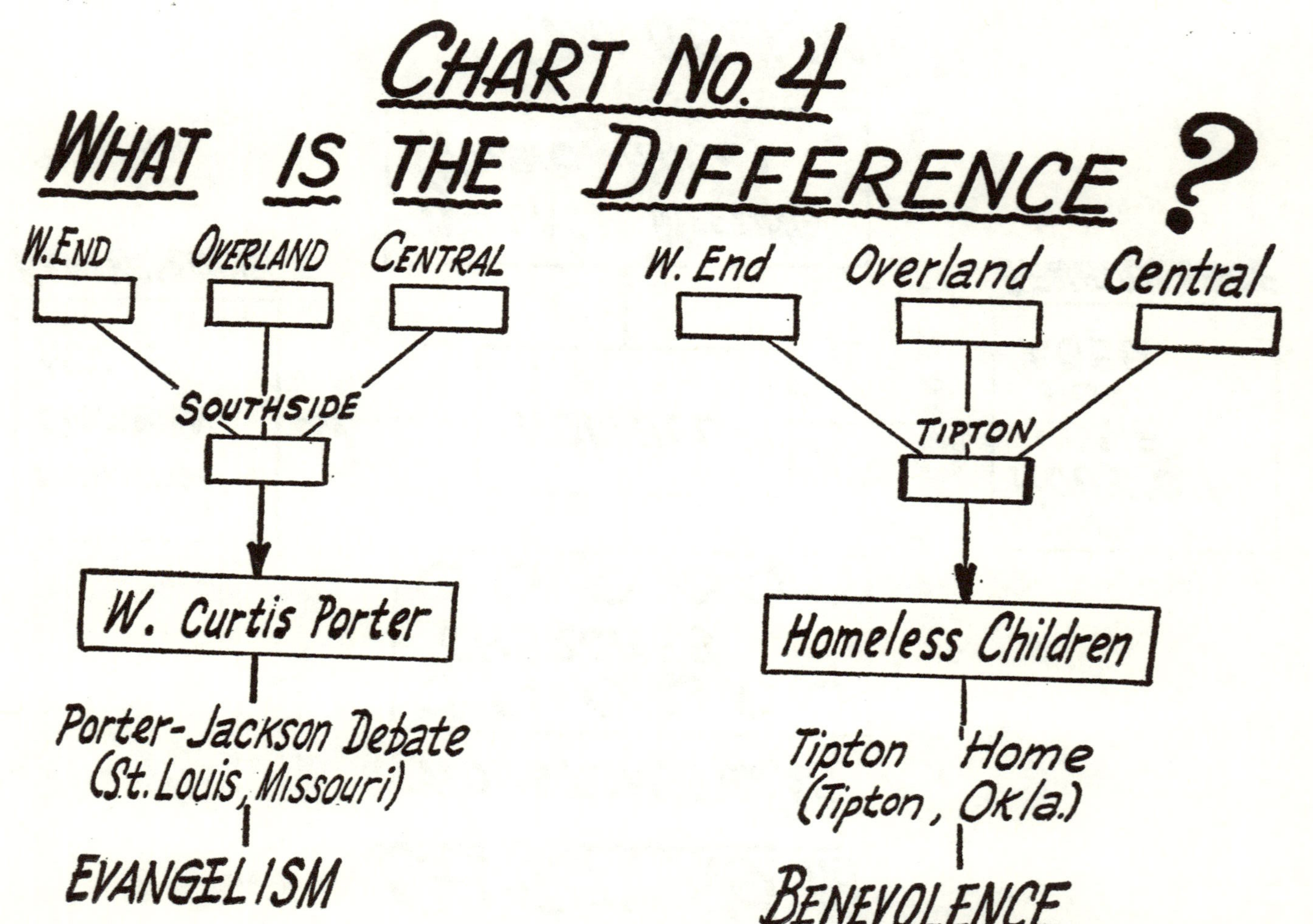
CHART NO. 4
WHAT IS THE DIFFERENCE ?
W.END
OVERLAND
CENTRAL
SOUTHSIDE
W. Curtis Porter
Porter-Jackson Debate
(St. Louis, Missouri)
EVANGELISM
W. End
Overland
Central
TIPTON
Homeless Children
Tipton Home
(Tipton, Okla.)
BENEVOLENCE

I shall start about where he left off. Of course, that chart number thirteen, the Houston meeting, has been discussed pro and con throughout a number of years—at least in recent years; and I presume there is no need to say more about it at this time. It is parallel with the one just preceding it; so we will take the one just preceding it, chart number four. Give us that on the screen, please.

This pertains to a debate that Brother Porter had with D. N. Jackson in St. Louis about 1945. And he said the different churches sent their money over to the South Side church, and it became the sponsoring church through which W. Curtis Porter was supported. I do not remember anything about the financial arrangements for that debate. I knew nothing about it then as I recall; I know nothing about it since. I don't know what their arrangements were; and if there was such an arrangement, I was in no wise conscious of it. And if it was so, why, I certainly do not accept that sort of arrangement as a scriptural arrangement by which the work is to be done. So if that was the method by which it was done, I would repudiate that kind of support. I do not know; I never knew of that kind of arrangement; and, therefore, it is entirely new to me.

On chart number twelve we come to his incidentals. I am backtracking here for a while. Chart number twelve.

We want to get to that, and this he gives as a parallel to the one we have over here on this chart: the ark, the gopher wood, the tools, the size of the trees, and the little ark, an addition. Work of benevolence: doing good, the essential; and money, food, and clothes, the incidental; and the orphan home and homes for the aged, the addition. And he came down to teaching. The truth is the essential; the incidental as the oral, written, radio, or tract; and that the Sunday school is an addition. Now then, Brother Woods, I want you to tell us—and I won't have any chance to reply to it—but I want you to tell us, Brother Woods, whether or not a centralized Sunday School Corporation, incorporated under the laws of the state, set up under a Board of Directors, after the same fashion you have the benevolent society, to do the work of edification of the church on Sunday morning, would be an addition. Now, you tell us. I would like for that to

CHART NO. 12

ITEM	ESSENTIAL	INCIDENTAL	ADDITION
Ark	Gopher Wood	Tools, Size of Trees, etc.	Little Ark
Benevolence	Doing Good	Money, Food, Clothes	Orphanages, Homes for Aged
Teaching	Truth	Oral, Written Radio, Tracts	Sunday School
Preaching	Gospel	Pulpit, Radio, Bldg.	Gospel Guardian!
	(1)	(2)	(3)

Where is the Private Home?

1. ______?
2. ______?
3. ______?

go into the book. I want you to tell us about it. I am insisting that a Sunday School Corporation would be *an addition.* And if you say it would not be an addition, then you are going to have trouble meeting the anti-Sunday school brethren hereafter. I can just guarantee you that. So you tell us whether that's an addition or not.

And then to chart number one again. Let us have that. Take a brief look at it. Just this other here; I will mention that as we go along. He mentioned the *Guardian* in that connection, which is a private enterprise, and we are discussing the church—the work of the church, and not private enterprises, as far as that goes. Now then, chart number one.

The Federal Government argument. He said Porter seems never to have understood the argument. Oh, yes, I have understood it too well, Brother Woods. That's where the trouble is. And he said that this is not a rival—the Post Office Department is not a rival to the Federal Government; therefore, it is all right. And anything that is not a rival of the church of Christ, therefore, is all right. And he gave the Catholic Church, and those others in connection with it as parallels of it. And since the Catholic Church has orphanages that do not rival the Catholic Church, then that would be all right for them. On the same basis, the church of Christ can have orphanages because they do not rival the church. Well, he says, "I admit that the Catholic Church also has Missionary Societies and a lot of other things that are wrong." Well, I am wanting to know, Brother Woods, and you didn't tell me; you didn't even touch the question that I asked you. I asked you: "Do the Missionary Societies *rival* the Catholic Church?" And if they don't rival the Catholic Church, then you have them in the same category; and upon that same basis, then Missionary Societies *would not rival the church of Christ,* and we could have them just like we have the benevolent organization. Oh, he said, "On the basis of that, we could have the pope; Porter would endorse the pope." No, Brother Woods' argument would endorse the pope—not Porter. It is his systematic chart here that would endorse the pope. It is not Porter's argument at all. It is Brother Woods' argument that endorses the pope.

Chart No. 1

Organizations in Different Categories

Fed. Gov't. ----Post Office Dept.
State Gov't.---Highway Dept.
Masonic Lodge---Homes for Aged.
Catholic Church---Orphanages.
Church of Christ---Orphanages & Homes for Aged

Rival These? Do These

Now, then, we get back just a little more here to the "silly grin." He said he would erase the word "grin." And that's down further beneath the dignity of a man of your ability, Brother Woods. I don't know how much you could go below that now. That's beneath the dignity of a man of your ability to get up here and say, "I will just erase the grin and leave you silly." Now, I am actually ashamed of a man who would resort to tactics like that. He said, "The only time I have ever seen anything like that was on the face of Baptist preachers." Well, I have never had the Baptist preachers to grin when I had hold of them, Brother Woods. (Laughter.) It worked the other way.

To the matter of the Sunday school. He said, "The Sunday school is in the word 'teach'; but the word 'teach' does not necessitate the Missionary Society. Porter took this position in his debate with the anti-Sunday school brethren." I said the Sunday school, in the sense of our Bible classes, where there is no organization set up, where there is no corporation, where it is merely a systematic arrangement, is not in conflict with the New Testament teaching. But if you set up a human corporation under a Board of Directors, such as you have in this matter, it is in conflict with it. And I am interested to see in years to come just what the anti-Bible class fellows do with you when they get hold of you on that proposition again.

The matter of incorporation. He said the churches in California had to incorporate in order to exist; and Brother Cogdill shook his head; and he personated him and called him out and took a shot or two at him. He finally backed up and said they did not have to have it in order to exist. And that's what he was shaking his head about. Brother Woods turned right around and admitted he was shaking his head right. What? He was shaking his head that they did not have to have a corporation to exist, and you turned right around and said they did not have to have a corporation to exist—they just had to have a corporation to own property. They could exist without owning property, couldn't they? And so you turned right around and admitted that Brother Cogdill was right on the very thing he was shaking his head about—that that was true. Well, so much for that.

He said regarding these other things, this matter—hand me that. Right there. That right next to you, brother. Right there. He said the reason we have a corporation for these orphan homes is because we have to do it *in order to be legal*—that you can't have, you can't maintain, an orphan home without having a corporation, without its being incorporated. If you do, *it is illegal.* Well, it just happens, Brother Woods, that that one that you brought up a while ago, that you told about having a number of children they couldn't place in homes, *is not incorporated.* Did you know it? Did you know it? Here I have a letter from Brother John B. White, the Superintendent of that home; and he says, "The children's home at Lubbock is not incorporated, but it is under the direct supervision of the elders of the Broadway Church of Christ, as is the regular Sunday morning Bible classes, the Texas Tech Bible Chair and other work carried on by this congregation." Brother White says that home at Lubbock *is not incorporated.* According to Brother Woods, that home is *illegally operating.* It is not incorporated. Not only is that so, but I have here a letter from the office of the Secretary of State of Kansas; and this letter says, "The corporate statutes of the State of Kansas do not require that orphans homes organized by church organizations be incorporated under the provisions of our Kansas Corporate laws." I have also a letter from the office of the Secretary of State of Indiana; and this letter says that, "A church operating in the State of Indiana, whether a corporation or an unincorporated association, may operate as a church in all capacities. Thus a church may have and operate an orphans home in conjunction with its religious activities. To operate an orphans home it will be necessary to comply with our health laws and our safety protection laws." But they say that it does not have to have an incorporation. Brother Woods said they can't operate without being incorporated. And here is one from the Secretary of State in Kentucky, and it says, "It is up to the group to decide if they want to incorporate or not." All right, that takes care of that.

Now, regarding the Lubbock Home and the children that they could not place there, I have a statement here from a brother who said, "I tried to get a child from the children's home at Lubbock, Texas, a year ago; and they had none that I could get. I asked if they would let me know when one came in that was adoptable." Signed: Vernon Ripley, Ropesville, Texas. And another statement that Vandalia Village Church of Christ, in Lubbock, tried to get a family of seven children from the Lubbock children's home, and could not. Five of them had already been placed, and a member of the

Vandalia church had already taken the other two. And so a lot of things could be brought up about those matters.

Now, we go back to some other things I want to get to just a little more as my time allows me. He says he is aware of the fact that a house and an organization are different things. He is fully aware of that. But how can a home be operated, and how can you have a home that has no organization, no supervision, or anything? Well, I said there could be *systematic arrangement.* And that reminds me of this question over here that he said I had been ignoring. I simply let it slip my mind. Where is the private home on this? Well, this is dealing with the church, Brother Woods. This is dealing with the work of the church—not with the private home. We are dealing with the work of the church. The private home, you said the other night, is a divinely given institution—that it is a divine institution. God has two divine institutions: the church and the home. But the benevolent organization that you have set up is not a divine arrangement. That's a human organization; and so there is your difference. Well, then he wants to know who will take care of them in that home, and things of that kind. I showed you a while ago that a person may be hired to do the cooking, and the family that takes care of them does the cooking—takes care of them, and looks after them in that way. And so there is simply that arrangement. *But that is not a corporation,* Brother Woods. That is not a corporation. You just as well say that you can't hire a janitor to look after the building without setting up a corporation for him. And if he has any arrangement whatsoever, you have a corporation that is comparable to your benevolent organizations; and everybody knows that isn't true.

Well, he said, "Porter declared that the preacher's home is not an organization." I was replying to what you said about the preacher's home and referring it to the house where the preacher lived. You were saying that the preacher has a house that is furnished for him—that we furnish a home for him. Of course, the church does not furnish the man's family. The family is the home in the actual sense of the term. The church doesn't furnish that. But what you were referring to was the house. And you were calling the house the home. And I was showing that that thing isn't a corporation; and it isn't. There is a difference between a house, or a place, and an organization.

Then he said, "I never said that the church is not God's benevolent organization. I said that the church is not the orphan home." The church is not an orphan home. And then he turned around and said the orphan home is not in conflict with the church, because it is *the church doing its work*. One breath he says it is not the church, and the next breath he says the orphan home is the church doing its work. Well, draw your own conclusions. Then he got back to his laws regarding the incorporation.

I believe that covers about everything that was said. If I have missed anything, I have done it unintentionally. How much time do I have? About six or seven minutes?

BROTHER DOUTHITT: "You have about seven minutes."

All right, that is fine. Now, then, we want to take another look at this just a moment.

And in this we find a number of additions here, as another building that Noah might erect, and the Christian Missionary Society, the Christian Baptizing Association, the Singing Saints Society, the Christian Communion Confederation, the Christian Praying League, the Christian Fellowship Federation, and the Christian Benevolent Corporation. And Brother Woods said, "I will move this one over here" (pointing to "Inclusions"). I believe that's where you put it. I couldn't see from where I was sitting. Is that the place you put it, Brother Woods? All right, the best I could see, that was it. He said, "I will move this one over here." All right, he moves this one over there in the *inclusions*. Upon what basis, then, will you keep me from moving this one (pointing to "Christian Missionary Society") over here? And how will you keep me from moving the Christian Praying League over here? And how are you going to keep the Christian Communion Confederation from being moved over here? Or the Singing Saints Society? Or the Christian Baptizing Association? Or the Christian Missionary Society? Or the other building of Noah? If you can move one of them, you can move all of them. They are all separate buildings; they

Porter's Roll
Chart No. 2.

LAW AND EXPEDIENCY

To Be Expedient - Must Be Lawful. 1 Cor. 6:12.

COMMANDS	INCLUSIONS	PERVERSIONS	INCIDENTALS	ADDITIONS
Build Ark Gen. 6:14-16	Gopher Wood Three Stories	Cottonwood Ten Stories	Tools - Size Transportation	Another Building
Teach Mat. 28:19	Whole Counsel Truth	Human Traditions Doctrines of Men	Blackboard - Radio Charts - Press	Christian Missionary Society
Baptize Mat. 28:19	Water - Believers Burial	Wine - Infants Sprinkling	Ocean - River Pool - Baptistry	Christian Baptizing Association
Sing Eph. 5:19	Spiritual Songs Melody in Heart	Worldly Songs Melody on Harp	Books - Tuning Fork Voice Parts - Notes	Singing Saints Society
Partake Lord's Supper 1 Cor.11;Acts 20:7.	First Day - Bread Fruit of Vine	Midweek - Beef Buttermilk	Plates - Cups Place - Hour	Christian Communion Confederation
Pray Phil. 4:6; Jas. 1: 6.	To God In Faith	To Virgin Mary In Pretense	Length of Prayer Posture	Christian Praying League
Give 1 Cor. 16:1,2; 2 Cor. 9:6, 7.	As Prospered Cheerfully	Sparingly Grudgingly	Collection Plates Envelopes	Christian Fellowship Federation
Visit Orphans Jas. 1:27.	Food - Clothes Shelter	Oppress - Vex Neglect	House - Tent City - Country	Christian Benevolent Corporation

are all other buildings; they are all other bodies; and he has admitted that this is another body. And if you can move another body over there, why can't I move another body over there? Huh? Now, he hasn't told us; and I have been asking why. Why he can move one and not move the other? He hasn't made any effort to tell us. He just says, "I will move this one," and lets it go at that and says that answers the whole thing. Well, he has to move something else before he has answered the argument, or else put it back where it belongs.

Now, I want Brother Woods' chart number eleven, please. We want to take a look at this "component parts argument" that is one of the finest arguments Brother Woods has heard in twenty-five years and in approximately one hundred debates, that he considers *absolutely unanswerable* and *irresistible.*

This is the argument that he adapted from Brother Thomas Warren and Roy Deaver. And the "axiom" up here is: "the whole of anything is the sum of its parts." And he says, "The proof of my proposition requires: first, the care of orphans and aged; second, church support of the orphans and aged; and third, church cooperation in the support of the orphans and aged." And he said, "This we have already done—that is, we have already shown this." This is the idea he intended. And, "Porter concedes the foregoing anyway." Then his "syllogism" following says that: "First, all situations, the component parts of which are scriptural, are scriptural situations; second, the component parts of the whole work involved in my proposition are scriptural; third, the whole work involved in my proposition is scriptural." Then he says, "Porter's alternative" is: "first, he must deny the major premise"—that is, this one here, that "all situations, the component parts of which are scriptural, are scriptural situations." "Or he must repudiate his public statements." Now, he said this is absolutely *irresistable* and *unanswerable;* and upon this he is willing to rest the whole case. Whenever he does, the whole case is gone, world without end. Now, then, let us look at it. Notice here are three things. We believe in the care of orphans—we both agree upon that—and the aged. We believe the churches may sup-

CHART NO. 11

AXIOM: "The WHOLE of anything is the SUM of its parts"

PROOF MY PROP. REQUIRES:
- Care Of Orph. & Aged
- Ch. Support " " " "
- Ch. Cooperation in the Support of " " "

(a) This we have already done.
(b) Porter concedes foregoing anyway.

Syllogism:
(1) All situations, the component parts of which are scriptural, are scriptural situations.
(2) The component parts of the whole work involved in my prop. are scriptural.
(3) ∴ the whole work involved in prop. is scriptural.

PORTER'S ALTERNATIVE:
(a) Deny the major premise.
(b) Repudiate Public Statements.

port the orphans and aged. And we believe the churches may cooperate in the support of the orphans and the aged. And then he says, "That proves my proposition." That's the sum total of it. Those are the component parts of it. I showed you there is a *very important*, a *very necessary*, *component part* of his proposition that is *absolutely missing* from it. His proposition does not say that it is scriptural for orphans to be cared for. His proposition does not say that it is scriptural for churches to support the orphans and aged. His proposition does not say that it is scriptural for churches to cooperate in the support of such. But his proposition says that it is scriptural for churches to *build and maintain benevolent organizations* in which that is to be done. And so there is the component part of his proposition which is not on the chart —that that says benevolent organizations. And that does not set them up, and no conclusion and no syllogism that he can draw upon the matter, can bring that in, because he has left out the important part. The very center, the very heart, of his proposition is left out of his component parts.

Now, then, I want my chart number five.

BROTHER DOUTHITT: "Two minutes."

Two minutes. Fine.

Porter's Projector
Chart No. 5.

A "DEADLY PARALLEL" TO WOODS' CHART NO. 11

AXIOM: "The WHOLE of anything is the SUM of its parts."

PROOF FOR MISSIONARY SOCIETY REQUIRES:

1. Obligation to preach the gospel.
2. Obligation of church to support preaching of gospel.
3. Church cooperation in supporting preaching of gospel.

(a) This has already been done.
(b) Woods concedes foregoing anyway.

SYLLOGISM:

(1) All situations, the component parts of which are Scriptural, are Scriptural situations.
(2) The component parts of the whole work involved in Missionary Society are Scriptural.
(3) The whole work involved in Missionary Society is Scriptural.

WOODS' ALTERNATIVES:

(1) Endorse Missionary Society.
(2) Repudiate best argument of 25 years and 100 debates.
(3) Repudiate proposition and admit defeat.

Now, we look at this briefly. Here is the deadly parallel to Woods' chart. "The axiom: the whole of anything is the sum of its parts. The proof for the Missionary Society requires: first, the obligation to preach the gospel; second, the obligation of the church to support the preaching the gospel; third, church cooperation in supporting the preaching of the gospel. And this has already been done, and Woods concedes the foregoing anyway. The syllogism: all situations, the component parts of which are scriptural, are scriptural situations. The component parts of the whole work involved in the Missionary Society is scriptural; therefore, the whole work involved in the Missionary Society is scriptural. Woods' alternative: to endorse the Missionary Society, to repudiate the best argument in twenty-five years, or repudiate his proposition and admit defeat." And the component part here that is essential that is left out is the *organization.* This is a deadly parallel to his; and if he can take his, then this is *absolutely irresistible* in support of the Missionary Society.

Now, when Brother Woods comes to his final speech, any appeal to emotionalism, telling you how he believes in taking care of and defending the little orphans running around in the streets and living in boxes and eating out of garbage cans and things of that kind, is a pure appeal to emotionalism; and it is beneath the dignity of Brother Woods to come with a thing of that kind in his closing speech; and I hope he doesn't do it; but that he comes and deals with the arguments fairly and squarely as they have been presented.

(Time Called.)

And I thank you very kindly.

Woods' Sixth Negative

Brethren Moderators, Brother Porter, Ladies and Gentlemen:

I am before you for the final speech of the evening; and I may say that I have no intention whatsoever of making any appeal to prejudice, because it isn't necessary. I have the truth on this question. One doesn't need to resort to appeals to prejudice, or to the audience, as Brother Porter has done in his last speech, when one has the truth and the consciousness of that fact. Now, I propose to take up his speech, statement by statement, and then to conclude with a summary of what has been presented.

I gave you a chart on the Houston Music Hall Meeting. Brother Porter waived it aside and said, "I will not say anything about it." Now, why not? He did say that it is included in the next one, but it isn't. It is an entirely different proposition and on an entirely different basis. Of course, the conclusion to which it leads is the same; that is, church cooperation in the field of benevolence. But, he waived it aside. I wonder what you brethren would think if Brother Porter were debating with a Baptist preacher who put an argument on the board and Brother Porter just waived it aside and said, "Well, I won't pay any attention to that!" That's not his way of doing it when he is debating with a Baptist. The reason that Brother Porter waived that chart aside is that he didn't know *what* to say about it. He couldn't say *anything* about it, because he knows it is in direct conflict with their theory today, and it is in harmony with the practice which I am defending tonight. If I were to follow the pattern that this man has done in this, the brethren whom I represent in this debate would hang their heads in shame. Put the chart on the board again. That's chart number thirteen.

Here it is. These are the churches of Houston. The Norhill congregation sponsored a meeting. It was held in the Music Hall, and Brother Foy Wallace did the preaching. It was in the field of evangelism. To this very day, the preacher (Roy Cogdill) who was then working with the Norhill church endorses that plan. He doesn't say that it is unscriptural. He believes that it is right. Brother Porter, do you? Do you accept it? Now, I know you are silent; and I am not expecting you to answer; but you had a chance to answer, *and you didn't do it!* And every preacher in this audience knows the reason why. You know that that's not right, according to your present position. But you knew that it has not been repudiated; therefore, you didn't have the courage to come up here and say, "I will meet the issue."

Now, friends, suppose we change it from a meeting in the field of evangelism to an orphan home in the field of benevolence or to a home for the aged in the same field. If it is right for however many churches there were—I do not know the number—thirty, forty, or fifty, or however many there were, to combine their resources and turn the money over to Norhill, who sponsored the meeting and who oversaw the meeting, then why wouldn't it be right for Norhill to operate a Houston orphan home and a home for the aged by means of the same support? Why not? Every person in this audience tonight knows the reason why you didn't answer. It

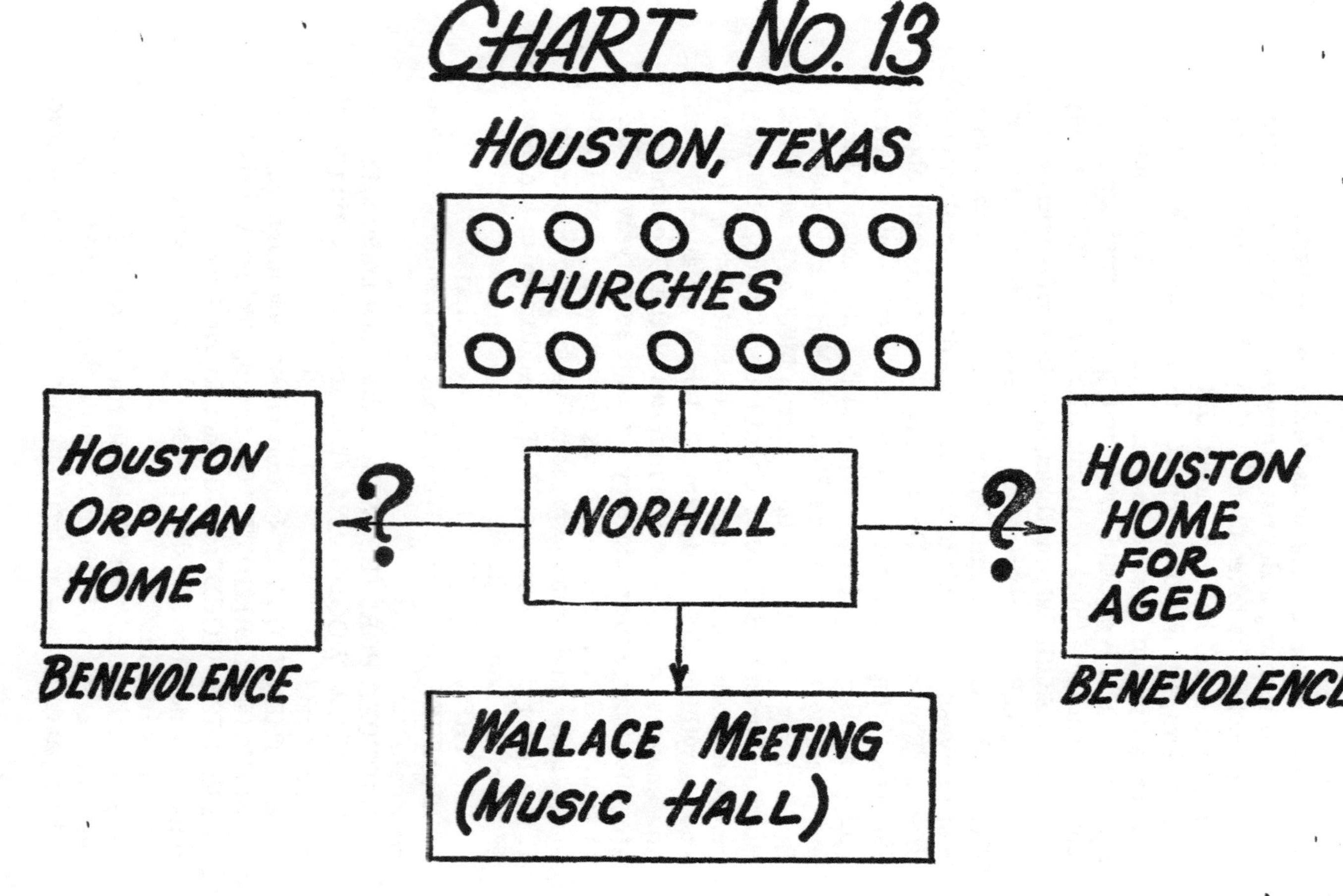
CHART NO. 13
HOUSTON, TEXAS
CHURCHES
NORHILL
HOUSTON ORPHAN HOME
BENEVOLENCE
HOUSTON HOME FOR AGED
BENEVOLENCE
WALLACE MEETING (MUSIC HALL)
EVANGELISM

isn't characteristic of W. Curtis Porter to pass arguments by. When he is meeting a Baptist or any sectarian or denominational preacher, he takes them as they come. But he didn't take this one, did he? He didn't, did he?

All right, let us look at chart number four. I called attention to the fact that some years ago he held a debate in St. Louis. The West End, Overland, and Central congregations—I just have these for illustration—turned their money over to the South Side brethren, who in turn supported the debate. I called attention to the parallel there; that the West End, Overland, and Central churches could then turn money over to Tipton's elders for benefit of homeless children in Tipton Home. Do you recall what he said about? He said, "I repudiate that." Well, all right then, if he repudiates this one, and this one is just like the Houston Meeting, then he repudiates the Houston Music Hall Meeting! But, Brother Cogdill says the Houston Meeting is scriptural. Brother Porter and Brother Cogdill are standing crossways before us here this evening. Brother Porter says, "I didn't know anything about this (the St. Louis) situation." Well, you know it now. I saw the minutes of the Overland congregation where they said they set aside seventy-five dollars to send to South Side for the Porter debate. And, I have here a letter, and I merely present this for your information. It is a letter dated October 29, 1955, addressed to Mr. Sterl Watson, St. Louis, Missouri.

BROTHER PORTER: "Is that new material?"

BROTHER WOODS: "Well, I am answering what you said here."

BROTHER PORTER: "Well, is that new material?"

BROTHER WOODS: "No, it is merely answering what you have said."

BROTHER TOTTY: "No, that is not new material."

BROTHER DOUTHITT: "Go ahead, Brother Woods."

BROTHER WOODS: "I do not know how to reply to what he said here if I do not use it. I don't want to deal unfairly with him."

BROTHER TOTTY: "That isn't new material; but if it were new material, in the last debate they printed three and a half pages of new material in our book after a contract

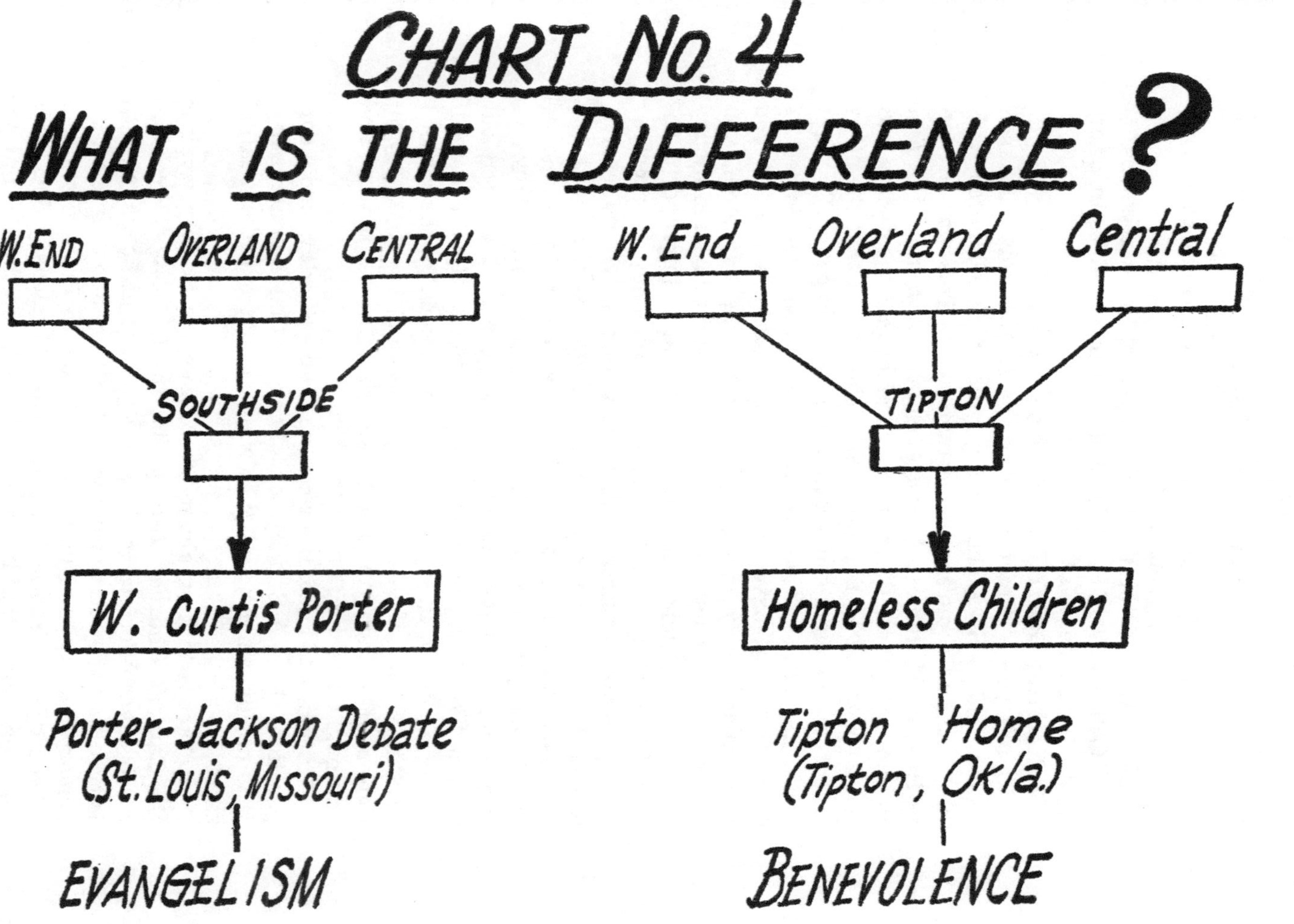
CHART NO. 4
WHAT IS THE DIFFERENCE?
W. END
OVERLAND
CENTRAL
SOUTHSIDE
W. Curtis Porter
Porter-Jackson Debate
(St. Louis, Missouri)
EVANGELISM
W. End
Overland
Central
TIPTON
Homeless Children
Tipton Home
(Tipton, Okla.)
BENEVOLENCE

was signed that it wouldn't be. But that is only answering his argument; so, go ahead."

BROTHER DOUTHITT: "Go right on, Brother Woods."

BROTHER WOODS: "Brother Douthitt, is this out of order to introduce this?"

BROTHER DOUTHITT: "I don't think so."

Thank you. "Reference is made to the Porter-Jackson debate held in St. Louis, during which time I labored with the West End congregation in that city." This was written by Brother M. Robert Adamson, signed by him. *"The first night of the debate I told Brother Porter that the debate was being sponsored by the South Side elders, and that the other congregations were cooperating in paying expenses."* Want to see the letter? There is more to it. You want to see it? Brother Porter, have you sent that money back? If you knew that you received money that somebody stole, you would send it back, because it is not right to have money in your possession that is stolen, or that is improperly obtained, is it? Brother Porter, you have money, or received money, in your possession that was wrong for you to receive, wasn't it? *Have you sent it back?* I was debating with Leroy Garrett one time and a similar situation arose, and he said he used it all in preaching the gospel. Maybe Brother Porter has used it in preaching the gospel. I pointed out to him, "Well, it would be all right then to steal a horse if you rode it to an appointment to preach!" (Laughter.) Brother Porter, if this is unscriptural, and it is if your position is right, then you owe those brethren that money; and you ought to send it back to them.

He wants to know if we could set up a Sunday school corporation. No. A Sunday school corporation is unnecessary. It is not expedient; and that which is not expedient is not right.

He keeps talking about the Missionary Society rivaling the Catholic Church. *I deny that the Catholic Church has a Missionary Society in the sense you are using it!* Now, it is true that they have missions. But they don't have a Missionary Society like you are talking about. In the first place, it would be an impossibility to have a Missionary Society in an organization that has a central head, and there is but one of them to start with. There is no such thing in the Catholic Church as that which he describes.

He doesn't like for me to refer to him; and I apologize if I offended Brother Porter's feelings, though I didn't intend any reflection. I was merely describing what I saw. And, if that was beneath my dignity, my dignity sometimes sees things that I ought not to see, because that's exactly what I saw; and that's what I said. He said that Baptist preachers do not grin when he debates them. Then, evidently he doesn't get Baptist preachers in the shape I had him last night, because he was certainly doing some of it last night. I meant no reflection upon him at all. I respect and honor Brother W. Curtis Porter, and think he is a fine, Christian gentleman. I am just sorry he has got over on the wrong side of the fence and has identified himself with a hobby and is destroying, in large measure, the great good he has done in the past.

He said that Brother Cogdill has said we cannot own property in California without incorporation. Well, that is correct; and, therefore, since a church can't exist without some place to meet, and since they do have church buildings in which to meet, then the brethren feel it is proper to have buildings and churches organized. Regardless of whether it is necessary to the existence of the church, it is necessary to the existence of the church *as it is out there.* Now, you endorse that. At least, you go out there and hold meetings. Therefore, you endorse organizations apart from the church, and even receive money from them.

Well, he says the Lubbock home is not incorporated. Now, it is entirely possible that I have inadvertently used the word "incorporated" to convey an idea that I had in mind when I intended to speak of the state supervision, or the conformity to the state law with reference to such. That's entirely possible. To show you that that is what I had in mind, I knew that the Lubbock home was not incorporated. I have here in my hand this letter: "Mr. Guy N. Woods, Memphis, Tennessee,"—dated December 9, 1955—"Dear Brother Woods: We have just received the following request from Brother W. Curtis Porter that I thought you would be interested in. 'Brethren: Under what name is the children's home in Lubbock incorporated? I shall appreciate the information. Brotherly, W. Curtis Porter.' In reply we stated: 'Dear Brother Porter: We have your request of December 6 for the name under which the children's home in Lubbock is incorporated. The children's home of Lubbock is not incorporated.' " Now there is where Brother Porter quit. Or he might have read one more phrase. "It is under the direct supervision of the elders of the Broadway church." He quit reading. Why didn't he read the rest of it? Because he didn't want you to know what they said. Now, listen to the rest of it: *"The children's home of Lubbock is not incorporated, but is under the direct supervision of the elders of the Broadway Church of Christ, as is the regular Sunday morning Bible classes, the Texas Tech Bible Chair, and other work carried on by this congregation." Now, Brother Porter, do you endorse the children's home at Lubbock? You said the only thing that is wrong with having a place and children in it is the fact that it is incorporated.* Here is one that is not incorporated. Will we shake hands on that—that we endorse that? Will we? Now, Brother Porter, we have at last found one that doesn't have the condition that you say makes it wrong. What has he said thus far? That it is right for churches to cooperate. Let us have chart number sixteen, the one that has the Memphis home on it.

He said that it is right for churches to cooperate. Here it is. Let this represent the churches of an area in the vicinity of Lubbock, Texas, and this represent the home out there. He says that his objection is that it is incorporated; that it is a corporation; and, hence, another body. Here is one that is not incorporated, and it has all the characteristics that you endorse in this, and it doesn't have that which you condemn. Will you accept it, Brother Porter? Will you shake hands with me on that one thing? Can we agree on that? Well, now, why not? I am willing for us to reach some agreement. Will you shake hands with me on that?

BROTHER PORTER: "I didn't say that, Brother Woods."

BROTHER WOODS: "You didn't say that?"

BROTHER PORTER: "I didn't say that was the only thing wrong."

Chart # 16

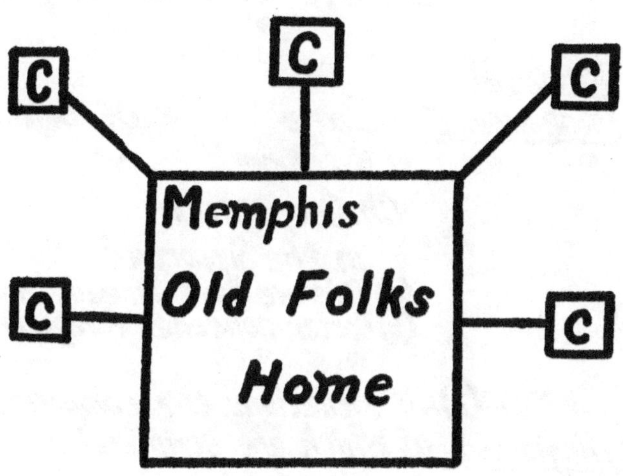

Pooling of Funds - Cooperation

Well, that's the only objection you have offered to it. Isn't it a fact that every time I have produced an argument he would say, "I admit the place; I admit there must be care; I admit that there can be supervision; but you have an organization that is incorporated"? Well, then, can we accept it? Can we agree on that? You see, friends, it is not the incorporation he objects to. The truth of the business is Brother Porter is opposed to the idea of church cooperation in the support of orphan children in a collective capacity. That's the truth upon it.

Let me ask a question or two: Where is the pattern of

CHART NO. 11

AXIOM: "The WHOLE of anything is the SUM of its parts"

•

PROOF MY PROP. REQUIRES:
- • Care Of Orph. & Aged
- • Ch. Support " " " "
- • Ch. Cooperation in the Support of " " "

(a) This we have already done.
(b) Porter concedes foregoing anyway.

•

Syllogism:
(1.) All situations, the component parts of which are scriptural, are scriptural situations.
(2.) The component parts of the whole work involved in my prop. are scriptural.
(3.) ∴ the whole work involved in prop. is scriptural.

•

PORTER'S ALTERNATIVE:
(a) Deny the major premise.
(b) Repudiate Public Statements.

New Testament teaching for the home that Brother Porter believes in? Where is the passage of scripture that justifies the Memphis home? Where is it? Where is it? I called for it repeatedly, and he has been as silent as the stars above us regarding it.

"Brother Porter says that I said this (the Christian Benevolent Corporation, on his chart) was moved over to the column headed "Inclusions." I did not move *this* anywhere, because I do not endorse this (the Christian Benevolent Corporation.) What I said is this: It is not in the column where the Christian Benevolent Corporation is that the orphan home should be placed; it is in the column designated on his chart as "Inclusions" and where "food—shelter—clothes" appear. And, that is exactly what you have at the Lubbock home, and that is what you have at the others. Exactly so."

Now, let us see chart number eleven. This, friends, is the one that Brother Porter has felt the force of throughout the entire debate.

His effort to meet it is this: I say that the essential characteristics of it are: care, church support, and church cooperation in such support. Now let us have his chart number five. We will see his effort to answer it.

Chart number five. He has in the place of the care of the needy, church support, and church cooperation in such care, the obligation to preach the gospel. Now, have the other chart ready to come right after this. The obligation to preach the gospel. The obligation of the church to support such preaching. And, church cooperation in supporting the preaching of the gospel. Look, friends: You can have all three of those characteristics and not have a Missionary

Porter's Projector
Chart No. 5.

A "DEADLY PARALLEL" TO WOODS' CHART NO. 11

AXIOM: "The WHOLE of anything is the SUM of it's parts."

PROOF FOR MISSIONARY SOCIETY REQUIRES:

1. Obligation to preach the gospel.
2. Obligation of church to support preaching of gospel.
3. Church cooperation in supporting preaching of gospel.
   (a) This has already been done.
   (b) Woods concedes foregoing anyway.

SYLLOGISM:

(1) All situations, the component parts of which are Scriptural, are Scriptural situations.
(2) The component parts of the whole work involved in Missionary Society are Scriptural.
(3) The whole work involved in Missionary Society is Scriptural.

WOODS' ALTERNATIVES:

(1) Endorse Missionary Society.
(2) Repudiate best argument of 25 years and 100 debates.
(3) Repudiate proposition and admit defeat.

Society. The Missionary Society is not implied, nor is it necessarily inferred in this statement, because you can do all this and not have a Missionary Society. I accept that without question. Now, let us have the other one.

CHART NO. 11

AXIOM: "The WHOLE of anything is the SUM of its parts"

•

PROOF MY PROP. REQUIRES: • Care Of Orph. & Aged
•Ch. Support " " " "
•Ch. Cooperation in the Support of " " "
(a) This we have already done.
(b) Porter concedes foregoing anyway.

•

Syllogism: (1.) All situations, the component parts of which are scriptural, are scriptural situations.
(2.) The component parts of the whole work involved in my prop. are scriptural.
(3.) ∴ the whole work involved in prop. is scriptural.

•

PORTER'S ALTERNATIVE: (a) Deny the major premise.
(b) Repudiate Public Statements.

Get it, please: You cannot exercise care for orphans, and church support for such care, and church cooperation in such care without having first a place, food, clothing. Let us have chart number nine.

You can't have this without having that which I have here described. Now, look at it. For the orphan: a place, food, clothing, education, supervision, and medical care. You

CHART NO. 9

"REMEMBER THE POOR"

Gal. 2:10

THIS REQUIRES

FOR THE ORPHAN:

- A Place
- Food
- Clothing
- Education
- Supervision
- Medical Care

FOR THE AGED:

- Shelter
- Food
- Clothing
- Medical Care

can preach the gospel, you can have church cooperation in such preaching without a Missionary Society; but you can't care for the orphan without having a place, and food, and clothing, and education, and supervision, and medical care, and without conforming to the law of the land in such care. And that's what I am defending here tonight. That's the reason why the two propositions are not parallel. That's the reason why the Missionary Society does not inhere in those three conditions. That's the reason why the orphan home, at least, *some kind of home,* does inhere in my position. Now, that's sufficient for that.

Basically, the issue in this debate is simply this: Shall we espouse a position that was popularized by Daniel Sommer, that has been given considerable advertising by Carl Ketcherside, and that is popularly styled (perhaps with a reflection upon the man) *Sommerism.* Daniel Sommer didn't claim to originate these views. He claimed to find them in the Bible, just as these men claim it. But let me tell you this, please. When men identify themselves with a movement, and propagate and preach that which is popularly styled under that designation, they cannot escape that designation themselves. Brother Allen Sommer, in the audience tonight —and I do not intend to address him or embarrass him because I have come to appreciate him highly—told me today that he and Ketcherside, after listening to this debate, had decided that one of two things would happen: Either these brethren identified with the *Gospel Guardian* would go all the way over and espouse all the positions that Daniel Sommer advocated, or else they would quit debating with us. And I say that that's right one hundred per cent. It isn't fair, it isn't ethical, for them *to steal Daniel Sommer's thunder and not give proper credit for it!* I maintain that they ought to be proud of their theological father, because that's exactly where the position traces itself in the Restoration Movement. And I say that, not for the purpose of prejudicing anybody, because these men were among those who said the same thing a few years ago.

Friends, I think it is sad that a man of Brother W. Curtis Porter's stature, one who influences so many people as he does, should have identified himself with a hobby and involve himself in the ridiculous position that has been characteristic of him in this debate. I have engaged in many debates. I have met a lot of men. I consider Brother Porter one of the strongest men I have ever met; but I say it without hesitation that I have never seen a denominational preacher more bewildered, more confused, or who resorted to more quibbling than that which characterized him in this debate. From beginning to end his approach has been negative; and, though we have called repeatedly for the passage or passages that justify the pattern—though we have asked him to tell us *how the church is to do it*, to this good moment nobody in this audience knows (from Brother Porter) how it can be done. Not only that, the positions he has espoused are in conflict with those which characterize these who endorse him. I make the prediction that until Brother Porter settles himself one place or the other—over with the *American Christian Review* or back to his former position—this is the last debate he will engage in on these matters. I recommend to him that he ground himself and that he identify himself with one or the other. (Time called.)

I thank you.

www.ingramcontent.com/pod-product-compliance
Lightning Source LLC
LaVergne TN
LVHW091031080826
845145LV00002B/438